ELEMENTARY AND MIDDLE SCHOOL

SOCIAL STUDIES CURRICULUM PROGRAM, ACTIVITIES, AND MATERIALS

James L. Barth
Purdue University

University Press
of America™

Copyright © 1979 by

University Press of America, Inc.™

4710 Auth Place, S.E., Washington D.C. 20023

ISBN: 0-8191-0667-4

Library of Congress Catalog Card Number: 78-71367

PREFACE

Social studies materials have generally had a hard time fitting into an elementary school curriculum. Granted there are a good many reasons, all legitimate, all compelling, but the fact remains that social studies is not hardly a favorite subject among most teachers or student, primary, intermediate or middle school levels. Primary teachers know full well that social studies is often not even a part of the organized curriculum kindergarten through third grade in many schools, including even elementary shcools where the state mandates the teaching of social studies.

At best elementary teachers may have experienced in their own education a fragmented social studies curriculum, a curriculum that seemed to be aimed at little other than the recall of the chief export of Turkey, the climate of North Africa, and the names of Columbus' three ships. Having endured the subject has not necessarily inspired a desire to repeat the experience.

Elementary teachers tend to believe that social studies is chronology of historical events and geography. I hope this book will persuade elementary teachers that the social studies they knew years ago is not what we would wish them to repeat. I want to convince teachers that there is a New Social Studies that aims at constructing an integrated developmental curriculum of courses, topics, activities, and materials. This book offers you an alternative, a different vision of social studies for elementary and middle school.

The book is designed for teachers in training, experienced teachers, and elementary supervisors who are looking for help on how to organize a systematic elementary social studies program. The activities, the materials are organized and classified into long and short range purposes and objectives. It is designed, in part, to be used as one might use a dictionary. <u>Elementary and Middle School Social Studies Curriculum, Program, Activities, and Materials</u> is not a methods text nor is it a substitute for a methods text. The book is a supplement to a methods text offering in detail the activities and materials that teachers seem to find most useful in the classroom.

For the past five years teachers in the classroom have been field testing the program, activities and materials in this book. Teachers often ask me two questions: Where do the materials come from? and Can a teacher follow the sequenced activities in this book without benefit of a classroom set of social

i

studies texts? The activities and materials come from a variety of places. Some come from state social studies curriculum guides, some are common well-known activities used in a number of subject fields, some come from classroom teachers, but most are original. On the second question: yes, teachers can use the activities and materials as sequenced because they offer a comprehensive program, but my assumption is that teachers normally would have a classroom set of social studies texts for their students. This book will help a faculty to organize a systematic program no matter what set of texts are used in the class.

The book is organized into nine chapters with a prologue called Person to Person. The reader is urged to read the prologue carefully for the program offered in the book is based upon the agreements about what ought to be taught among social studies educators. The prologue is followed by the first chapter which describes and illustrates a K-12 curriculum. Each succeeding chapter describes what courses are taught at that grade level and includes illustrative activities and materials.

I would like to acknowledge the hundreds of graduates and undergraduates who have read and critically evaluated the activities and materials for they are responsible for my belief that the book will help the Teacher. Special thanks to Brenda S. Naugle for typing the manuscript. In particular I am indebted to Barbara Bauhof Barth who was the illustrator for this book and who helped to organize the activities and materials in many of the chapters.

Purdue University   James L. Barth
1978

To the Bauhof family, in particular Florence S.,
Florence C., Adelaide C. and Rudolf, this book is
fondly dedicated.

TABLE OF CONTENTS

PERSON TO PERSON

I wonder if you realize that the field of social studies is less than seventy years old. Some of the original founders of the social studies movement which later became the field of social studies are still alive, and in some cases still academically productive. O, but you say, schools have been teaching history and geography in American schools ever since colonial days. Yes, of course you're right, but then that teaching was not social studies. Social studies as a field is not just history and geography. So what's the point? Well, the point is that social studies as a field has just begun to develop. If there is considerable misunderstanding about the role of social studies between parents, administrators, and teachers, then don't be dismayed, for what would you expect from a young, growing field but disagreement and hesitation.

What is social studies?

There is substantial disagreement within the field as to first, what social studies is and second, how social studies ought to be taught. Please don't think because I raise these problems about disagreements that authorities in the field have not made attempts at clarifying and re-ducing the size of the disagreements. What is social studies? In a recent publication the field has been defined as:

> The social studies is an integration of experiences and knowledge concerning human relations for the purpose of citizenship education.[1]

One part of that definition is particularly significant for our purposes in this book for the definition tells us that the reason for teaching social studies is citizenship education. Simply the goal of teaching social studies is citizenship. Suppose the goal is citizenship so what must a teacher do to achieve that goal? This is a point at which social studies educators seemingly have substantial agreement.

The four purposes for teaching social studies

Educators seem to agree that to achieve the goal of citizenship the teacher should practice the following four purposes:[2]

1. Knowledge about the human condition which includes past, present, and future.
2. Skills necessary to process information.
3. The skills to examine values and beliefs.

4. The application of knowledge through active participation in society.

For purposes of this book the four purposes are shortened to:

1. Gaining knowledge (work, roles, services, define, identify)

2. Processing information (interpreting symbols, map skills, fact from fiction)

3. Valuing (evaluation, divergent, clarify, rank)

4. Participation (find and solve, social action, establish rules)

I don't wish you to get lost in the agreements and disagreements above. Perhaps it is sufficient to know that the social studies field is young and changing. What I do wish you to know are the four purposes above. I have told you that social studies teachers generally accept the four purposes. Just what does this mean? It means that a teacher will practice all four purposes when teaching social studies whether in kindergarten or twelfth grade. So in practice you (teacher) should help students gain knowledge, process information, develop the skill to examine values, and finally help student apply knowledge through an active civic participation. The argument is that, if you practice the four purposes, you will be teaching your social studies course as citizenship education.

Is it important?

Why is it important that you know the four purposes before reading this book? Very simply all activities and materials found in this book are categorized under one of the four objectives. In other words at each grade level all activities and materials are organized to accomplish one of the purposes. At each grade level there are activities designed to gain knowledge, process information, develop valuing skills and encourage participation.

You might ask "Even if activities are identified for each of the four purposes by grade level, why is this different or unique?" This book is one of the first attempts to organize a kindergarten-eight social studies curriculum that says to teachers--the objectives for which you teach kindergarten are the same as those used in each of the succeeding grades right up through the eighth grade. For the first time you could know that what you taught was part of a developmental social studies program. That each teacher, though the courses and topics differ, were following the same objective and purposes as you were. No longer need you feel isolated, alone, seperated

vi

from others who are teaching social studies.

I want to encourage you to teach a social studies that is part of an organized curriculum. You and I both know that social studies is almost in Primary education an after thought--after reading, language arts, math, etc. Hopefully you will be more likely to use social studies content if you knew that the lessons taught in your class were to be followed up next year by lessons that build upon the concepts and skills you taught. If you know that the social studies curriculum was developmental, you would be more likely to teach the curriculum.

Some Activities and Materials Include all Four Purposes

You could argue that the absolute best type of social studies activities should be organized to provide knowledge, process information, valuing, and participation. As the activities become more complex in the fourth, fifth, sixth grades and middle school, distinctions between the four purposes blur. The important point is that all four purposes should be part of a social studies program, that all four purposes be part of each activity is not important, that activities and materials at least incorporate one of the four purposes is important, that all four purposes be part of a K-12 social studies curriculum is essential.

Social Studies Integrated with Other Fields

The social studies is a distinct subject field, but that does not mean that social studies should not be integrated with fields which do offer opportunities for integration. Many of the activities suggested in this book could be and should be found in methods and activity books in other fields. Some of the social studies materials will look familiar and I suspect that as you read through activities at each grade level you might say, "I saw that in science methods," or about valuing, "That's talked about in health, I didn't know that's social studies." It is no accident that activities are designed to be integrated with lessons in other fields. Common sense alone tells us that elementary teachers with limited time to teach all subject fields, will look for opportunities to integrate some of the fields with the hope of concentrating on those for which they are held accountable.

Social Studies Ask The Important Questions

It is natural to suppose that one's field is the most important. Surely without math, science, reading, music the world would be different. But for a moment consider the social studies educator's point of view. In other fields questions are asked that have to do with why and how things work.

In social studies the really important questions are asked that must be answered otherwise there would be no family, culture, or human life as we know it. Social studies questions are: Who am I? Who are you? How are we related? How did we get this way? What was the past? What is the future? Shall we live for the present? Trying to find answers to these questions takes a lifetime. These are the important questions that have to do with the quality of life. Your task as an elementary and middle school teacher is to help your students use social studies to start the search for answers.

A Final Word on how to Read this Book

Frankly I do not anticipate that teachers will read straight through this book. What I think will happen is that teachers will identify their grade level: primary, intermediate, middle school. Because I have anticipated how teachers might read this book, I have designed each grade level to be self-contained. The fact that teachers really ought not to read the book piecemeal probably has little to do with what they will actually read. I have purposely written each chapter following the same pattern so that to know the pattern of one will be to know the pattern of all chapters on activities and materials. These final thoughts complete our Person to Person. Use this book as a dictionary, use it as a text, use it to coordinate a consistent social studies program, and finally you use it because some of the best ideas about teaching social studies are here.

A SOCIAL STUDIES KINDERGARTEN THROUGH
TWELFTH GRADE CURRICULUM

Though this book focuses on elementary social studies, I think you might
agree that conceiving social studies as a subject in elementary grades only,
would be a narrow perspective. As in any other field, knowing the whole program is undoubtedly necessary so that you can more easily spot your part in
that total program. What is a social studies kindergarten through twelfth
grade curriculum supposed to do for a student? One answer is that the curriculum
should help students integrate their life experiences including knowledge
gained from a study of the social sciences and humanities for the purpose of
performing as effective citizens. Fine, you say, so what we want is an
effective citizen. But just what specifically should an effective citizen be
able to do? I as a teacher have to know this otherwise I cannot very well
prepare the student for a task without knowing what skills are needed. You
surely can answer this question assuming you have read the preceding Person
to Person. Of course the answer is that the task of preparing effective
citizens is best accomplished by preparing the student to perform the four
purposes of gaining knowledge, processing information, examining values, and
knowing how to participate.

A Systematic Curriculum

Am I saying that at each grade level social studies should be taught so as
to emphasize those four purposes? Yes, absolutely. Those four purposes plus
some common activities and concepts such as interdependence, scarcity, group
control, offer the best chance for a systematic kindergarten/twelfth social
studies curriculum. If for the moment you agree that a systematic curriculum
should be built primarily upon the teaching of the four purposes at each grade
level, then you know that each of the four purposes must be carefully planned
at each grade level. If you can conceive of a funnel as it spirals and broadens
upward from the base, then you can imagine how the four purposes are passed from
one grade to another deepening and broadening the child's ability to understand
the world.

Fragmented Bits and Pieces[1]

Now, be honest when asking yourself this question. What pattern of social
studies topics and courses did I follow elementary through high school? Think
about this question for a minute. Odds are that you can't recall the course
topics or whether there was a pattern. If your experience was similiar to
most college students', you remember social studies as history (with emphasis
on events and dates) and geography (with emphasis on land forms and exports).

Believe it or not there was supposed to be all three--courses, topics, and patterns--throughout your scholastic years, and together they were to be called the social studies curriculum. Every school has a social studies curriculum. The fact that you probably don't know this and also that you don't remember the course, topics and patterns practiced on you for 12 years suggests that the school system was not particularly interested in having you know that a prescribed social studies pattern existed. If you are curious at all, you must be wondering why you don't know much about a curriculum that you spent considerable time in school completing.

There are many reasons why you don't know. One reason among many is that teachers--both elementary and secondary--don't know that there is a prescribed social studies curriculum. We've said above that most all school systems have a kindergarten through twelfth grade social studies curriculum, a part of which is mandated by the state. That curriculum often is designed by a kindergarten through twelfth grade school system curriculum committee that has produced a study guide that each social studies teacher in the system is supposed to follow. The practice has been for each teacher to ignore the study guides, then proceed to teach whatever course, topic and pattern that fits their individual interests. Of course, the consequences of such liberties have been that little or no continuity exists between courses or topics, and patterns don't emerge, giving the social studies program the apperance of being disjointed, fragmented bits and pieces of government, history and geography.

Social studies, according to authorities in the field, was never meant to be fragmented bits and pieces. The intent was for a carefully planned curriculum that set forth a pattern of courses and topics which built a logical progression of concepts. In this chapter you are introduced to the rationale for and the demonstration of a kindergarten through twelfth grade social studies curriculum. You should become convinced that the social studies you may teach should not be taught as disjointed, fragmented bits and pieces, but rather should be taught as part of a total social studies curriculum aimed at the goal of preparing citizens.

Social Studies Curriculum Chart

The following chart is a fair representation of a curricular pattern that generally exists throughout the United States. However, take note that this national curricular pattern may not exactly fit your state pattern. Instruction:

Examine the national representative curricular pattern in column 1,[2] then in column 2 try your hand at identifying your state's approved (mandated) pattern, then try in the third column identifying your school's approved kindergarten-twelfth grade pattern.

Column 1 National K-12 Social Studies Curriculum	Column 2 Your state's K-12 Curriculum. Fill in your state's approved curriculum	Column 3 Your school system's K-12 Social Studies Curriculum. Fill in your school's approved curriculum
Grade Basic Theme	Grade Basic Theme	Grade Basic Theme
K-2 Individuals and Families K & Individuals and Families 1 Locally and in the U.S.A. 2 Individuals and Families in Selected Parts of the World.	K 1 2	K 1 2

3-4 Communities
3 The Local Community and
  Selected Communities in the
  U.S.A.
4 Selected Communities of the
  World.
	3
	
	4
		3
		
		4

5-6 Countries
5 The United States Today and
  Yesterday (Postholing cer-
  tain periods in our history
  in the second half of the
  year)
6 Selected Countries of the
  World (to be studied in
  depth)
	5
	
	6
		5
		
		6

7-8 Basic Problems and Decisions
  in the U.S.A.
7 Problems and Decisions in
  the U.S.A. Today
8 Problems and Decisions in
  the U.S.A. Yesterday
	7
	
	8
		7
		
		8

9-10 Cultures
9 Studies in Depth of the 8
  Major Cultural Areas of
10 the World "Today and
  Yesterday," Western and
  Non-Western
	9
	
	10
		9
		
		10

11-12 The United States and the
  Emerging International
  Community
11 United States History
12 Contemporary Problems in the
  U.S.A. and in Other Parts
  of the World
	11
	
	12
		11
		
		12

Comment

Possibly your state does not have a suggested kindergarten-
twelfth grade social studies curriculum. The probability is that even if your
state does have a suggested social studies curriculum, like most of your col-
leagues, you just do not know either your state's or your school system's curriculum. It is an interesting question to ponder. Why is it that school administrators, social studies teachers, and students who obviously are required
to pass through a social studies mandated curriculum do not know what their
state's or their school's kindergarten-twelfth grade curriculum is?

Social Studies Course Content, A Brief Overview

Just what content is included in a total social studies
curriculum? The chart above lists, under the national curricular pattern,
course titles. Though the titles are suggestive, they give only a hint as to
content. Remember there is no one prescribed national social studies curricular pattern. Each state established its own pattern. There are literally
fifty different patterns, but as suggested in the chart above there are similar
state patterns. What follows is only a suggestion of a particular pattern of
course offerings and content, but the courses do illustrate what a systematic
program might be like.[3]

Kindergarten - The child and his investigation of himself, his family, home,
school, and neighborhood and the accompanying living and working functions of each in which the child learns to work in
groups, to use classroom tools, to share materials, to use
simple inquiry skills and social participation.

Grade 1 - Individuals, families, schools and social institutions of the
neighborhood, ways of living and working together using available resources at home, and in other parts of the world (in
other environments); yesterday and today with extension of,
or introduction of, cooperative and problem-solving skills.

Grade 2 - Local school neighborhoods, neighborhoods in other countries;
how local communities meet common interests and needs of individuals and institutions through human interaction and
through services basic to mankind; the introduction of valuing skills and simple map reading skills; the development of
skills of responsibility.

Grade 3 -   Development of the local community, other communities, states
             and regions in other parts of the world; ways they adjust to
             the environments, develop and use technology and human and
             natural resources, and adapt from other cultures while ex-
             tending student interests; knowledge of occupations, values
             and value systems, map skills, organization, inquiry and other
             skills.

Grade 4 -   State (History), region, nation and world communities in-
             fluenced by the past; present use of environment, distribution
             of human and natural resources, use of societal controls,
             ever-present problems, and the influence of geography on
             development with extension of research skills, problem-solving
             and valuing activities.

Grade 5 -   The United States, Canada and regions of the world; the
             growth and development of nations and regions of the world
             as influenced by geography, history, physical and cultural
             environments, and the roles and relationships which develop
             and exist among them while comparative study, problem-solving,
             and awareness of how to affect change as an individual are
             emphasized.

Grade 6 -   Western Europe, Latin America and other regions of the world
             with comparative studies on the growth and development of
             nations and regions of the world, influenced by geography,
             history, physical and cultural environments and the roles
             and relationships which develop and exist among them; also
             stressing pupil-teacher planning and decision-making.

Grade 7 -   Area studies of World Civilization (global studies) including
             the Middle East, Asia and Africa.

Grade 8 -   United States history (including instruction in the Constitu-
             tion of the United States of America).

Grade 9 -   Course offerings of 9-12 are allowable at any level but must
Grade 10   provide: United States History (2 semesters required);
Grade 11   United States Government (2 semesters required or 1 semester
Grade 12   of U.S. government or civil government and 1 semester of an
             acceptable citizenship course). The classes must deal with
             the historical, political, civic, sociological, economic and
             philosophical aspects of the Constitution of the United
             States. In addition to the required courses, each commis-

sioned high school shall include in the curriculum:
ancient, medieval or modern history and economic or physical
geography. Courses approved for the foregoing additional
elective offerings and for other electives are: African
Studies, Early World Civilizations, Psychology, Sociology,
Urban Affairs, Western Civilization, Anthropology, Asian
Studies, Economics, Ethnic Studies (U.S.), Latin America,
Area Studies, Modern World Civilization, World Civilization,
World Geography, Current Problems, Introduction to Social
Science, and Values and Issues.

Expanding Horizons

There are several ideas about the organization of social
studies courses and basic themes which you should note from the above kindergarten through twelfth grade curriculum. Notice that social studies starts
with individuals, families and school the first years and ends twelve years
later with contemporary problems of the social system with special interest in
the emerging international world. This approach is called expanding horizons--
starting with oneself and expanding through the school years to an understanding of the social, political and economic problems of family, neighborhood,
community, state, nation, and the world.

Spiral

American history is taught three different times throughout the curriculum at grades five, eight, and eleven. Also content about
other cultures, that is global studies are taught at grades two, four, six or
seven, ten, and twelve. This repeating of topics at ever greater levels of
complexity kindergarten through twelfth grade is called a spiral. That is, at
specific grade levels certain topics and themes are repeated but at a more complex level each time. If you can imagine what the funnel of a tornado looks
like, the small end of the tornado on the ground is kindergarten with an in-
crease in the size of the funnel as it reaches for the sky representing the
higher grades. In practice, if you are teaching about non-western societies
in the sixth or seventh grades, you should be building on topics and themes
developed in grades two and four and preparing students for further study in
grades ten and twelve.

Current Events and Comparative Studies

Though current events was not listed as part of the basic
themes of recommended curriculum, since 1916 it has been strongly recommended

as a supplementary part of any social studies instruction. Readiness for
current events should originate in grade one and in each succeeding grade
should be emphasized. Each succeeding year students should gain both experience and skill in learning where to find information on current events
and in processing that information. So, another common thread throughout the
entire kindergarten through twelfth grade curriculum is current events along
with comparative studies. You are encouraged to remember expanding horizons,
and the spiral, both of which help to keep social studies content from being
seen as fragmented bits and pieces. The spiral holds the bits and pieces
together; the expanding horizons provide the depth.

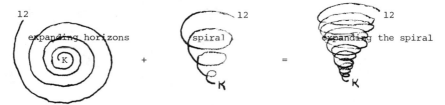

Summary: Expanding the Spiral

Yes, there are social studies goals, purposes, themes and concepts that
should be taught in a common kindergarten through twelfth grade social studies
curriculum. No matter what grade level, kindergarten to twelfth, at least the
following should be basic threads holding all social studies courses together
in a common curriculum. Just to be sure that I am not misunderstood, yes,
absolutely the following ideas should be part of any social studies curriculum.

spiraling themes and concepts		gaining knowledge
expanding personal horizons	(plus of	processing information
comparative studies	course the 4	examining values & beliefs
current events	purposes	participation

I suspect the notion of practicing the above ideas in one social studies
course is nothing less than frightening. I can hear you saying, "No way!"
Well, there is a way, not the only way, but a way to make such a complex
curriculum come true. The following chapters on activities and materials,
in part, offer some hope of helping teachers find purpose for teaching
social studies.

NOTES

CHAPTER KINDERGARTEN/FIRST GRADE

ACTIVITIES AND MATERIALS FOR KINDERGARTEN/FIRST GRADE

CHAPTER KINDERGARTEN/FIRST GRADE

I. Advanced Organizer

Each of the proceeding chapters represents a particular grade level, in this case kindergarten and first grade. These two grade levels are combined because in some schools formal social studies does not start until first grade, and therefore what would normally be taught in kindergarten is not begun until first grade. Each chapter consists of four parts, and this is why the introduction is called an "advanced organizer." In other words you ought to know before reading the chapter how it is organized, for such knowing may help you to remember. The four major parts to this chapter are: part 1 is a brief discussion on topics taught and national trends in teaching kindergarten and first grade throughout the United States. The second part is an illustration of a state kindergarten/first grade program. The third part has activities and materials which conform to topics taught in kindergarten/first grade and are categorized by the four purposes of teaching social studies; knowledge, processing, valuing, and participation. Fourth part of the chapter is an interest form.

II. Topics Taught and National Trends
in Teaching Kindergarten and First
Grade[1]

Courses, Topics, and Themes
most Frequently Covered in Kindergarten:
"Living Together in a New Environment."

The emphasis in kindergarten is on the child (a study of the self). The study includes how the child identifies his role in the family and the school with special emphasis on living and working with other children. Some teachers prefer to see social studies in kindergarten as a concentration on immediate surroundings. This includes an examination of what the family is, what the relationships between the child, home, and school are, and what functions the members of the home, school, and neighborhood environment perform. The kindergarten social studies program should be integrated with the first grade which as you will find emphasizes not only the topics of living and working at home and in the school, but also extends to comparisons of living and working in other parts of the world and to topics such as the various ways families make a living.

Courses, Topics and Themes
most Frequently Covered in First Grade:
Self, Home, and School.

<u>Purpose</u> <u>of</u> <u>the</u> <u>Course</u>: Preparing the pupil for school life and community liv-
ing. Speical emphasis is on developing attitudes of self-reliance and cooper-
ation at home and school. The course introduces the concepts of interdependence and variety in human life--in family, school, neighborhood, etc.; providing readiness experiences for skills and concepts related to understanding
of space and time relationships (map skills, chronology).

<u>Basic</u> <u>content</u> <u>of</u> <u>the</u> <u>course</u>: The family--its members, the work of various
members, rules, recreation; School--the physical plant, "helpers" at school,
such as the principal, nurse, custodian, patrol persons, bus drivers, parapro-
fessionals, school rules and reasons for them; safety--in home, at school, en-
route to and from school; experience with simple maps of the neighborhood and
with diagrams of the school and its ground; holidays--Thanksgiving, Christmas,
birthdays of patriotic heroes.

Just as a reminder, where there is a kindergarten program in social studies,
the above content will be treated there and then reinforced in grade one.

In addition to the above, schools include one or perhaps two
of the following topics: Pets--emphasis on caring for them; the Farm--atten-
tion to farm animals, work of the farmer, seasonal changes in farm work and
life, farm products. Transportation--in daily life of the family and neighborhood and food for the family--kinds needed for healthy diet.

Kindergarten and First Grade Course,
Topic and Themes for Advanced Students:
Home, School, and Neighborhood or Community.

<u>Objective</u> <u>of</u> <u>the</u> <u>course</u>: Basically, the same as for "Home and School" but
with an additional dimension: neighborhood.

Basic content of the course: In addition to the topics family, school, safety,
maps and national holidays the course includes selected neighborhood or community helpers and the services they provide: policeman, fireman, postman,
milkman, newsboy, doctor, nurse, librarian, bus driver, garbage collector, and
repairmen of various types. This is content that was formerly reserved for
grade two and still is in many schools.

Trends in Teaching Kindergarten/First Grade Social Studies
1. More emphasis on current events readiness. Calling attention to media,
newspapers, radio, TV, popular news magazines (<u>Time</u> and <u>Newsweek</u>) that carry

current events.

2. More emphasis on geographic concepts, including more intensive readiness experiences for map-reading and map making.

3. Systematic development of economic concepts, in connection with study of the family. Division of labor, specialization in production, role of the consumer, budgeting limited resources to meet family needs, making choices among the many ways the family can use its resources. Example: Our Working World series.

4. Emphasis on variety in family patterns and ways of living. Some guides for the first grade unit on "family living" develop these main ideas:

> Families differ in size and composition.
> The composition of a family may change.
> Homes may be different in many ways.
> Families are supported in many ways.

5. Perhaps the most important trend is toward the use of comparative studies. Comparing the child's own self, home, and school with alternative life styles in America and in Asia, Africa, and Europe, in other words developing readiness for global studies.

III. Illustration of a State Kindergarten/
First Grade Program.[2]

Realize there are 50 states and therefore 50 different state departments of public instruction, descriptions of courses, topics, and themes. There is no one prescribed social studies program throughout the United States. However, one state's description of its social studies kindergarten/first grade program will illustrate the content which the state expects to be taught. This illustration is included so that you can identify how a state mandates the teaching of social studies in the first grade.

> Children examine how they learn in different envi-
> ronments, primarily within family, peer, educational and social
> institutions. They also begin to develop their self concepts,
> group and social participation skills. Reading skills are de-
> veloped while learning about families in various parts of the
> world. Students learn how families differ in composition, life
> style and role expectations. Studying the multiethnic nature
> of societies, children learn how in different environments groups
> of people use resources available to them, earn a living, and
> discover how basic social structures sustain themselves.[2]

IV.   Activities and Materials Categorized by
Knowledge, Processing, Valuing, and Participation.

I realize a rather common practice is to skip purposes and
specific objectives which precede the activities, but in this case the objectives are extremely important for an objective in the first grade will be
found in proceeding grades. This is a <u>developmental</u> program with objectives,
activities, and materials organized to build from one grade level to another.

KINDERGARTEN ACTIVITIES AND MATERIALS

1. Purpose: to <u>gain</u> <u>knowledge</u> about oneself and one's family.

Specific objective: Develop a concept of self.

1. Activity & materials

<u>Up</u> <u>and</u> <u>Down</u> <u>the</u> <u>Ladder</u>

(<u>or</u> <u>stairs</u>)   (identifying self)

when: recurring

what: tape outline of ladder on floor

tape labels on steps of ladder or use
school stairs.

how: introduce the children to the game
"Up and Down the Ladder (or stairs)"
to knowing oneself. Explain that each
child will climb as high on the ladder
or steps as child is able to recall the
specific information. This activity should
be continued from time to time until the
child has successfully climbed the ladder
or stairs.

telephone number

city
county
state
country

Street
house number
last name
first name

2. Activities & materials

<u>Here</u> <u>Is</u> <u>My</u> <u>House</u> (identifying self)

when: recurring

what: yarn, construction paper

how: construction paper is cut in the general shape of
the student's house (A frame, rectangle, square) and

is pasted on manila paper with room to write name,
address, and telephone number as the child learns
them.   Houses are placed on a construction paper
street with paper telephone poles attached to houses
with yarn to show how houses in the neighborhood are
connected to each other.

3.   Activity & materials

My Birthday (identifying self)

when: recurring

what: calendars (free from businesses)

how: help child find birthday and mark it on child's own
        calendar. Also mark it on the room calendar. Children
        can look for birthdays and holidays. May wish to start
        in January to illustrate entire year.

4.   Activity & materials

Birthday Cake (identifying self)

when: recurring

what: large paper cake and paper candles

how: label paper cake with current month. Children
        with a birthday in that month put name and date
        on candle and put on cake. May reuse same cake each
        month or make a new cake, posting previous cakes in
        another part of the room. This has the advantage of
        showing the months, the passage of time and the
        relationship of the child's birthday to the month.

Specific objective: Develop a concept one's family relationships.

5. Activity & materials

Who's Who (identifying family)

when: two periods

what: magazines, catalogues (Sears, Penneys, Wards)

how: each child finds pictures of figures that represent own family members, cuts them out and pastes them on separate sheets of paper. Child or teacher prints label on sheets. Fasten sheets into booklet for each child.

6. Activity & materials

Who's Home (identifying family)

when: two periods

what: paper cut into window shapes by teacher

how: child draws a house on paper. Child takes from teacher a paper window for each person in house, draws face of that person on window and pastes it on house. Names are written under windows. This activity is particular appropriate for children who have people living in their home who are not necessarily relations.

7. Activity & materials

Relationship Clothesline (identifying close family and other relationships)

when: two periods

what: clothes line, clothes pins (or string and paperclips) paper

how: children draw pictures of family members and cut them out. Hang them on lines marked: brothers, aunts, fathers, grandmothers, and others who may be living in the home but not necessarily related.

8. Activity & materials

Routing my Roots (identifying family)

when: one period

what: dittos of geneology root form

how: have each child route own family roots with names

and pictures.

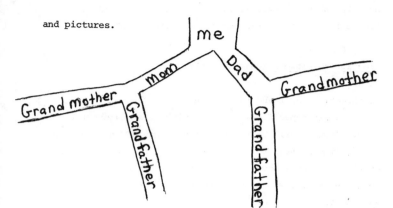

Specific objective:

Identifying one's immediate world and how it changes.

9. Activity & materials

Our Class Roots (identifying school classmates)

when: one period

what: tree branch (or small tree) paper leaves

how: child prints name on leaf and fastens on photo.
       Leaves are taped to tree branch.

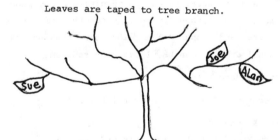

10. Activity & materials

Our Book[3] (identifying school people)

when: recurring

what: paper

how: -make booklet of children's experiences of going to
       school for the first time.
       -after visiting with different school personnel
       (nurse, principal, etc.) have children draw pictures
       of these people and dictate experience stories to

go with the pictures. i.e., "I will not be afraid to visit Mrs. Jones, the nurse, if I get hurt."

11. Activity & materials

Flourishing Flowers (changing self)

when: recurring

what: construction paper and tape measure

how: fasten a big paper flower to wall with tape measure for stem. Fasten small leaf with child's name at child's height (may be necessary to make a stem if several leaves overlap). Leaves move up during year as child grows (measure every few months). May make new flower for each month.

12. Activity & materials

Seasons (changing weather or seasons)

when: recurring

what: material scraps and construction paper

how: label four separate sections of the room for each season. Use tree branch for little tree. Have children color leaves appropriately for each season and fasten to tree. Dress large girl and boy paper dolls in the clothes appropriate for the current season. Move tree and change dolls' clothes as seasons change. Seasonal stories can be placed near section.

First Grade Activities and Materials

Specific Objective: Identify family relationships

13. Activity & materials

Me and Mine[4] (identifying self and family)

when: one period

what: large manila paper

how: students make booklet pages by folding paper in half. On first page they put title "Me and Mine" and one sentence on each page which they illustrate; i.e., "This is my house." "This is my animal." "This is my mother."

Specific objective: Identify family members' roles and
compare with other cultures.

14. Activity & materials

Family Helpers[5] (identify work roles of the family)

when: two periods

what: chart or questionnaire

how: children fill out family members including self on
chart, what they do at home, and how it helps the
family.

family member	what member does	how it helps
1. grandmother	washes dishes	dishes ready for next time.
2. older brother	mows grass	keeps lawn neat.
3. father	paints house	makes home look nice.

If children cannot fill out chart they may take it
home. Compare and contrast jobs, i.e., Are certain
jobs done by the same people in each family?--
Do all older brothers cut grass?

Specific objective: Identify how weather and surroundings
affect (change) what we eat and wear and where we live.

15. Activity & materials

Weather Person (identifying change)

when: recurring

what: large cardboard doll, cloth or paper clothes
teacher cuts out doll and various pieces of
clothing, i.e., boots, shirt, skirt.

how: Each day a different child dresses the doll according
to the weather. (stick clothes to doll with rolled
masking tape.)

16. Activity & materials

Weather Chart (identifying change)

when: recurring

what: large weather chart, cards printed with days of week
and weather symbols

how: each day a different child fills out the chart

according to the weather.

17. Activity & materials

    Playhouse (identifying different environments)

when: recurring

what: large packing carton

how: make a playhouse out of carton and have children decorate it using a certain theme: holidays, different cultures, life styles.

18. Activity & materials

    Houses Around the World (identifying different environments)

when: two weeks

what: resource materials, art supplies, boxes

how: discuss houses in own community and other climates and cultures, how they are made, and how they help people.

    -make houses: shoe box houses

                clay igloos and pueblos

                cloth tent

    -make paper dolls dressed to go with houses.

Specific objective: Identify National Holidays.

19. Activity & materials

    Holidays (identifying one's culture)

when: recurring

what: resources, art supplies

how: use holidays to identify with history.

Thanksgiving--discuss first Thanksgiving.

    -make Pilgrim and Indian costumes using construction
    paper to make paper headbands and feather, collars
    and hats, cardboard shoe buckles covered with
    aluminum foil.

    -sculpture Indian and Pilgrim faces on bottom
    of paper plates, pasting on hair, hats, etc.

    -log cabins made from Lincoln logs or rolled
    brown paper.

Specific objective: Define neighborhood/community and
examine different communities.

20. Activity & materials

A Walking Tour[6] (identifying neighborhood)

when: three days

what: boxes, art supplies

how: take a walking tour of community. Have students listen
to sounds (machines, traffic), look at houses, stores,
pools, parks, places to worship, streets, trash, etc.
Using what children learned make a scale model
community on table or floor of their community.

21. Activity & materials

Communities Chart (identifying neighborhoods
and communities)

when: two periods

what: chart

how: have children help fill out chart with things common
to all communities: homes, transportation, schools,
food, etc. Children can collect illustrations or
tell about where they have visited.
May want to concentrate on a community in another
part of world.

22. Activity & materials

Early American Community (identifying
historical communities)

when: two weeks

what: Lincoln Logs, boxes, art supplies

how: use the children's understanding of their neighborhood
and community as compared with historical American
community, relating the present needs to the past.
Have children plan and build an early American
table top community, use Lincoln Logs, paper scenery,
people. May be play area when finished.

II. Purpose: Develop skills necessary to process information.
KINDERGARTEN ACTIVITIES AND MATERIALS

Specific objective: One skill of processing information is
learning to locate places such as home, land, water on model,
map or globe and compare distances (shorter, longer).

1. Activity & materials

Head to Feet (develop readiness in measurement, a
skill in processing information)

when: recurring

what: art supplies

how: use distances from one object or area in room to another
to identify concepts of longer than or shorter than. Pick
area of room for home (teacher's desk). Lay blue paper for
sea going to the art supplies, lay brown paper for land to
block play area.

Have two lines of children lay down on paper (head
of first child against teacher's desk on brown paper with
toes pointing to blocks, second child head at feet of first
child and so on, same for blue paper.) Which line had the
most children so was longer? shorter? Teacher should make
map of layout for children to color. Students can measure
distances with yarn. Simple teacher drawn maps for similar
activities.

2. Activity & materials

   Arrows (developing readiness in measurement
             a skill for processing information.)

when: recurring

what: colored or masking tape, simple teacher made floor

       plan of school or kindergarten wing of school, yarn

       or string

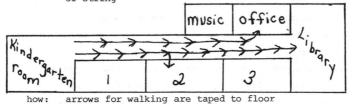

how: arrows for walking are taped to floor

       Have the children walk the arrows, then study arrows

       drawn on floor plan map. Children can measure

       distances with yarn or string and compare to see

       which is longer, shorter.

Specific objective: Learning to group and classify.

3. Activity & materials

   Let's Line Up (developing the concept of
                    classifying, a skill in processing
                    information.)

when: recurring

what:

how: When class must line up to leave room (library, recess)

       use categories. Teacher says "I'm taking a potato."

       Each child must name another item in the category

       (vegetable) or go to back of line. Different

       categories are used so each child has a chance to

       succeed in classifying: fruits, colors, games, clothes.

Specific objective: Learn to distinguish fact from fiction.

4. Activity & materials

   Keep Your Ears Open (developing readiness skills
                          for classifying information)

when: three periods

what: stories

how: Read fairy or fantasy story to children and then

raise specific questions, i.e., Can birds talk?
Can people fly by themselves? Can objects do things
people can do? Read another story and have children
make a sign (clap, raise hand) when events are not
based on fact.

5. Activity & materials

Strangers (identifying community safety)

when: three periods, good at Halloween

what: stories

how: Read story of your choice such as "Hansel and Gretel".
Discuss story in terms of present day situations:
witch was stranger who allowed children to eat house,
Discuss strangers today who might offer candy or
toys to children.
Have children make up, draw, or tell modern versions
of fairy tales. Share stories.

FIRST GRADE ACTIVITIES AND MATERIALS

Specific objective: Learning to group and classify.

6. Activity & materials

Fish Pond[7] (developing the processing skill of
classifying and categorizing.

when: recurring

what: sticks with magnets attached, boxes or buckets

how: Cut pictures from magazines, attach paper clips
and place in box called "Fish Pond." Children
fish with poles and separate what they catch into
correct box or bucket by categories (food, animals,
transportation, etc.)
May also use things people use or make such as artwork,
food, clothes, and have children categorize in
buckets as to country or culture.

7. Activity & materials

Toys from Home (developing the processing skill of
classifying and categorizing.)

when: one period

what: toys from home

how: Children bring a favorite toy. Children name

categories. Categories should be discussed and

voted on: games

wheeled toys

dolls

etc.

8. Activity & materials

What We Need[8] (developing the processing skill of
classifying and categorizing)

when: three periods

what: magazines, catalogues (Wards, Penneys, Sears)

how: Divide children into committees. Have each member

cut out pictures of things child thinks are necessary

in order to live. Committees place like things

(i.e., clothing) in construction paper folders. Label

one folder "Committee Problems", do not label other

folders yet.

Have class meeting. Each committee shows folders to

entire class. Are there similarities? Put all like

pictures together and name group, i.e., food, tools.

Committees discuss "problem" pictures and see if they

fit a category, need a new category, or if item is

not necessary.

Teacher should help committees as they work.

9. Activity & materials

Grouping (developing the processing skill of
classifying and categorizing)

when: one period for each activity

what: materials for each activity

how: groups--

foods--use paperplates to hold cut out pictures

of foods grouped by breakfast, lunch, dinner.

Group by color, by likes and dislikes, by

holidays, by hot and cold.

clothing--plan a fashion show and include

categories such as work clothes, school clothes,
party clothes, play clothes, costumes, adult
clothes. Invite another class or parents
for audience.

Make puppets and dress by categories.

shelter--

transportation--

Specific objective: Interpreting symbols, a skill in processing
information.

> NOTE: This is an extremely important skill because
> children do not necessarily recognize that
> symbols represent a real object.

10. Activity & materials

Symbols (symbolizing: a processing skill)

when: two periods

what: classroom objects

how: begin with maps and globes and the colors for land and sea
Take a large piece of paper and place small objects on
it (pencil, chalk, paper clips, block, etc.) and let
children examine it. Remove objects and ask a child to
replace them exactly as teacher had them. Children will
argue about placement and end up not being sure.
Replace articles and have children draw around each one.
Remove articles and have same child replace them.
Discuss use of symbols and how paper is a simple map.
Trace 6 rulers and 6 scissors on a paper. Remove and
place legend in corner of paper:

Show as map.

11. Activity & materials

Floor Plan (symbolizing: a processing skill)

when: two periods

what: doll house furniture or little boxes to represent
furniture

how: same activities as "Symbols" above

Make a room plan of furniture and then decide
on symbols you will use to represent furniture.

[ ]bed [ ]table ◯chair etc.

Make a new floor plan using only symbols.

Specific objective: Learn to distinguish fact from fiction.

12. Activity & materials

Is It True? (process of identifying facts)

when: two periods

what: copies of commercials heard or seen by children

how: Discuss how commercials may influence people.

-did you beg mother to buy cereal because of prize
and then did not want to eat cereal?

-are brand name toys better than other toys? Toys
brought from home might be compared (would help if
parents could recall price of toys)

-do special brand name shoes make children run faster?
Have a fast child without brand name shoes race child
with brand name shoes. Did brand name shoes help?

III. Purpose: The skill to examine values and beliefs.

KINDERGARTEN ACTIVITIES AND MATERIALS

Specific objective: Valuing the knowing of oneself.

1. Activity & materials

Put Me Together (valuing the uniqueness of self)

when: three weeks

what: brown (butcher) paper, masking tape

how: Trace around each child naming parts of the body,
then have child paint or color tracing. Cut portrait
outline and then cut into separate body parts (one
person at a time). Attach little rolls of masking
tape to the back of each piece. Have child stand
in front of mirror and reassemble parts working from
head to feet. Remove tape and place pieces in envelope
for further practice away from mirror.

hair

face

ears

neck

arm

wrist

hand

thumb

fingers

trunk

legs

thigh

calf

ankle

foot

shoe

2. Activity & materials

Me, Myself, and I (valuing the uniqueness of self)

when: two weeks

what: coat hangers, paper

how: -make a booklet including sheets for: my name, my
      picture, my hand, my footprint, my house, my
      friend, my room, my toys, etc.
      -make a mobile using a coat hanger.

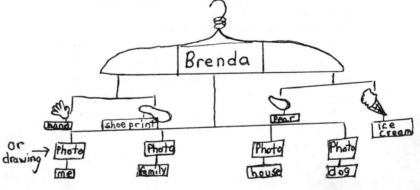

Specific objective: Identify actions or feelings that are
similar or different from story book characters.

3. Activity & materials

Reactions (valuing feelings)

when: recurring

what: stories, films, etc.

how: read story or show film and ask questions, i.e.,
"What would you have done or felt if 'it' had
happened to you?"
Have children draw pictures about what they liked
best and then let child dictate sentences about
drawing, i.e., "I liked the part where. . ."
Make papers into a book.

4. Activity & materials

Feelings (valuing feelings)

when: recurring

what: stories

how: read stories showing emotions (fear, love, etc.)
Choose a feeling such as "I felt angry........"
Have children draw pictures of themselves in a
situation that made them angry (friend broke favorite
toy, etc.) and then have child dictate story that
goes with picture. Vary emotions.
Discuss how all people have similar emotions.
Discuss mixed emotions, i.e., want to start kindergarten but afraid to go to school.

FIRST GRADE ACTIVITIES AND MATERIALS

Specific objective: Realize people in different societies
may behave differently but have many things in common.

5. Activity & materials

Glad or Sad (valuing other cultures)

when: one period

what: ditto or stencil questionnaire

how: after studying other cultures, children could do
a value rating on the questionnaire.

like or
agree

dislike or
disagree

neutral or
mild
feelings

Sample questions:

1. I like German sauerkraut_____.

2. I like Chinese fortune cookies_____.

3. I like Dutch cheese_____.

Discuss the fact that though people may disagree on what they like to eat, they all still eat.

6. Activity & materials

What to Choose (practicing evaluating questions)

when: two periods

what: teacher prepares stencil of ditto of questions that require child to make a choice between several alternatives.

| The weather I like to dress for is_____ and I wear_____. |
| On Halloween I would like to wear a costume from another country. I would be_____. |
| If I were in a play about the first Thanksgiving, I would dress as_____. |

how: Have children fold and cut large manila paper into booklet. Have them cut stencil and paste each evaluation question on a separate page of booklet. Then they can illustrate their answers on those pages.

Use after studying other cultures, times, and weather.

Specific objective: Identifying "advantage" and "disadvantage" value judgments.

7. Activity & materials

Our Classroom[9] (practice valuing on real problems)

when: one period

what: chart

how: Use classroom to identify meaning of advantage and disadvantage. Discuss good and bad things about classroom and then make a chart.

```
┌─────────────────────────────────────────────────────────────┐
│                      Our Classroom                          │
│ Disadvantages                    Advantages                 │
│ 1.  Plants don't grow well       1.  Shady side of building │
│ 2.  Noisy                        2.  Close to playground    │
│ 3.  Late lunch schedule          3.  Short afternoon        │
│ 4.  Can't chew gum               4.  Don't get "stuck-up"   │
│                                      with gum.              │
└─────────────────────────────────────────────────────────────┘
```

8. Activity & materials

What Can We Do About It?   (practice valuing on
real problems)

when: several periods

what:

how: refer to classroom chart on advantages and disadvantages. Discuss ways disadvantages might be
changed where possible. Some things cannot be
changed but list suggestions and try. For example
let children chew sugarless gum. If they are
responsible for carefully throwing it away, they get
to keep the privilege.

9. Activity & materials

Improving the Neighborhood (practice valuing on
real problems)

when: several periods

what:

how: Discuss advantages and disadvantages in neighborhood,
such as crossing streets, safety, facilities for play,
library.
Discuss suggestions for improvement that children
might do: pick up litter, get permission to do some
planting.

IV. Purpose: The application of knowledge through active participation in
society.

KINDERGARTEN ACTIVITIES AND MATERIALS

Specific objective: Participate with others to solve

problems and find solutions.

1. Activity & materials

<u>Award</u> (practicing participation by
achieving goals)

when: recurring

what: paper tree and ladder, paper made awards

how: Teacher helps child decide on area which needs
personal improvement such as putting toys away.
On large paper draw a tree with kitten stuck high
up in the branches. Draw a ladder reaching up to
cat. Put child's name on little paper. Each time
child succeeds in task child's name moves up a rung of
the ladder. When child reaches the top, child gets the
kitten award. The award is a kitten and a paper blue ribbon
which the child gets to wear for the rest of the day and
then take home. Repeat with new goals.

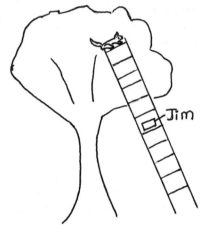
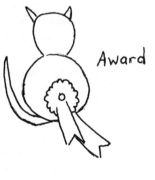

Specific objective: Preparation in developing rules for
classroom behavior.

KINDERGARTEN AND FIRST GRADE ACTIVITIES AND MATERIALS

2. Activity & materials

<u>Trusty Tricks</u> (developing readiness for
practicing participation)

when: recurring

what:

how: 1) during first days of school teacher circulates

giving praise where good behavior is observed. "I
like how Tim and Mike are sharing the Lincoln Logs.
I like how Sue and Jane are sharing the doll house."
If child is not using good rule (behavior) help to
correct it on the spot. "I like to use a clean
paint brush when I start to paint. Help me clean the
brushes you just used so that they will be ready
to use again."
2) appoint child of the day to be line leader,
announce show and tell, etc. Child will pick
theme: "We will all be kittens." Children pretend
to be kittens when walking in halls, etc. They
evaluate if they were quiet as a cat. Let
child use imagination.
3) discuss possible problems with total group.
Suppose two people want to use all long blocks
at the same time. Let them offer solutions.
No need to write all rules down because "class
members are so considerate and know what to do."

V. INTEREST FORM

You have just completed the Chapter Kindergarten/First Grade
and in an effort to have you identify activites and materials
that seem most promising at this grade level to you, please
fill out the following interest form.

Instructions:

Identify two activities from this chapter. Name the activities
and briefly describe why these particular activities are of
interest to you.

ACTIVITY 1

ACTIVITY 2

CHAPTER SECOND GRADE

ACTIVITIES AND MATERIALS FOR SECOND GRADE

CHAPTER SECOND GRADE

I. Advanced Organizer

Each succeeding chapter represents a particular grade level, in
this case second grade. Each chapter consists of four parts and this is why
the introduction is called an "advanced organizer." In other words you ought
to know before reading this chapter how it is organized for such knowledge
can help you to remember the major parts. The four parts are: part I is a
brief discussion on courses, topics, and national trends in teaching second
grade throughout the United States. The second part is an example of a state
second grade program. The third part is activities and materials for the
second grade categorized by the four purposes of teaching social studies:
knowledge, processing, valuing, and participation. The fourth part of the
chapter is an interest form.

II. Topics Taught and National Trends
in Teaching Second Grade[1]

Courses, Topics, and Themes
most Frequently Covered in Second Grade
"Neighborhood and Community"

Objectives of the course: Continuing from the first grade emphasis should be
upon a concept of interdependence, the notion that we are not alone. High-
light the services and activities in the neighborhood community that affect
every day life and processes of living with the purpose of teaching a comparative study of communities other than the child's own. Also continue from
the first grade emphasis on fostering the positive attitude of cooperation
among people. Encourage current events-mindedness and lay foundations for a
systematic geographic study.

Basic content of the course: Second graders study community helpers with emphasis on names and places, type of work, i.e., fireman, policeman, postman,
milkman, store keeper (grocery, drugstore, bank), librarian, transportation
workers, doctors, repairmen of various types (TV, electrician, plumber, gas,
telephone) and others who affect daily life. In addition one or more topics
such as transportation within the community, communication within the community, food types required for good health are usually studied in the second grade. Besides the study of the community, second graders often have
units of work on the relationship between types of clothing and seasons of
the year, the difference between city life and country life, and special ob-
servance of national holidays and the birthdays of national heroes (Washington,

Lincoln, Martin Luther King).

> Note: As you surely have already noted, second grade objectives, topics, courses, and content may seem not to be significantly different from those suggested for first grade. There is a difference. The difference is in the depth of the topic to be studied and in the breadth to which the study should be expanded to cover more people, places, and things than were covered in first grade.

Second Grade Course, Topic,
and Themes for Advanced Students
"The Community"

Objectives of the course: Essentially the same as for neighborhood community with emphasis on basic needs of people.

Basic content of the course: How needs of people in the community for goods, clothing, shelter, protection, transportation and communication are met. A typical illustration of a curriculum guide that emphasizes community living is the following:

> Geographic overview (relating to the community as a whole, and to basic needs of food, clothing, and shelter)
>
> Our Community (background of geography; homes; types of stores; factories; places of interest)
>
> Food (kinds, balanced diets)
>
> Clothing (traced from raw material to product; wool, cotton, flax, silk, synthetics)
>
> Shelter (how a home is built--planners, workers, materials, utilities).

Trends in Teaching Second Grade Social Studies

1. The chief trend is toward an indepth study of neighborhood and community. Some programs approach this by moving the "food, shelter, clothing" themes from the third grade into the second and including in them the treatment of "helpers" who have not already been studied in grade one. Comparative studies of food, clothing, and shelter in communities in other cultures and/or in an earlier period of time (as in pioneer days) are often topics at the second grade level.

2. A popular trend is to study each "helper" and his job more fully, and to include a greater variety of helpers, such as the street cleaner, the shoe

repairman, the TV repairman, the bus driver, the filling station attendant, the librarian, the playground director, as well as the traditional fireman, policeman, etc. Helpers may be studied through such questions as these: What is his job and why is it important to us? What education and training does he have to have? What special skills? What special equipment does he use? Who pays him (leading into some study of local government)? How are the services this helper gives us provided for in other communities, in other cultures and in different types of rural, suburban, or city communities, and how were they provided for in past times--as in pioneer days?

3. A continuing trend is toward emphasis on basic social science concepts, such as specialization of labor and production, how goods are distributed in our economic system through private business organizations, etc., as the various services and institutions within the community are studied.

4. Some teacher's guides and textbooks are beginning to suggest units on the study of local government. Partly this is an attempt to stimulate a positive and constructive civic attitude, and partly an attempt to show how the political system delivers neighborhood and community services. It is a continuing effort to demonstrate that garbage pickup, paving and fixing of roads, street lights do not just happen, they are the consequences of political decisions.

5. Recall that current events in the first grade was limited to readiness exercises. By second grade current events should be a regular part of the social studies program. Teachers are being encouraged to continue readiness experiences for map reading and in other geographic skills such as symbol interpretation.

6. As in the first grade a popular trend is toward comparative studies with emphasis upon global studies. Comparisons are often made between climates and family roles in other cultures. Again the emphasis is on broadening the child's outlook. Within recent years the emphasis has become more possible because children view TV programs that are filmed in other nations and in consequence are exposed to other cultures.

III. Illustration of a State
Second Grade Program.

There is no one prescribed social studies program throughout the United States. However, one state's description of its social studies second grade program will illustrate the content which the state expects to be taught. This illustration is included so that you can identify how a state mandates the teaching of social studies in the second grade.

Students study the role of the individual in the neighborhood community in which they live and how needs are met through human interaction and communication. Neighborhood and world interdependence are studied while examining how needs are met for transportation, learning government, and the market place. Students continue to develop self concept, reading, group and social participation skills within this context.[2]

IV. Activities and Materials Categorized by Knowledge, Processing, Valuing, and Participation

I realize a rather common practice is to skip purposes and specific objectives which precede the activities, but in this case the objectives are extremely important for an objective in the second grade will be found in proceeding grades. This is a developmental program with objectives, activities, and materials organized to build from one grade level to another.

SECOND GRADE ACTIVITIES AND MATERIALS

I. Purpose: Gaining knowledge about the human condition which includes past, present, and future.

Specific objective: Learning about roles and services performed by people who live or work in neighborhood/community.

1. Activity & materials

Prop Box[3] (identifying work roles in neighborhood/community)

when: recurring

what: sturdy boxes and various items students contribute.

how: a prop box is composed of specialized items combined to foster a specific type of play. This combination of ordinary housewares can afford a child hours of enjoyment while providing an educational experience. A prop box contains the kinds of things which prevent play from becoming stale or from stopping altogether. Watch the play. Where is it going? What will keep it going?

What does a mechanic need when he/she wants to repair cars or bikes, trains or planes? Tools, parts, wires, flashlight, etc. What does an astronaut need when he/she is about to visit the moon? Proper clothing, instruments, a space panel, food containers,

camera, etc. What might a nurse require in order
to tend an emergency case? Bandages, medicine bottles,
hot water bottle, uniform, etc.

Boxes of props may be started as children need
materials to extend their play (electrical switches,
wires and pliers for the electrician; plastic flowers
and vases for the florist). The props are real and
that is their appeal. Or they are made to order by
the players over at the art center or the carpentry
table. And so they are meaningful because they are
made the way a child thinks they should be made.

As an open-ended material, prop boxes can be developed
for children to use at home or at school. At home
they may be joint creations of parent and child, or
created as a gift for a young child. At school they
are developed by children and staff together. They
constantly grow. They fill up and probably start to
spill over as everyone finds things or makes things to
add. Since these are really separate boxes for various
kinds of role-playing, they can be made easily identifiable
to children by appropriate pictures cut from magazines or
drawn by children and/or adults and pasted on boxes.

Specific objective: Identify family member roles and compare with
other cultures.

2. Activity & materials

What Is It and Who Uses It? (identifying work roles in
                                  other cultures)

when: three periods

what: articles from other cultures, perhaps brought from home
       by children. Other cultures means foreign lands (such
       as Canada, Mexico, Europe) but it also means other cultures
       within the United States (such as ethnic groups, American
       Indians, New England, Appalachia, the South, etc.). Remember
       that grandparents and older relatives may very well represent
       a different age of cultural development in the United States
       and therefore qualify as having articles from "other cul-
       tures."

how: separate class into groups and divide the articles
between the groups. Move articles from group to
group so that each group can see all articles.
Questions to ask: What is it? What does it do?
What is it made of and how (by hand)? Does it have
a name? Who uses it? Do we have anything like it?
Can you tell anything about people who use it?
Is it useful?
Have class separate articles into various displays
as to who in family they think uses it.
Study information about articles used by people in
other cultures and then see if articles had to be
moved from one display to another. Have children
explain moves.

3. Activity & materials

    <u>Picturing</u> <u>Cultural</u> <u>Difference</u> (identifying work
                                        roles in other cultures)

when: one week

what: painting supplies

how: after studying roles of people in other cultures,
have each child pick a person in another culture to
paint, showing role that person plays. May also
paint whole family engaged in activity typical to
their culture.
Have children write stories to go with paintings.

Specific objective: Define neighborhood/community and
examine different communities.

4. Activity & materials

    <u>Ants</u> <u>and</u> <u>Bees</u>[4] (identifying another community)

when: two or three weeks

what: ant colony and/or bee hive or audiovisual aids.

how: study an ant or bee community either by bringing
them into the classroom or by using pictures and
films. Questions could include: Is there a group?
Do they all do the same work? Do they share anything?
Do they have similar problems? Do they do any activities

together? Is there a sign of individual initiative?
How do you feel about the ants and bees community;
suppose you could join such a community, would you?

5. Activity & materials

Community Criteria (identifying community)

when: two periods

what: identify four or five pictures; one of city, one
of plains, one of a farm, one of a small town.

how: post the pictures then have children identify which
are communities and which are not. The important
part of the exercise is listing under each picture
why it is or is not a community. Out of the reasons
will come the criteria for identifying what is or is
not a community. The final step in this exercise is to
apply the criteria to communities near the school. One
additional exercise might be for the children to collect
pictures from magazines showing different types of communities throughout the world. Be sure they apply the
criteria they have learned above to their magazine "scrap-
book" communities.

Specific objective: Learning about services performed by
community members.

6. Activities & materials

Who Will We Be? (identifying different
                        kinds of work)

when: three periods

what: large paper, art supplies

how: make a display of workers in the community. Separate
children into two groups. Groups must se   worker
they want to depict.
Have group of children trace one other
Figure of child on paper is then color
clothing or uniform of their chosen w
Variation: make puppets instead of
children.

7. Activity & materials

What Would Happen? (identifying different
kinds of work)

when: one period

what: paper

how: choose a worker in community and ask "If all workers
were bakers....." Children must finish sentence and
tell what would happen if there was no variety of
workers in community. Children could also draw
pictures to illustrate their description. To
illustrate a community with only bakers and no other
services, draw people without cars, shoes, clothes,
houses, etc.

8. Activity & materials

Play Time (identifying different kinds of work)

when: recurring

what: materials needed for each activity listed

how: Pantomime: one child or a group of children pantomime
work done by a specific worker. Class tries to guess
the worker. Discuss what training this worker needs
and whether worker is needed in neighborhood community.
Envelope: place picture of worker cut from magazine
or drawn by children in envelope (one worker to one
envelope). Have child pick envelope. Class must try to
guess worker by asking questions that can only be
answered by yes or no. One who guesses worker gets to
draw next envelope.

Specific objective: Learning to distinguish between
urban, suburban, and rural communities.

9. Activities & materials

From City to Farm (identifying contrast
between communities)

when: four or five periods

what: resource materials, pictures

how: give children plenty of time to examine resource
materials and pictures then make a chart on the

differences between rural, suburban, urban.

COMMUNITIES

	Urban	Suburban	Rural
Buildings			
Transportation:	taxi, bus truck	cars, school bus commuter train	car, truck horse
Homes			
Pollution Etc.			

Discuss similarities and differences and list
items that are interdependent. Pick one topic such
as bread and describe how each community might be
involved in making or using it.

Have children categorize pictures of communities
into urban, rural, suburban.

10. Activity & materials

Clean Clothes for Everyone (identifying community service
                          showing interdependence)

when: five or six periods

what: field trip

how: visit a service type industry such as bakery, food
     processing or canning plant, small factory, dry
     cleaning plant. Almost all neighborhoods have a dry
     cleaner. Have children prepare questions to ask on
     trip such as: Where do workers live who work at dry
     cleaning plant? How far do they commute? Who are
     cleaner's customers (individuals, restaurants,
     businesses, etc.)? Where does cleaner get its supplies
     (chemicals) to clean clothes? After field trip discuss
     answers and plot answers on a map showing interdependence
     of urban, suburban, and rural people, products, etc.

Specific objective: Learning to distinguish between
characteristics of different climates and how one lives
in each.

11. Activity & materials

Let's Visit (identifying climates)

when: three or four periods

what: shopping bags or suitcases made from cartons
children plan make believe trips to places having
different climates. Children can cut out or draw
pictures of items (clothing, etc.) they will need
in new climate and "pack" them in suitcases. They
will be staying a long time in new climate so they
should include shelter, tools, etc. Children can
show suitcases to class explaining relationship
between clothing, shelter, tools and climate.

12. Activity & materials

This Climate Calls For... (identifying climates)

when: two or three periods

what: magazines, several tree branches or paper made
trees

how: spread trees around room, labeling each tree
with a different climate. Children cut out pictures
that show ways of life for different climates and
hang on appropriate tree.

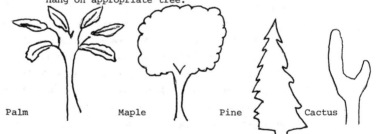

Palm   Maple   Pine   Cactus

II. Purpose: Develop skills necessary to process information.

Specific objective: Learning to group and classify.

1. Activity & materials

Recall and Categorize [5] (developing the concept of
classifying, a skill in processing
information)

when: three or four periods

what: collection of small objects, tray

how: teacher arranges small objects such as pencils, paperclips, thumb tack, plant on tray. Children view the
tray for one minute. Remove tray and have children
draw or write down all the items they can remember.
Discuss how categorizing things (food, writing materials)
helps you remember. Winners are those children who
remember the most items.

Specific objective: Interpreting symbols, a skill in
processing information.
Note: This is extremely important skill because children
do not necessarily recognize that symbols represent a real
object.

2. Activity & materials

Our Own Symbols (symbolizing, a processing skill)

when: three periods

what: paper, crayons

how: discuss symbols that could be used in landscape
pictures; hills, mountains, roads, bridges, trees.
Children decide what symbols should be and draw them
on a chart. Label symbols.
Each child draws a landscape picture and then he
makes a map of picture using only symbols.

/M mountains   tree   road

Specific objective: Learning to locate areas on
community map.

3. Activity & materials

Mapping our School and Neighborhood (developing
                                     map skills)

when: four or five periods

what: large paper, little blocks or pieces of cardboard
or colored paper.

how: take a walk around school and neighboring area,
having children take notes or make sketches of
what they see. Separate class into groups and

give each group a large piece of paper to be used
as map. Children place school (using blocks or
cardboard) on map, and then draw in or use colored
paper for grounds of school, surrounding streets,
buildings, area (pool, woods, etc.) If children
cannot remember or disagree, repeat the walk.
Continue until map is complete.

Same activity could be done for neighborhood
shopping area.

4. Activity & materials

   Tracing Our Community (developing map skills)

   when: three or four periods

   what: prepare transparency that shows the streets, buildings,
          and major land forms around the school and immediate
          neighborhood and/or community.

   how: project that transparency from projector on to a
          large piece of butcher paper. Have children trace
          in streets, land forms, buildings, etc. Then each
          child should locate his own home and label it.
          Have children locate and label stores, schools, etc.

5. Activity & materials

   Planning New Community (developing map skills)

   when: two or three periods

   what: art supplies, boxes

   how: cover large table with paper. Children decide what
          community needs and use milk cartons, boxes, etc.
          and lay out what they believe to be a good community.
          Then each child makes a map of the new community that
          includes a legend which symbolizes land forms, buildings,
          parks, shopping centers, etc.

Specific objective: Learning our nation is composed
of states and locating states and their capitals.

6. Activity & materials

   Same States Game[6] (map skills)

   when: two or three periods

what: large map of U.S.

how: using children's initials, match them to first letter
of state and/or state capital names. For example:

      Ivy, Irene - Iowa, Indianapolis

      Matt, Mike - Massachusetts, Montana

       Tim, Tom - Texas, Trenton

Have students write their names on states that have
the same first letter.

After students have written names on map, discuss
those states that have no student names on them.
Identify for those states without students' names
people that the students might know by name such
as national figures and community and school people.

7. Activity & materials

    Multiethnic Map (map skills)

when: one period

what: large U.S. map, magazines

how: have children cut out pictures of people (all kinds
of people) from magazines and cover the map with the
pictures (collage). Teacher places state outlines over
collage with magic marker. Display the collage and
title it: "Each of the 50 States and Its People Are
All Part of the U.S."

The pictures of people probably represent the
multiethnic character of the country. This exercise
reinforces the notion that this is a pluralistic nation.

8. Activity & materials

    State Songs (location and direction skills)

when: recurring

what: records, song books

how: add music to your program by listening to or
singing songs that mention states or particular
parts of the country.

      Rocky Mountain High

      My Old Kentucky Home

      Deep in the Heart of Texas

      This Land is Your Land

Sidewalks of New York

Fifty Nifty States--the best one for learning
all the states. It begins "Fifty nifty
United States from thirteen original colonies..."

Specific objective: Learn to distinguish fact from
fiction.

9. Activity & materials

Addled Ads (process of identifying facts)

when: three or four periods

what: paper

how: have children draw an advertisement then tell or
write about it.

Make up a funny commercial such as "Dirty Dishes
are Delicious." Can use TV set (below) to show
commercial.

Place emphasis upon importance of identifying
commercials noting that commercials are not
necessarily interested in offering facts but
rather stimulating interest. The funny commericals
the children make up should point up the difference
between stimulating interest and the giving of
accurate information.

TV SETS: Make TV by cutting part of side out of carton
and covering the hole with cellophane. Make
holes in top and bottom in back of cellophane
screen big enough for two sticks to pass through.
Draw pictures in order on long paper and roll
from one stick to another to give the effect
of a moving picture.

Make TV set the same as above but use puppets
attached to popsicle sticks stuck through holes
in top.

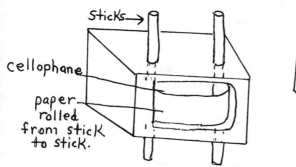

TV sets can be used for <u>showing</u> <u>commercials</u>, <u>current</u> <u>events</u>, <u>summarizing</u> field trips, and other experiences.

10. Activity & materials

<u>How</u> <u>Do</u> <u>They</u> <u>Do</u> <u>It</u>? (process of identifying facts)

when: one or two periods

what: visits from people who create special effects

how: to explain how some of the "super heros" such as Superman do things they do, invite someone who works with or understands special effects to demonstrate how things are made to look real on TV and in movies. The best place to find people who create special effects is in the theater where the set designers are required to simulate the real. The point being that in part the world of TV, movies, theater (entertainment) are created fiction and that it is important to learn to distinguish between the real and the unreal, between fact and fiction, for in the end we are talking about belief and disbelief. The very essence of processing information is at times identifying those things which are true and should be believed.

III. Purpose. The skill to examine values and beliefs.

Specific objective: To encourage an attitude that people

around the world are both alike and different.

1. Activity & materials

Would You Like...? (practicing evaluative
                              questions)

when: two periods

what: paper, ditto made by teacher that. questions what
        other cultures (of those studied) children would
        like to visit:

> Would you like to visit a family who lives
> in a high rise, on a farm?
> Would you like to visit a family who lives
> in an igloo?
> Would you like to visit a family who lives
> in a pueblo, kibbutz?

how: have children fold paper and cut into pages.
        Children should cut ditto so that they can
        paste one question on each page, then on that
        page they can anwser question, tell why, and
        make an illustration. Fasten pages into book.
        Using same format have children make book on roles:

> If I were a builder, I would make _____
> for a house. Why?
> If I were a man or woman, I would like to
> work in a _____. Why?

Specific objective: Practicing value judgments by
identifying "advantages" and "disadvantages."

2. Activity & materials

Questions, Questions, Questions (practicing valuing
                                  on real problems)

when: four or five periods

what: valuing questionnaires prepared by teacher

how: prepare questions for children to answer individually
        concerning what they think are good and bad things
        about their community. Example:

        1. In my neighborhood I like _____ best.

2. In my neighborhood I like _____ best.

3. In my neighborhood I would like to see _____ changed.

4. If I were a worker in my community I would _____.

5. The job I would like least in my community is _____.

Prepare similar questionnaire for children to take home for parents to answer.

Prepare survey sheet for community members and have children interview people. Survey should have people rank what they think the community's three greatest advantages and three greatest disadvantages are.

Compare children's parents' and community members' answers. Do they agree, disagree? Why?

3. Activity & materials

What Can We Do? (social action, practicing valuing on real problems)

when: two or three weeks

what: data from questionnaires in previous activity

how: using answers from questionnaires have class choose a social problem that they identify as a real problem to them. Discuss the different responses the class might make to the problem. If the children perceive the social/community problem as real to them, they might wish to not only study but to act upon the problem. The teacher's role is to help students identify and if possible to act through some form of participation. What is important for the children at the second grade level is to know that they are capable of identifying and participating.

An illustration of a real problem for second graders might be something like this: Suppose stray dogs were menacing the children while they were walking to and from school, barking, chasing

and generally frightening children off the side-
walk into the street. Having identified this as
a real problem to some members of the class, the
class could consider what would be appropriate action
to deal with the problem. The children might
well identify such problems as: How did the dogs
get there? What happens to dogs when they are not
cared for? What might happen if the dogs were
captured and sent to the Animal Shelter? What
officials in the community are responsible for
dealing with this problem? The class might
decide to ask the appropriate official to visit
the class and discuss the problem. The children
may discover that what seems like an easy solution
to their problem may represent a fatal solution for
the dogs. What decision will the class make?

IV. Purpose: The application of knowledge through active participation in
society.

Specific objective: Participate with others to solve
and find solutions.

1. Activity & materials

We've Got Problems (practicing social action through
participation)

when: recurring

what: puppets

how: two or three children plan and present a puppet
show on a problem situation or conflict. (may
wish to use TV set made and used in an earlier
activity) The children can stop the show before
the problem is resolved. Class discusses possible
solutions. Children presenting puppet show pick
solution they will use to complete show.

Specific objective: Preparation in developing **rules** for
classroom behavior.

2. Activity & materials

Looking Over the Rules[7] (participating in establishing rules)

when: one period

what: copies of school rules and class regulations

how: after identifying and discussing the rules of

school with the class, use the following strategy:

(1) Discuss by reviewing and evaluating the rules:

(a) Are there any complaints about the rules?

(b) Did we follow the rules?

(c) Are there times when you feel we shouldn't
follow the rules?

(d) Did following/not following the rules help/
hurt us in any way? (accomplish more, being
held after school, length of recess, etc.)

(e) Would you change any rule?

(f) Add rules?

(g) Do you follow rules without being told?

(h) Do you need to be responsible to follow rules
others make?

(i) Are you responsible to follow rules you help to
make?

(2) Evaluate pupil progress during report period
conference.

(3) Role play fairy stories or true stories
where people fail to follow rules.

Emphasize with the children participation in evaluation
and the practice of real rule making. The point should be
made (repeatedly) that along with participation goes
responsibility.

3. Activity & materials

Why Rules, Can They be Changed?[8] (participating in
establishing rules)

when: two or three periods

what: newspaper and magazine pictures

how: (1) Have children tell, write or draw:
If I could change the school, I would _____.
Discuss with class.

(2) Have children act out illustrations of people
following or breaking rules.

(3) Compare and contrast pictures of people at home,
school, in community who are following rules.

(4) Take a field trip to find examples of rules for all people, i.e., traffic light, no parking sign, no smoking sign.

V. INTEREST FORM

You have just completed the Chapter Second Grade and in an effort
to have you identify activities and materials that seem most
promising at this grade level to you, please fill out the following
interest form.

Instruction:

Identify two activities from this chapter. Name the activities
and briefly describe why these particular activities are of
interest to you.

ACTIVITY 1

ACTIVITY 2

58

NOTES

CHAPTER THIRD GRADE

ACTIVITIES AND MATERIALS FOR THIRD GRADE

CHAPTER THIRD GRADE

I. Advanced Organizer

Each succeeding chapter represents a particular grade level, in this
case third grade. Each chapter consists of four parts and this is why the
introduction is called an "advanced organizer." In other words you ought
to know before reading this chapter how it is organized for such knowledge
can help you to remember the major parts. The four parts are: part I is a
brief discussion on courses, topics and national trends in teaching third
grade throughout the United States. The second part is an example of a state
third grade program. The third part is activities and materials for the third
grade categorized by the four purposes of teaching social studies: knowledge,
processing, valuing, and participation. The fourth part of the chapter in an
interest form.

II. Topics Taught and National Trends
in Teaching Third Grade[1]

Courses, Topics, and Themes
most Frequently Covered in Third Grade

"Living in the Community"

Objectives of the course: The continued development of the concept of interdependence with emphasis on an indepth examination of the community. That
indepth treatment includes local history of the community and government with
special emphasis upon how the community delivers services such as water, power,
and waste disposal. Along with this indepth study is the continued emphasis
upon current events, the development of geographic skills and concepts, and
the stressing of a constructive civic attitude through responsible decision-
making.

Basic content of the course: Food, clothing, shelter, communication, transportation, government in the community; how education is provided in the community; and how the community grew (local history). A typical third grade
teaching guide might include the following units:

    Man's dwellings (influence of geography, customs: materials,
            tools, and workers involved; buildings of early settlers
            and Indians; how children can take care of the home and
            help at home)

    Where we get our foods (from plants and animals; from different
            geographic areas; workers who produce, transport, and

process food; food-getting today and long ago)

Clothing materials (materials from plants and animals, and
from man-made fibers; different geographic areas that
produce different raw materials for clothing; the
many people who work to provide clothing--the workers
and their interdependence; producing clothing long ago
and today)

Responsible civic citizenship (emphasis is upon decision-
making with reminders that responsibility is an
obligation that goes with making decisions. Participation
in decision-making is intended to encourage the attitude
of cooperation and constructive civic-mindedness)

Our city, past and present (local history which examines
why the community was created, why the community
has persisted, were there native Americans living on
the community site first, how has the community
changed through the years, what do you suppose the future
of the community to be)

Ways of travel (transportation used within the community and to
take goods and people out of the community; transportation
workers; travel today compared with pioneer days)

Keeping in touch with you (CB radio, postal service,
telephone, radio, movies, television, newspapers, books,
magazines).

Third Grade Course, Topic
and Themes for Advanced Students
"Comparative Study of Communities"

Objectives of the course: Similar to those cited for "Living in Our Community" but with emphasis on comparative study of how people meet basic life
needs. This course develops a global studies view by comparing communities
in other cultures as well as in other regions of the United States with the
child's community. The primary objective is to broaden the child's concept
of community in a world of many different communities.

Basic content of the course: The comparative study of communities course
usually has a beginning unit on a community familiar to the child, followed
by community studies in different regions of the United States. Additional
units emphasize communities around the world. These units of study usually

center on geographic factors, technology, cultural traditions, and in recent years upon the interdependence on earth of all peoples and communities upon each other.

Trends in Teaching Third Grade Social Studies

1. The strong trend is toward comparative studies. However, what is new in recent years is the increasing attention to basic social science concepts as these concepts are applied to the study of community life. For example, a portion of the elementary social studies texts are organizing their comparative content on such basic social science concepts as among others interdependence, scarcity, environmental adjustment, and social control. This is an important trend to note because it illustrates a recent tendency to move topics from higher grades to lower grade levels. Content and concepts are becoming more pronounced in kindergarten through third grade with the advent of the new social science elementary materials.

2. There is little question that third grade materials are aimed not only at comparative studies but at higher levels of thinking such as analysis, synthesis, and evaluation with the goal of preparing students for decision-making.

3. Some of the more recent curriculum materials for third grade include units such as: Primitives of Africa, Peoples of the Hot Dry Lands, The Boat People of Hong Kong, The People of Switzerland. What is particularly noteworthy about these units are the questions that students are expected to answer about each of the comparative communities: How do these people provide their basic needs? What rules govern the family? How do the people educate their children? What traditions do they pass on to their children? What evidences of change are there? The study of foreign cultures is no longer the traditional study of land forms and exports, the emphasis in on people and life styles.

4. As in grades one and two the trend is toward systematic instruction in geographic concepts and emphasis upon current events as a regular part of any social studies instruction, because current events are a reflection of the past but put into contemporary times making the past and present relevant.

III. Illustration of a State
Third Grade Program

There is no one prescribed social studies program throughout the United States. However, one state's description of its third grade program

will illustrate the content which the state expects to be taught. This
illustration is included so that you can identify how a state mandates the
teaching of social studies in the third grade.

> Children examine how different communities around
> the world develop based on environmental, cultural and tech-
> nological factors. They study similarities and differences
> in cultures and how contact between cultures often brings
> about changes in social institutions. The present condition
> of people is an outgrowth of the way human and natural re-
> sources are developed. All skill development is continued.
> The state may be studied within these contexts. Students
> read about people who specialize and contribute to society
> in a unique way by developing their own potential to the
> fullest.[2]

IV.   Activities and Materials Categorized by Knowledge, Processing, Valuing, and Participation

I realize a rather common practice is to skip purposes and
specific objectives which precede the activities, but in this case the objectives are extremely important for an objective in the third grade will be
found in proceeding grades. This is a developmental program with objectives,
activities, and materials organized to build from one grade level to another.

THIRD GRADE ACTIVITIES AND MATERIALS

I.   Purpose: Gaining knowledge about the human condition which includes
past, present, and future.

> Specific objective: Identify how weather and surroundings
> effect (change) what we eat and wear and how we live.
>
> 1. Activity & materials
>
> > Keeping the Weather   (gathering and gaining Knowledge
> > about environment)
>
> when: recurring
>
> what: outdoor thermometer, weather chart for graphing
>
> how: keep a temperature chart for each month. Have
> children check temperature each day at a set time
> (when school starts or after lunch), record it on
> a chart. Once a week have two or three children
> illustrate what clothes we should wear and what
> activities are going on (boots, shovel snow).
> Attach illustrations to chart.
> Alternative: give each child a big calendar to
> record temperature, special activities, seasons,

special events.

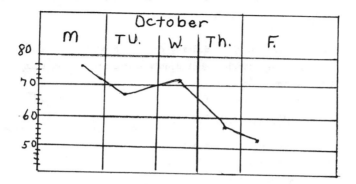

Specific objective: Identify different types of climate
and ways of living in those climates.

2. Activity & materials

<u>Climate Center Activities</u> (gathering and gaining knowledge
about environment)

when: two or three weeks

what: art supplies, scraps, resource materials, clay

how: the activities listed below are designed to encourage
children to think about the relationship between climate
and different ways of living. One's environment has a
direct personal affect upon the child's daily life.

1. Teacher prepares cards giving climate
conditions. Child picks card and makes
picture, diorama, using whatever materials are
available.

2. Children make collage of something "wrong"
with climate (snowsuits in summer, swim suits
in snow).

3. Children study pictures and see what can be
observed about climate by looking at landscape,
people, in pictures.

4. Papier mache (newspapers soaked in paste of
equal parts flour and water) sculpure of landscape scene can be molded, allowed to dry and
painted. Clay landscape scene.

5. Paper dolls dressed for climates around the
world.

Specific objective: Identify causes of pollution (air,
water, noise, etc.) in children's community and what is
being done about it.

3. Activity & materials

Gathering Your Own Trash (gathering and gaining
knowledge about environment)

when: two or three periods

what: art supplies, gallon containers (ice cream store might
supply these free)

how: clean and dry containers. Have each child decorate a
container to take home to use as wastebasket. Spray
completed container with commercial fixative to protect
decoration.

4. Activity & materials

Learning to Conserve Your Environment (gathering and
gaining knowledge
about environment)

when: one period

what: two shallow boxes or flats obtained (usually free)
from a nursery.

how: line boxes or flats with aluminum foil so water cannot
leak through the holes. Fill with soil, using finger
or pencil make furrows in dirt in one flat crosswise,
in other flat lengthwise. Cut one end of each flat in a
▼ shape.

Tip flats on a slant and water slowly with sprinkling can.
Which flat lets most water run off quickest?
Discuss how contouring is important to farmers in
conserving rain water for their crops. The point of this
activity is that by learning to work with our environment
we can conserve it, but first we must learn how nature
works.

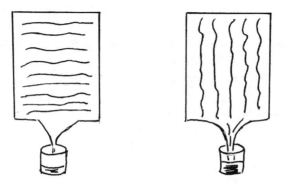

5. Activity & materials

   Action to Take (gathering and gaining
                    knowledge about environment)

when: two or three weeks

what: pictures, tape recorder, camera

how: identify problems by taking a walk around neighbor-
      hood and school, watching work at home, taping noises
      in school and out, inviting older person to discuss
      pollution, visit sewage treatment plant.
      Action: Children make personal decisions, i.e. I will
      clean my table after lunch, use only returnable bottles.
      Take picture of pollution conditions in community,
      and talk to officials who are responsible for this and
      discuss solutions.
      Other activites to examine the effect of man on the
      environment:
      noise: using tape of noises made earlier, have one
      group of children read under normal conditions and
      have other group read while tape of noises is being
      played. Which group was able to read the best?
      auto exhaust: must be done with teacher. Put a few
      earthworms and beetles in a plastic bag and hold it
      over the exhaust pipe of a car while the motor is
      running. When bag is full, tie it closed. Watch effect
      of exhaust on bugs. What did you think would happen?
      What actually did happen? Try first with leaded gas

and then with unleaded gas, was there any difference?

Specific objective: Learning about work performed by
community members.

6. Activity & materials

Interviewing (identifying different types of work)

when: two or three periods

what: tape recorder, cassettes

how: interview different workers. This may be done by
inviting people to the classroom (principal, nurse)
or by making an appointment to interview them in
their office (maybe after school). Help children
prepare questions to use in interview such as:
What kind of work do you do?
Did you need special training?
How does work help community?
When you were little did you plan to be what you are today?
How did you get this job?
If you had a chance would you choose this type of work again?

7. Activity & materials

Workers and Jobs (identifying different types of work)

when: two or three periods

what: chart for workers and jobs

how: chart workers and their jobs using people
children know or people they have interviewed or
people they make up.
Do certain jobs seem to be for only men or women?
Does it have to be that way? Why or why not?

Worker	Job	What is made	What is done for someone
Dr. Smith	doctor		keeps people healthy
Mr. Olsen	baker	breads, cakes	provides food
Mr. Phillips	Pres. of power co.	electric power	power to run labor saving devices
Mrs. Jones	bus driver		helps children get to school and home
Miss Jacks	bank president	loans	a place to keep money and to borrow money

8. Activity & materials

Workers and Job Fair (identifying different types of work)

when: two periods to plan, day for "fair"

what: booths

how: hold a "Workers and Job Fair". Invite parents and
community members to come to school and man a booth
to tell about their job, including training they need,
products or services they provide. Children should
visit as many booths as time allows using a "job
interview card".

After fair is over children can draw pictures or
tell about work they would like to do when older.
This is a good activity for several classes to do
together.

Job Interview Card

Occupation_____

Training_____

Will the job be available in the future when I grow up?_____

_____

Specific objective: Learning to identify criteria
for good work habits.

9. Activity & materials

How Do We Do? (identifying good work in school,
gaining knowledge about oneself)

when: recurring

what: bulletin board, children self-portraits

how: place bulletin board on section of wall accessible to
children. Put the title at top "How Do We Do?". Post
five self-portraits of children and underneath each
portrait put writing paper. During the week any class
member can write any positive statement about the work
done by one of the five children under that child's
portrait: "Barbara colors good pictures." "Jim read
well today." Each week teacher posts new portraits.

Start with five children who are easy to complement,
then as children understand procedure, mix less successful students in among other more popular ones.
At times it is difficult to identify those things that
we do from day to day that tend to make us successful at
a task. Sometimes we just don't stop to think about those
things that work for us. Sometimes we see only the negative.
Occasionally we may need others to point out what went right.
This may help us to identify and repeat good work habits.

10. Activity & materials
Letters (identifying good work in school,
gaining knowledge about oneself)

when: recurring

what: stationery, envelopes, box containing children's
names (each name printed on a separate card).

how: child reaches into box and pulls out a child's
name, uses stationery to write a note complementing
that child on some job or thing he has done well.
Do not replace name in box until all cards have been
used.
This type of activity tends to strengthen our concept
of self by pointing out those things which went right.
"Letters" may help us to identify and repeat good
work habits. In a sense we gain knowledge about
oneself.

II. Purpose: Identifying skills necessary to process information.
Specific objective: Using map key to interpret and read maps.
1. Activity & materials
Salt Maps (developing map skills)

when: two or three periods

what: salt mixture (1 cup flour, 1 cup salt, ½ cup water)

how: discuss topography in class using whatever
resource materials are avaiable.
Have groups or each child individually make a salt
map.
Discuss how others can read map and have children

make a key for map.

2. Activity & materials

    Mapping our Classroom (developing map skills)

when: one period

what: construction paper, paste

how: give each child a 9" X 12" piece of construction
paper on which to map the classroom. Children
decide on symbols, cut them out of scrap paper and
paste onto map, include key.
Be sure children try all items (symbols) before they
paste to make sure they fit.

Specific objective: Locating areas and places on maps
and globes.

3. Activity & materials

    Working with Maps (developing map skills)

when: two or three weeks

what: post world map so that it is accessible to children

how: 1. Each child makes a flag with his/her name one it
and pins it to location where he/she was born. Children
place markers on places they have lived or visted and
make paper planes to place on oceans they have crossed.
Place gold stars on capitals of countries. Locate item
on globe that you have labeled on map.
2. Outline continents in yarn using a different color
for each continent. Make a key for this. Have children
pick continent for imaginery trip. Have them tell or
write what cities they would visit and what countries
and oceans they would travel over to get there.
3. Divide children into groups. Each group lines up
flat on floor so that the line of their bodies forms a
continent. Class guesses what continent it is.

4. Activity & materials
   Using a Key (developing map skills)

when: one period

what: ditto of an imaginary place prepared by teacher
including key which includes countries, oceans,
capitals, continents.

how: have children locate areas marked by key on map
and name them. Children can make up imaginary
place maps of their own using their own key or
that of teacher.

5. Activity & materials
   Name Game (developing map skills)

when: one period per game

what: maps or globes as aids

how: 1. first child says place name such as "Indiana".
Second child must say a place that begins with the
last letter "a" of the name said before. "Arkansas".
Third child then finds place that begins with "s"
"Syracuse". If child cannot find name he/she is out.
Last person out is winner. Could also be played with
teams.
2. Have one child leave room. Class picks country,
city, etc. Child returns and tries to guess place by
asking twenty questions that can only be answered by
yes or no. Is it small? Is it water? If not successful
in guessing, then another child becomes it.

Specific objective: Learning to use cardinal (north,
south, east, west) and intermediate (northeast, northwest,
southeast, southwest) directions.

6. Activity & materials
   Directions (developing map skills)

when: four or five periods

what: sunny day

how: pick a sunny day and take children outside early and
line them up facing north. The sun should be on their

right (east). Repeat at noon (sun-overhead)
and as late as possible in afternoon (sun on left-
west). After each trip return to classroom and label
direction on correct wall.
Pick a starting point in room and give child oral
directions: thirteen steps north, four east.
Where did child end up (art center, etc.)?
Prepare cards that give child starting point and
directions. Did child end up on correct spot?
May begin to use intermediate directions (five
steps southwest).
Set up small community map and have children follow
directions (using hot wheel or matchbox cars brought
from home) to drive to location.

7. Activity & materials
Treasure Hunt (developing map skills)

when: one or two periods

what: cards written by teacher with instructions using
cardinal and intermediate directions, possible treat

how: divide children into groups and give each group a
card. Have them follow treasure hunt directions on
cards.
Children could plan own treasure hunts using directions.

```
+--------------------------------+
| Treasure   Hunt                |
| 10 steps   S                   |
|  4 steps   E                   |
|  2 steps   N W                 |
|  5 steps   N                   |
|  7 steps   W                   |
+--------------------------------+
```

8. Activity & materials
Footprints Up the Wall (developing map skills)

when: two periods

what: construction paper

how: have children trace around feet on construction paper

and cut out footprints. Have children print directions
on each footprint and place in a traveling pattern around
room even on walls.

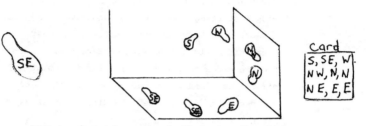

Have teacher make up cards that give directions
which children then follow laying out a new printed
cutout footprint every two feet. As a reinforcement
have each child walk his/her footprints giving directions
as he/she goes.

9. Activity & materials
     Graphing (developing graphing skills)
when: one or two periods
what: ditto a graph (one inch squares)
how: give each child a ditto and have him/her plan a city
       including things specified by teacher (hospital,
       lake, airport, hills). Children place items on
       graph as they wish along with symbols. Include
       symbols in map key on bottom of graph.
       After children learn to graph, they plan a city
       on a grid. Have them make key and tell area
       where things are located.

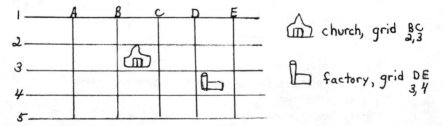

III. Purpose: Developing the skill to examine values and beliefs. Many
judgments call for values and beliefs first. For example. 1) ranking, and
2) identifying advantages and disadvantages and 3) examining similarities and
differences imply a set of values.

    Specific objective: Learning to rank based upon a set of
criteria.

1. Activity & materials

    Ranking Jobs   (the skill of ranking)

when: two periods

what: ditto made by teacher listing ten jobs in ten boxes

how: discuss with class a criteria for establishing the
      desirability of a job, i.e., What must a job provide
      me with? Such a criteria might be: 1) working hours,
      2) money, 3) job satisfaction, 4) location of job, 5)
      working conditions, 6) others. Give each child a ditto
      and have them cut out boxes. Have each child individually
      arrange boxes in row from most desirable job on left to
      least desirable job on right in order of preference.
      Tally class results. Discuss results with class. If
      group disagrees on two lowest or two highest ranks, ask
      children for reasons.

Specific objective: Identifying "advantages" and "disadvantages."

2. Activity & materials

    Keeping a Record   (advantages and disadvantages)

when: two or three weeks

what: resource materials

how: have each child pick a community to study.
      Child keeps a diary as he/she does research on the
      community recording:

          1. Things I like in this community.

          2. Things I do not like in this community.

Specific objective: Identifying similarities and differences
in all communities.

3. Activity & materials

    Finding New Friends   (identifying foreign communities)

when: .recurring.

what: letters, art work

how: teacher can write to a minister of education in a foreign
country to secure name and address of school with which
the children can exchange letters. Have children exchange
letters and art work that shows what each community is
like. Look for similarities and differences.
Invite foreign exchange students enrolled in local
high schools to visit the class to talk about their
countries. The foreign student can be helpful by
identifying schools to write. Also American exchange
students who have returned to school are an important
source.

Specific objective: Identify how values affect solution to
personal social problems.

4. Activity & materials

    <u>Watches</u> (developing the skill to identify values)

when: one period

what: story told by teacher, for example:
Cindy and Jack are brother and sister. Cindy is in
the fourth grade, and Jack is in second grade. For
Christmas their grandparents gave them each a watch.
The grandparents wanted to be fair so the watches
were identical. Cindy put her watch on after she
opened the gift. Jack who hadn't learned to tell
time put his back in the box but left the box on
the floor. While cleaning up the Christmas wrappings
Cindy accidently picked up Jack's watch box thinking
it was her empty one and threw it out in the trash.
Who should get the watch that is left? Cindy threw
Jack's watch away, but Jack left his watch on the floor.

how: Teacher now stimulates discussion that leads to moral
development. Encourage disagreement in children's choices.
If most feel Cindy should keep her watch, teacher could
ask: Couldn't Cindy have been more careful about what she
threw away? Cindy should have looked in watch box to make sure
it was empty, shouldn't she?

If most think Jack should get the watch, teacher
could ask: Shouldn't Jack have put the watch somewhere
safe like on a table? Shouldn't he have checked what
his sister was throwing out?

Teacher should make children stick to problem and not
choose easy solutions like getting another new watch.
Have children role play by pretending they are either
Cindy or Jack and giving reasons why they should have
the watch, then reverse roles. Look for compromises.
Valid compromises (sharing watch) should be treated as
moral choices. When class reaches agreement on what
should be done have them pick best reasons to support
their view.

Once children have expressed their preference for a
solution, the teacher's responsibility is to encourage
valuing by asking "What are your beliefs (values) that
are the basis of your solution?" In other words the
teacher will want the children to identify (go beyond
their reasoning) what they value. In this case their
values may be rooted in concepts of honesty or fairness
or perhaps the Golden Rule (Do Unto Others...). The
point is that we have opinions and reasons that are
usually rooted in value. A step in the process of moral
development is that we identify and evaluate our values,
for our judgments are based on our values.

5. Activity & materials

   Valuing the Feelings of Others (developing the skill
                                    to identify values)

when: one period

what: the situation: often children are in conflict with each
       other in class. Sometimes the conflicts become so marked
       that a child or children are isolated by their peers. The
       usual reaction is that the teacher intervenes by attempting
       to modify the situation and this may mean modifying both
       the isolates and the dominant group. The following
       technique is one promising way to intervene.

how: establish a Socratic small group

purpose: to bring students and instructor together
to discuss a problem posed by the teacher for which an
answer can best be determined through the open and
honest exchange of informed opinion.

guidelines: begins in stage 1 with teacher encouraging
free and uninhibited discussion of the problems children
identify and their feelings about those problems. For
example the teacher asks "How do you act that encourages
people to respect you?" "Are there things that classmates
do that you don't like?" "Have you ever been in conflict
with a classmate?"

In stage 2 the teacher does a lot of good hard listening,
then becomes a leader and participant by probing, stimulating, challenging, synthesizing. For example the
teacher might ask these questions in the second stage:
"Can you think of reasons why you behave in a way that
puts you in conflict with others?" "How does it feel to
be in conflict?" "Suppose you wish to act differently,
could you?" "What would be some of the different ways you
could act?" "Are there people who could help you."

This activity "Valuing the Feelings of Others" should
help the children to examine their behavior, increasing
some children's ability to control themselves and help
others identify the problems and feelings of others.

IV. Purpose: The application of knowledge through active participation
in society.

Specific objective: Identify problems of communities and cities.

1. Activity & materials

Plan a City (participate in the process of decision-making)

when: two or three weeks

what: large board, carton, boxes, art materials, film strip.

how: show film strip showing a city, discuss what makes a
city establishing categories such as homes, stores,
schools, services, parks, industry. Assign groups to
make things for each category. Prepare board by pinning on
pieces of torn construction paper. The torn paper re-

presents trees and the whole board represents unsettled
territory. Class must now settle area using categories
decided upon previously. Children must think seriously
about what type of community they are building (fishing,
seaport, lumber, industry, farm community). They must
realize that removed trees are gone forever. Children
should see some need for organization as groups compete
to place their categories. They may need to elect mayor
or planning commission to approve roads, buildings, etc.
Discuss how community grew. Did it remain small or
become a city with suburbs? Do some communities remain
small? Why?

After children work for a short time teacher should
start to hurry them by saying "We need a hospital, a
baby is about to be born." We need a bakery, shoe store,
etc. The idea is to rush children so they don't have
time to plan where things go and the city grows hap-
hazardly (the way most cities grow).

Have children examine city and list good and bad features.
Suggest ways to improve city.

Plan a new city without hurrying--use blocks for buildings
so that children can experiment by moving them around.
When good working model has been established make map by
tracing around blocks and drawing in streets and landscape.
Color it using an agreed upon color code. Attach key to
map and display it.

2. Activity & materials

Problems Right Here[3] (participating in the process of
                        decision-making)

when: three or four periods
what: newspaper articles on community problems.
how: after using strategy Plan A City (previous activity)
       try to discover and offer solutions to local problems.
       For example: (1) How would you redesign your own community?
       (2) Visit local library--look up any plans for community
       changes. (3) Our community needs a super highway, or sewage

treatment plant, or new hospital-where would we locate
it? Why or why not? (4) Check newspapers--bring in
articles about problems in the community. (5) At home,
have children take snapshots of smog, etc. or draw
illustrations. Share with the total class. Compare these
problems to other communities. Are they similar, different?
(6) Invite speakers such as civic association president,
chairman of retail associations, highway department leaders,
etc., to give opposing views to problems in local community.

Specific objective: Participate with others in deciding on
directions to be taken in improving community and then taking
action to do so.

3. Activity & materials

Social Action on Real Problems[4] (participating in acting
on problem)

when: three weeks at least

what: materials as below

how: have class identify a real community problem. A real
       problem means that the children actually recognize it as
       a problem to them. Remember that because the teacher
       announces something as a problem it does not necessarily
       mean that the children accept this as a problem. For
       example, many elementary teachers identify ecological
       problems, i.e., smog, noise, waste disposal including
       litter as community problems. However, it seems that
       studying a social problem does not necessarily enhance
       the children's personal awareness of that problem in their
       own lives. Problems which children might identify as
       real: being bullied by older students after school, no
       place to play after school, no bike lanes on the streets,
       a lot of trash and litter along the sides of streets and
       in vacant lots.
       Suppose the children decide to participate on the problem
       of rubbish on school property and in surrounding neighborhood.
       The class might elect to participate in a trash pickup by
       taking one period to walk about the school and school grounds
       collecting and properly disposing of trash. Even though the

class trash pickup temporarily helps, the point reeds
to be made that other activities need to follow that help
in maintaining a cleaner environment which apparently
the students value.

Possible actions:

1. Make posters to display in halls such as
    "Help Snoopy beat the trash problem" with a
    picture of snoopy trying to put trash in
    containers. Suggest trash containers be
    painted in bright colors.
2. Set up trash contests--award for class that
    collects most trash.
3. Award to cleanest classroom of the week, cleanest
    desk of the week.
4. Invite school custodian to class to talk about
    rubbish and give him recognition for his work in
    keeping school neat.
5. Invite someone from city sanitation department
    to speak to class about problem and what they can do
    to help.

Specific objective: Participating with teacher in changing
classroom procedures.

4. Activity & materials

    Contracts (creative participation)

when: recurring

what: dittos of contracts

how: teacher has conference with each child individually.
      They discuss what the child would be interested in
      trying. They can fill out a contract card.
      Often children express desires to try different ideas,
      new things, but those occasions may not happen if the
      teacher or parent does not allow for new interests.
      This is one way to stop the daily routines and provide
      time for reflection. The contract is a means of
      stimulating the child to try different ideas. Of course,
      the contract could also be used to increase the children's
      attention to those areas in which they need to improve.

Contract date_____

I agree to_____

_____

_____
student's name

_____
teacher's signature

Suggestions for contract: to attend a play, to try a hand
at carving, to take some time for special reading, to leave
home a little earlier in morning, to take an interesting trip.
Both teacher and student should have a copy of contract.

Making Things

The formula for making salt maps was offered in Activity 1 under
Processing. Several additional recipes on creating "inexpensive" playdough
are:

Salt Clay: 1 cup salt

½ cup cornstarch

3/4 cup water

food coloring if desired

1. Put the salt and cornstarch in top of double boiler and place
   over boiling water.
2. Add water slowly, stirring constantly.
3. When the mixture has thickened (i.e. difficult to stir) spoon
   onto a cookie sheet to cool.
4. When completely cool, knead to remove lumps and air bubbles.
   Store in an air-tight container as air will harden the mixture.

Craft Clay: 1 cup cornstarch

2 cups baking soda

1½ cups water

food coloring if desired

1. Combine all ingredients in a pan or pot.
2. Cook over medium heat stirring constantly.
3. Turn out on a pastry board and knead slightly.
4. Cover with a damp cloth until cool to keep it from hardening.

V.   INTEREST FORM

You have just completed the Chapter Third Grade and in
an effort to have you identify activities and materials
that seem most promising at this grade level to you,
please fill out the following interest form.

Instruction:

Identify two activities from this chapter. Name the activities
and briefly describe why these particular activities are of interest
to you.

ACTIVITY 1

ACTIVITY 2

CLARIFICATION AND SUMMARY OF SOCIAL
STUDIES CURRICULUM DEVELOPMENT
KINDERGARTEN THROUGH THIRD GRADE

This is the appropriate time to take a break between grade
levels for the purpose of clarifying and summarizing the major points discussed over the last three chapters. The suggestion was made in Chapter 1 that
it is not at all unusual for elementary teachers and for that matter those
who are specially hired to teach the social studies program not to know what
that program is. Yes, they know of courses taught a grade behind and perhaps
a grade ahead but they do not know of the total program. It is no small wonder then that teachers in the primary grades are reluctant to teach social
studies content which in many cases is not specially identified as a testable
part of the primary program. To put matters simply, the primary teachers are
not particularly held responsible for the content of their social studies
program.

Hopefully, having read through the courses trends, activities,
and materials in the last three chapters, you have identified why it is important that there be a primary social studies program. Imagine the severe
limitations that a fourth grade teacher would face if the students had no
background in current events, comparative studies, or geographic skills.
Suppose further the students lacked any acquaintance with a concept such as
interdependence or had never been exposed to themes such as identifying the
self and the relationships between home, school, neighborhood and community.
A good many primary teachers might react to some of the activities materials
by saying "Yes, I recognize some of those activities and in fact use a few of
them already, it's just that I never thought of them as being social studies.
I never really thought that the study of self or of the school as being part
of a social studies program. I never really thought of social studies as an
integration of the social experiences of the children. I always thought
social studies had to do with history and geography." Well, now you know that
social studies is an integration of life experiences with the goal of citizenship education, and further you know that the goal is achieved through the
purposes of gaining knowledge, processing information, valuing, and participation. Surely those four purposes need to be taught systematically kindergarten
through the twelfth grade for the expectation is that as citizens our students
having graduated ought to be effective decision-makers.

Up through the third grade the notion of a "spiraling expanding horizon" where we start with the self and methodically work through the child's relationship with each new part of his environment probably makes reasonable sense to most teachers for this pattern has persisted over the years, even though there have been concerted efforts at revision. After all, some educational authorities say that children's environments do not expand in neat concentric circles, and in fact the contemporary child with travel, TV, and increased exposure to a number of alternative life styles is able at an earlier age to be more national and global minded. Therefore, topics which were traditionally taught in upper elementary are now appearing more frequently in the primary grades. Without question the social studies texts for first through third grade have increasingly emphasized the integration of basic social science concepts and comparative studies between American and foreign cultures. All things being equal, this trend will carry into the 21st Century.

Even though there may not be complete agreement there is at least a consensus about what social studies ought to be taught in the primary grades. So in a sense, it is relatively easy to imagine the spiraling expanding horizon but that concensus does not continue to hold after the third grade. You will find in the fourth, fifth, and sixth grades a wide variety of different courses. Up through the third grade the student is being prepared to spiral off into a number of directions. Having completed an indepth study of one's own community with comparisons of other communities both in and outside the United States, the curriculum could logically spiral to a regional study of cultures throughout the world or could stay closer to home to emphasize state and regional studies. In other words the neat, clean progression personal expanding horizons of the primary grades no longer dictates particular topics and themes. The social studies curriculum beyond the third grade resembles a branch with many leaves, with only the state legislature or some state department of public instruction determining the proper order of the leaves.

NOTES

CHAPTER FOURTH GRADE

ACTIVITIES AND MATERIALS FOR FOURTH GRADE

CHAPTER FOURTH GRADE

I. Advanced Organizer

Each succeeding chapter represents a particular grade level,
in this case fourth grade. Each chapter consists of four parts and this is
why the introduction is called "advanced organizer." In other words you ought
to know before reading this chapter how it is organized for such knowledge
can help you to remember the major parts. The four parts are: part I is a
brief discussion on courses, topics and national trends in teaching fourth
grade throughout the United States. The second part is an example of a state
fourth grade program. The third part is activities and materials for the
fourth grade categorized by the four purposes of teaching social studies;
knowledge, processing, valuing, and participation. The fourth part of the
chapter is an interest form.

II. Topics Taught and National Trends in Teaching Fourth Grade[1]

Fourth grade social studies usually follows one of these
three courses: state and United States history, state and communities around
the world, or communities around the world. If you recall, the third grade
curriculum, the children have studied their own community in depth and have
compared that community with other communities including pioneer communities,
other communities in the United States, and some selected communities around
the world. The children supposedly enter the fourth grade with graphing,
mapping, and map interpretation skills and have studied the interrelationship
between climate, homes, neighborhood, and communities, and finally they have
a basic mastery of the four purposes: gaining knowledge, processing information, valuing, and participation.

With this foundation a social studies curriculum can logically
spiral in a number of directions. The student is ready to move on to a study
of the state and from the state to the nation. Or the student could proceed
to study the state as a region, and then compare it to other selected regions
around the world (people of the state of Indiana and the Midwest region in
contrast with the peoples of Nova Scotia and the people of Mysore State, India).
Or students could just as well be launched into a study of the interdependence
of people and places throughout the world with emphasis upon Africa, the Middle
East, Southeast Asia, and Asia. No one pattern of courses seems to absolutely
dominate the teaching of fourth grade social studies in the United States. It

is not unusual for one state to mandate the teaching of its state history at the seventh grade level while preferring to teach global studies in the fourth grade. In another state the reverse may be true. What is of importance at this moment is not the dwelling upon disagreement over what ought to be taught but rather noting what is taught and in consequence, being prepared with activities and materials which will help you to be flexible enough to teach any one of the three curriculums.

Courses, Topics, and Themes
most Frequently Covered in Fourth Grade
"State and United States History"

Objectives of the course: Introducing the child to his home state with special emphasis upon geography, history, and government and stressing the events, places, and people important in the establishment of the state. Usually state history is taught in this course as it directly relates to the development of the United States as a country so that state and national history will tend to flow together to tell the story of how the country has grown and changed. A state objective might sound something like this: examine the state's physical geography and relative geographic position, where the people live and why, how people lived in the past, and the present as part of the regional and national community.

Basic content of the course: Authors of state history at the fourth grade level will often stress that "history content is to be enjoyed," that the study of heritage will help students to develop a better understanding and appreciation of who they are as the new generation of citizens of the state. To develop that understanding and appreciation the following are illustrations of typical topics: Our State, a Place on the Map; How the Ancient Indians Lived on our Land; The White Man Comes to America, Our State and the American Revolution; Indian Wars and Early Settlements; Trails and Rivers, Roads and Canals; Our State in the Civil War; People in Government; Our State's Environment. Also within the state history book there is an attempt to show how the state was affected by national issues with such topics as the French and British Fight for the New World, The Black Man Comes to America, The Fight to be Equal. In other words American history is not taught as a separate course but only as it relates to specific important events in the state's history. American history when taught as part of the state history is usually intended to prepare students for the formal study of American history in fifth grade.

Courses, Topics, and Themes
most Frequently Covered in Fourth Grade
"State and Regions Around the World"

Objectives of the course: The course is intended to provide systematic instruction in geographic concepts and skills with emphasis on the influence of
geographic and cultural factors on the ways people meet needs: work, shelter,
food, clothing, transportation. Though the course focuses on state and other
regions around the world, it is intended to provide an overview of world geography.

Basic content of the course: Keep in mind when thinking about this course
that the emphasis is upon certain basic life processes. The regions are studied to show how these basic life processes are viewed from different cultures.
The effort is made not to isolate and study each region separately but rather
to show how each region deals with a particular process: work, food, transportation, etc. Typical units on the combined state-world regions approach
are: An Interdependent World, A World of Different Regions (essentially a
map skills study), People at Work, World of Buyers and Sellers, Transportation,
Cities, and Their People, Cities around the World. Though the unit headings
suggest the broad outlines of a region study, to identify the essence of regional studies it would be useful to look at what would be covered in one of
the units. For example the unit Cities Around the World might well include:
Chicago, Illinois; Rotterdam, The Netherlands; Osaka, Japan; and Nairobi,
Kenya, with emphasis on such topics as transportation, manufacturing, trade,
shipping, port cities grow and change, and how the cities were made.

Courses, Topics, and Themes
most Frequently Covered in Fourth Grade
"Regions Around the World"

Objectives of the course: As in the case of the preceding course the intent
is to provide systematic instruction in geographic concepts and skills with
emphasis on the influence of geographic and cultural factors on the ways people
meet needs connected with basic life processes: work, food, clothing, shelter,
recreation, transportation. This course, though it focuses in depth upon a
few regions around the world, is expected to give an overview of world geography. As distinct from the other two courses, the objective of this course
is to focus exclusively on cultures outside the United States and in some cases
exclusively on non-Western cultures.

Basic content of the course: The content of this course is usually designed
to show sharp contrasts between the students' life style and those of other

cultures, but that "the aspirations of all people have much in common." Very
often contrasting cultures are chosen to demonstrate the influence of environment, custom, traditions in under-developed countries and the effect technology
can have on the lives of people. For example typical units might sound like
this: The World and Maps, By a Fiord in Norway, On a Desert in Saudi Arabia,
In the Mountains in Ecuador; or The People of Mysore State, The People of
Osaka Prefecture, The People of Serbia, The Peoples of Nova Scotia.

Trends in Teaching Fourth Grade Social Studies

1. Of the three approaches "State and United States History," "State-World
Regions," and "Regions Around the World" the course "State-World Regions"
is becoming the most popular. This trend will undoubtedly continue. Teachers
view this approach as a compromise between the other two, that is being able to
link some of the fourth grade content directly to third grade, and yet provide
preparation for American history in the fifth grade.

2. Continued emphasis upon current events with special attention to world,
state and local affairs.

3. Increased attention to key social science concepts. In the first three
grades students learned such concepts as interdependence, differences, cultural change. In fourth grade such concepts as causality, tradition, social
control, institutions are being emphasized in some social studies texts.
Though both teachers and students are experiencing some problems with identifying these social science concepts, there remains a strong trend toward
using these concepts. The argument in favor of using these concepts is that
they lend substance (hard content) to the course.

4. The more traditional world culture materials tended to stress regions
within the western civilization: Norway, Holland, Greece, perhaps a Latin
American country. The most recent trend is away from western civilization to
reflect a more modern world affairs approach which focuses on part of the
non-western world: SubSahara Africa, Middle East, Asia.

III.   Illustrations of a State
Fourth Grade Program

There is no one prescribed social studies program throughout the United States. However, one state's description of its fourth grade
program will illustrate the content which the state expects to be taught.
This illustration is included so that you can identify how a state mandates
the teaching of social studies in the fourth grade.

The world as the home of humans provides opportunities
to compare and contrast how we live in our state, or within a
region of our state, and how people of other cultures and regions
live and how we are alike and different. Students examine how
different cultures and ethnic groups within our state influence
the ways in which similar geographic and environmental conditions
are utilized. Students note the ways in which human and natural
resource distribution affect people's life styles, and how peaceful
interaction among humans is related to social control amidst changing requirements and problems. Reading for context clues, map and
globe skills and social skills are all emphasized.[2]

IV. Activities and Materials Categorized
by Knowledge, Processing, Valuing, and Participation

I realize a rather common practice is to skip purposes and
specific objectives which precede the activities, but in this case the objectives are extremely important for an objective in the fourth grade will be
found in proceeding grades. This is a developmental program with objectives,
activities, and materials organized to build from one grade level to another.

FOURTH GRADE ACTIVITIES AND MATERIALS

I. Purpose: Gaining knowledge about the human condition which includes past,
present, and future.

Specific Objective: Gaining knowledge about the roles people play
in society.

1. Activity & materials

What's My Role   (identifying roles and practicing graphic
and interview skills)

when: three weeks

what: materials as needed for activity

how: 1) Divide students into groups. Have them discuss
and list activities, jobs (roles) they undertake in
a typical day. Have groups classify activities
under categories such as homes roles, school roles,
recreation, living, "just messing around".

Home roles: babysitting raking leaves making bed wash dishes deliver papers take out trash feed pet, walk dog	School roles: writing reading homework watch film take test

Recreation:
    play basketball
    TV
    ride bike
    sew
    read
    stamp collecting
	"Messing Around":
	    talking to friends
	    playing around
	    watch the world go by!
	Living:
	    eating
	    sleeping
	    bath, shower

Alternative: list categories on the board and have class as group fill in activities under each category.

Alternative: make a checklist of activities and have students check ones that apply to them.

> ☐   read
> ☐   TV
> ☐   feed pet
> ☐   deliver papers

2) Have students make a chart that shows how many hours each day on the average are devoted to each of the categories of activities.

3) Have students make a pie, bar, and line graph that shows their use of time.

Pie graph
(24 hours)

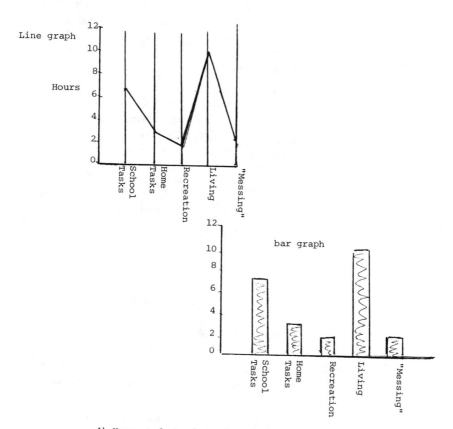

Line graph

Hours

School Tasks | Home Tasks | Recreation | Living | "Messing"

bar graph

School Tasks | Home Tasks | Recreation | Living | "Messing"

4) Have students interview adults (relatives, neighbor) to find out what kind of work role they had or have. Decide on questions students should ask at interview.

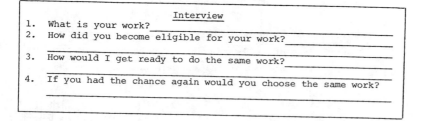

Interview

1. What is your work? _____

2. How did you become eligible for your work? _____

3. How would I get ready to do the same work? _____

4. If you had the chance again would you choose the same work? _____

2. Activity & materials

 Crafts from Pioneer Days (identifying work roles and
 skills of past cultures)

when: three or four periods

what: materials as needed for activity

how: have students choose pioneer crafts they would like
to try. They may spend several periods on one craft
or use each period for a different craft.

1) Cooking: make corn bread, gingerbread cookies, pumpkin bars.

2) Sewing: make a sampler out
of burlap. Use cardboard
bar from coat hanger (dry
cleaner type) to hang burlap.

Quilting Bee: sew cotton squares together and
attach to quilt backing.

3) Candle making: (Best to do with teacher or aide
supervision) Tie candle.wicks to narrow piece of wood.
Melt paraffin in deep pan (crayons add color) and dip
wicks in paraffin, let dry and dip again--repeat until
thickness wanted is obtained. Some parents may have
candle molds they would let class use.

4) Wig making: shape heavy paper to fit student's head like
a helmet. Cover paper with yarn or cotton glued to stay
put.

5) Printer: carve one side of styrofoam block, cover with
ink or paint and press on paper. May carve cut side of
potato sliced in half to use as printing block also.
Print design on edge of paper, use quill pen and ink to
fill in words; announce town meeting, ship sailing dates,
etc.

6) Weaver: wrap string or yarn about 21 times around a
stiff piece of cardboard. Use knitting needle or popsicle
stick with hole cut in end and yarn tied to it to use as a
shuttle. Cut strings at top and bottom and tie.

Alternative: have a colonial day where students
dress in colonial clothes, eat foods eaten in
colonial days and play colonial games or dance as
they did in colonial days.

Specific objective: Categorizing information about cultures.
3. Activity & materials

Student Groups and Clubs[3] (identifying youth roles in
present day society)

when: three periods

what:

how: 1) have students list groups or clubs they belong to:
Boy/Girl Scouts, Brownies/Cub Scout, choir (church)
band, team sports (swim, football, track, gymnastics,
volleyball, etc.) student council.
2) make a bulletin board of groups listing
qualification, goals, records, or achievements,
advantages of joining.
3) divide students into groups. Have groups invest
a club with rules for membership, an emblem, and goals.
They may make posters to encourage others to join.

Remember the purpose of this activity is to help students
to note that their membership in organizations includes
belonging to a grade and class in school. It is not unusual
for children to conceive of society as the "society page" in
the newspaper. This exercise should help students understand
that their role in society includes membership in family,
school, and organizations. In part to understand society is
understanding how one is bound to that society.

4. Activity & materials

Adult Groups and Clubs[4] (identifying adult roles in present
day society)

when: three periods

what: questionnaire

how: 1) have students decide on questions to be included on
an interview sheet. Questions should be about what

groups or clubs adults belong to. Interview parents or neighbors using questionnaire.

QUESTIONNAIRE

1. What is the name of organization?_____
2. What are the qualification for membership in this
   organization?_____
3. Suppose you were me would you join the organization?

   _____

---

2) discussion after interview: Do parents join groups for same reasons students do? Would you like to belong to any of the adult groups? Why or why not?

Have students draw emblems of youth and adult groups on board and let the other class members try to guess what club the emblem stands for.

3) make a bulletin board of adult <u>groups</u> under categories such as professional, social, political, recreational, civic, etc. Use art supplies to draw symbols to display with each <u>group</u>.

5. Activity & materials

<u>Suggest</u> a <u>Club</u> (identify characteristics of group roles)

when: one period

what: teacher prepared paragraphs describing cultures,
       but without naming cultures or countries.

how: have students read paragraphs and suggest groups
      or clubs that might be formed for those cultures.
      Would people in other cultures have the same reasons
      for joining clubs that students have?
      Sample paragraph:
      1. There is a country that is flat and low as sea
      level. The land is bisected with canals that are

used much like roads are used in other countries.
In winter the canals often freeze and people can skate
on them. They use windmills for power. The country
is known for its fine cheese and for a certain spring
flower. The bulb is exported so plants can be grown
elsewhere.

Suggestion on groups or clubs they might form: skating,
cheese maker, cooperative flower export association.

Sample paragraph:

2. There is a group of people who live in rural
communities in the east and midwest. Most of them
farm for a living. They use no modern or electrical
machinery, preferring a horse to pull a plow or pull the
buggy for any traveling (trips to town). The adults wear
mostly black. The men usually grow beards.

Suggestion on groups they might form: sewing, quilting
bees, preserving food, harvesting groups to help each
other, barn raisings.

The point is, of course, that membership in organizations
is based on where we live, what we do for a living, and
what our needs and interests are.

Specific objective: Identifying features of the environment
for the purpose of discriminating between similarities and
differences.

6. Activity & materials

Look Around You (practicing cataloging the environment)

when: one period (homework)

what: check list

how: have students look at features of their community and
record what they see.

____trees	____river	____fast food place
____flowers	____lake	____coffee house
____parks	____pool	____book store
____houses	____church	____drug store
____apartments	____school	____grocery store
____gas stations	____fire station	____ } students
		____ } own ideas

This activity is meant to call the students'
attention to the environment around them. It
is a cataloging exercise building toward identifying
similarities and differences.

7. Activity & materials

<u>Discriminating</u> <u>Between</u> <u>Environments</u> (identifying character-
istics of similarities
and differences)

when: two or three periods

what: sketches or pictures that fit activity
record form

how: 1) show students three sketches or pictures of natural
environment (pastoral scenes--woods, prairie, sea shore)
As students examine pictures have them begin to realize
that all three pictues have something in common. Have
students answer the questions in part I of Record Sheet.
(see below)

2) show students three more pictures, this time have
two pictures of man-made environment (Indian camp,
pioneer town, modern factory city) and one of natural
(pastoral) environment. Number the sketches 1, 2, 3.
Have students answer questions in part II of record sheet.

3) have students do part III of record sheet.

RECORD SHEET

I.

(1) Identify the similarities and differences in the three
pictures._____
_____

(2) What are the characteristics that describe the similarities
in the three pictures?_____
_____

II.   Which picture of the second set of pictures fits the
characteristics identified above?_____
_____

III.   Make your own picture using the characteristics identified
in parts I and II.

Specific objective: Identifying dilemmas in solving
personal social problems.

8. Activity & materials

Personal Social Problems (making decisions)

when: three or four periods

what: case studies and questions below

how: divide the class into groups and give a different
case study to each group. The group may role play
the case study and then act as a panel to ask the
audience selected questions. The group may role
play again using audience suggestions.

Alternative: entire class may read same case study
and discuss questions.

Case 1

My little brother does dumb things without
thinking and then gets in trouble. Last week his friends
dared him to throw a rock at a window, so he did. They
all ran but a man who came out of the house may have seen
my brother's face. My brother came running to where I
was playing football. He wanted me to say he had been
with me and my friends playing football all afternoon.
Promising he wouldn't do it again, he said he would do my
paper route for a week if I would lie for him. What am I
going to do?

Questions:

1. What are the facts?

2. What did little brother want from big brother?

3. Suppose you were the little brother what might
you have done about the broken window?

4. How would you feel about lying for someone else?

Case 2

I felt pretty good when I found the watch at
the bus stop. The strap was broken so it must have dropped
off of someone's wrist, but it was still running. I
figured I could keep it, sell it, or trade it for something
really neat. While I was waiting for the bus this strange

looking guy came by and was looking all around.
He muttered something about losing his watch and
asked if I had seen it or seen anyone pick it up.

Questions:

1. What are the facts?

2. What does the student want to do?

3. Suppose you found the watch, what might you
   have done with it.

4. How would you feel about keeping the watch?

Case 3

I was tagging along with a group of older
kids that I wanted to be friends with. On the way
home from school they sometimes stopped at a discount
drug store. They said it was easy to steal candy bars
and if I would talk to the clerk to keep his attention,
they would take the candy bars and get one for me. I
want to be friends with them. What should I do?

Questions:

1. What are the facts.

2. What do the older boys want the younger boy to do?

3. Suppose you were the younger boy, what might you do?

4. How would you feel about eating the stolen candy?

II. Purpose: Develop skills necessary to process information and to
work with others.

Specific objective: Students will process questions by
differentiating between open and closed.

1. Activity & materials

Questioning Skills   (identifying open and closed type
                      questions)

when: two days training and then as regular part of activities.

what: question preference form and class text books

how: questioning is a skill. Students can learn to ask
       good questions. Asking good questions is important
       to many of the activities found in teacher's guides--
       but rarely are students taught the skill. The

assumption is that students will learn from adults and peers through trial and error. Some do learn, some don't. There is a relationship between questions asked and creative behavior. For creativity both forms, open and closed are required. The usual practice in school is for texts and teachers to ask mostly closed questions. The higher the grade the more closed are the questions--so as the student proceeds through the grades less creativity is demanded. Learning about questions starts with identifying and then differentiating between open and closed type questions. Prepare a form that asks these questions. The form will help students identify their preference and strength of feeling for certain types of questions.

QUESTION PREFERENCE FORM						
I. Preference: for each group of questions below, tell which one you would most like to ask by placing a "1" in front of it, a "2" in front of the next, a "3" in front of the next, and a "4" in front of the question that you are least interested in.		II. Strength of Choice: After each of the questions below, circle how you feel about that question as follows: A=strongly like, B=like, C=neutral, D=dislike, E=strongly dislike.				

Teacher Key							
closed	___1.	Name the...	A	B	C	D	E
closed	___2.	Compare the...	A	B	C	D	E
open	___3.	Suppose the...	A	B	C	D	E
open	___4.	Why do you think...	A	B	C	D	E
closed	___1.	Why did the...	A	B	C	D	E
open	___2.	In your opinion...	A	B	C	D	E
closed	___3.	Describe...	A	B	C	D	E
open	___4.	What would happen...	A	B	C	D	E

After the students have finished marking the form discuss their preference and choice with them: identify each question as to whether it is open or

closed. The students will not know the difference at
this point, but in filling out the question-preference
form they may have marked one type of question over
the other. If students do prefer one type over
closed or vice versa, ask the students why?
Disclose the meaning of open and closed questions
and discuss this with the class.

In brief: Open questions are those that do not have
answers. Open questions require speculation such as
suppose and evaluation such as opinion. Examples:
Suppose you were Washington, what might you have done?
In your opinion was Washington a good president?

In brief: Closed questions have answers. Examples:
When did Washington become president?
Explain how he became president?
Identify the name of his home?
What was his wife's name?
What did he do that was important to the American Revolution?

Follow through activities:

a) have students look at the questions in back of
   their social studies and other text books. Have
   them classify questions as to open or closed.

b) on the social studies topic being studied ask
   students to write out at least two open questions
   and two closed questions.

c) when designing a test, written or oral, be sure
   to include both types.

Note: to help you continue using and developing this
skill the remainder of the activities in this book are
designed to illustrate the use of both open and closed
questions.

Specific objective: Identify scale of miles on maps and
globes and learn to locate places.

2. Activity & materials

Treasure Hunt (identifying geographic concept--
                direction)

when: one period

what:

how: tell students they are going to play a game of
       treasure hunt. Have one or two students leave the
       .room and while they are gone the .class decides on
       an object to be the treasure. Students are called back
       in and given clues by the class to tell them where the
       object is. Clues can only be given in terms of
       direction (north, south, east, west or front of room,
       back, door side) or in distance (i.e., four feet from
       teacher's desk). Class members give directions in
       turn until object is located. The object is to
       give such accurate clues that "it" students will
       not have to leave their chairs to locate treasure.

3. Activity & materials

    Working with Scales   (identifying geographic concept--
                           measurement and scale)

when: two or three days

what: paper, masking tape, yard stick, chalk, twist
       ties or pipe cleaners cut in four inch lengths.

how: desk: have students measure their desks with the four
       inch twist tie. Have them draw the exact size on a large
       piece of paper and cut it out.
       On a second piece of paper have students draw their desk,
       but first cut the twist tie in half. (drawing should be
       one half size of desk).
       Cut twist tie in half again and draw desk again.
       (drawing should be one-fourth size of desk).

       floor: mark the classroom floor in a yard square
       grid with chalk and then cover with masking tape
       to make it more permanent. Have students make a
       grid on paper with one inch to equal one yard
       (same number of squares as floor).
       Students can see where grid objects are on floor
       grid (desks, chairs, bookcases, etc.) and then draw
       them in the corresponding grid on their paper grids.

Specific objective: Learning to research for information
from a variety of sources, organize the information, and
report it.

4. Activity & materials

Research "Know How" (identifying historically important
persons, places and events, organizing
and reporting)

when: three or four weeks

what: materials as need for activity

how: 1) have students make a list of famous Americans
or people from the state. Teacher can list
names on the board and add others that the
students may not have thought of.

Names or events appropriate to early American history:	Names or events appropriate to state history:
Washington	explorer of territory
Jefferson	territorial governor
John Adams	Indians--local
Boston Tea Party	Transportation in a pioneer
etc.	state
	etc.

2) have students decide on the questions they wish
to answer in a report they will write on one of the
above names.

(1) Why is this person remembered?

(2) What were his/her major contributions?

(3) Suppose you had a chance to talk to this
person, what might you ask, what would
he/she answer?

(4) Do you still think this person should be
remembered?

3) have the librarian review with the students how
to use the card catalog to locate information on
the subject for their reports.

4) spend one period in the library for the students
to use the card catalog and check out books they
find that would help them in writing their reports.

They should be encouraged to use all types
of materials: books, encyclopedia, magazines,
records, tapes, filmstrips. A simple card
catalog form will help:

Film strip	Record	Tape	Magazine	Encyclopedia	Book	Information from Card Catalog		name		
						title	author publisher for filmstrips, records, tapes	page	mag.	issue

5) when students have selected book, they should
be encouraged to note the important information
about the book. The following information sheet
asks for essential information.

Information Sheet

Title_____

Author_____

Illustrator_____   Copyright_____

Publisher_____ Place of publication_____

Table of Contents Chapter name that would be interesting
_____

Use index in back of book to pick out information that is of
interest._____

---

6) review how to use index with students using
the following example of an index. Then have
them fill out the index questionnaire.

INDEX

crops, 12, 13, 97, 107, 115, 117,
        180, 181, 184, 186, 192, 240,
        247, 253, 255
    and air pollution, 234-235
        fertilizing 181; harvested by
        Spanish speaking people, 170;
        historic Indians, 24; Hopewell
        Indians, 20; in New Switzer-
        land, 265; Middle Mississippi
        Indians, 21, 23; rotating, 180.
Crusades, 25, 28, 29
Cuba, 269, 271
    and slavery, 37
Cubans, 269, 27
Cumberland, 272
    Gap, 56, 82; Road, 114, 272
Czechoslovakia, 269

da Gama, Vasco, 30, route to India,
    map, 30
Davis, Jefferson, 159
Dawes, William, 54
Debs, Eugene V, 187, 202-203
deer, 248
Deleware Indiana, 131
Democratic Party, 208, 212-214
Depression, 187, 205, 207, 214, 223
Dutch colonies, 31

earth, changes in, 10, 12, 17
education, 67, 164
    changing world of, 172-174;
    church, 172; in Middle Ages,
    26, 27; La Salle's, 40; New
    Harmony, 145
    see schools
Eisenhower, Pres., 216, 226
electric power plants,
    and air pollution, 230-231;
    and water pollution, 237-239
Ellis Island, 263-264
Emancipation Proclamation, 158
    161, 162
England, 47, 48, 49, 50, 82, 104
    107, 144, 151, 154, 159, 266,
    268, 269
environment, 227-244, 247, 248,
    249, 250, 252, 253, 258,
    261, 262
Europe, 15, 26, 29, 31, 34, 37,
    40, 46, 47, 117, 144, 151,
    190, 201, 205, 217, 263,
    265, 266, 267

INDEX QUESTIONNAIRE

1. In index do you look for a person's last name or first name?_____
2. If you were doing a report on Ellis Island what page would
   you look on?_____
3. If you were doing a report on crops and wanted to know what
   historic Indians planted, what page would you look on?_____
4. If you were interested in education in the Middle Ages, what
   page would you look on?_____
5. If you wanted to know about electric power plants (and water
   pollution) what page would you look on?_____
6. If you were looking up the Cumberland Gap, what page would
   you look on?_____

7) students need to learn how to read to gather information and facts for their reports. The paragraph
below and the questions following it should help students
learn how to look for information.

EARLY PIONEER TRANSPORTATION

The earliest transportation was on streams, rivers, and lakes where Indians used <u>canoes</u>. The waterways became the Indians' roads. Another early means was by <u>horse</u> down trails cut by animals, Indians, and early-pioneers. The horseback rider was soon followed by <u>wagons</u>, conestoga wagons pulled by four to six horses down the newly cut roads. Along with wagons came the <u>flatboats</u> that could only float downstream on the Ohio River.

Questions:

1. Name the four means of transportation indentified in the paragraph?_____

2. What form of transportation did the Indians use on rivers and lakes?_____

3. Suppose you were a pioneer moving west by yourself, what means of transportation might you use?_____
   _____

4. Would you enjoy traveling west as the pioneers did?
   _____ Which form of transportation would you
   have used?_____

    8) using index cards: students should have one
       card for each question asked in (2) above
       where students decide what information is
       needed for their reports. Have students
       answer questions by using resource material
       in the library that they have already identified.

    9) after students have gathered their information
       they must put that information in a written report
       form. The following is a form example that might
       help them write a paragraph. A paragraph writing
       exercise:

PRACTICE PARAGRAPH FORM

name_____

_____
Title

_____ is remembered because _____.
    Person's name   reason

His/her major contributions were/are_____
_____.

If I had a chance I would like to talk to_____
about_____and ask him/her_____?

I think he/she would answer?_____

This person should/should not be remembered because_____
_____·reasons_____.

5. Activity & materials

Puzzles (identifying historically important persons,
         place, events; organizing and reporting)

when: two or three periods

what: puzzles to do during or following research above.

how:

simple crossword puzzle

word search puzzle
find the hidden word

FLATBOAT
CANOE
CONESTOGA
PIONEER

F	Z	E	N	C	O	N	E	S	T	O	G	A	L	Y
C	A	N	O	E	W	R	U	I	V	M	B	S	A	T
A	B	E	L	C	D	Q	N	O	P	T	X	C	G	H
E	C	V	T	Y	H	J	F	L	A	T	B	O	A	T
O	I	W	P	I	O	N	E	E	R	M	A	Q	E	P

FLATBOAT

CANOE

CONESTOGA

PIONEER

crossword puzzle

ACROSS

2 Abraham_____, a backwords lawyer who became ·president.
3 The _____Gap was a way through the mountains discovered by
  Daniel Boone.
8 Many pioneers moved west carrying their belongings in a _____ wagon.
11 In early days the only way to cross a river was by _____.

12 Early trappers sold their furs to trading posts many of which were
_____ forts.
13 Daniel Boone made a famous trail west called the_____Trail.

DOWN

1 George Rogers_____was an early settler and helped fight
the British during the American Revolution.
3 A _____road is made up of logs laid side by side one
right next to another.
4 Daniel_____was an early settler in the west
5 Many Indians and explorers and settlers made clothes out of_____.
6 William Henry_____was the first governor of Indiana Territory
and became President of the United States.
7 Early settlers were often called_____.
9 The_____River was an important waterway for Indians and for
settlers moving west.
10 When a territory became a_____it became one of the United
States.

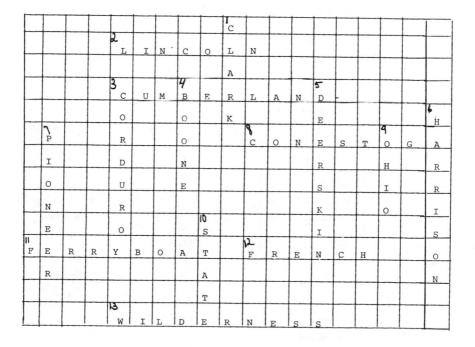

6. Activity & materials

   Creating and Presenting   (identifying historically im-
   a "Write-On" Filmstrip   portant persons, places, events;
                               organizing and reporting)

when: one period

what: special filmstrip kit (The Write-On Filmstrip),

      overhead projector

how:

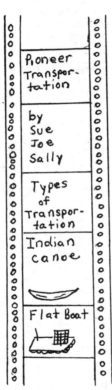

filmstrips are available that can be
written on by the students with colored
pencils. Students can create their own
pictues and captions on the filmstrip
to be shown on an overhead projector.
These filmstrips are ideal for helping
students organize, create, and present
reports. The special filmstrips are
available in a number of school supply
catalogs. One supplier is Prima Educational Products, Irving on the
Hudson, NY 10533. The students may
work up their presentation on a story-
board guide first then transfer their
pictues and captions to the film. The
film can be erased and used over again.

7. Activity & materials

   Personal Pin-ups   (identifying historically important
                       persons, places, events; organizing
                       and categorizing)

when: one period

what: pins, names of famous people being studied written

      on papers

how: pin the name of a famous person to the back of
        each student without letting them see who it is.
        They must guess the name of the person on their back
        by asking yes or no questions of the other students.
        Alternative: The students should mill around and treat
        each other as the person they represent. (King George
        III, Abraham Lincoln, George Washington, Benedict
        Arnold). Students try to guess who they are by the
        way they are treated.

8. Activity & materials
        Aiding Reports (identifying historically important
                         persons, places, events; organizing
                         and categorizing)
when: one period per activity
what: materials as needed for activity
how: 1) have students make a transparency about the
           person or event they researched.
        2) have students who wish to dress up as the person
           they researched.
        3) have students locate on a map where the person
           they researched lived or where the event they
           researched took place. A little flag with the
           event or person's name might be pinned to a
           United States flag.

III. Purpose: Develop the skill to examine values and beliefs.
        Specific objective: Examining one's own beliefs and values.
        1. Activity & materials
                We Like... (identifying similarities in values and
                             beliefs)
when: one period
what:
how: have each student pair with another student who has
        the same interest (model ship building). Have them
        touch in some way (lock elbows, hold hands). Each
        pair then tries to join with another pair on another
        shared interest or an expansion of the earlier one

(model building of any kind). The four lock elbows,
hold hands or touch somehow. The foursomes try to
join on a shared interest. Continue until whole
class is one big circle that shares an interest.

2. Activity & materials

Beliefs[5] (identifying similarities in values and beliefs)

when: three or four periods

what: materials as needed for activity

how: 1) pick a TV show (Grizzley Adams, Gentle Ben) a movie
the whole class has seen (Wizard of Oz) or show a
movie to class. Discuss one of the major characters
in the movie: what the character did and why, and what
beliefs or values the character might hold that would
cause the character to act the way he/she did.
Discuss what students would do in a similar situation.
Are there similarities and differences between what they
would do and what the character did and what they value
as compared with what the character seems to value?
2) clean the toy box: teacher makes a list of toys and
objects that might be stored in a toy box (books,
baseball cards, football, skates, clay, ball and jacks,
broken alarm clock, toy telephone, toy cars, trucks dolls,
etc.) Give each student a copy of the list and have them
pick toys they would discard and tell why. What do the
lists revel about students' values and beliefs? Are there
similar lists between students?

3. Activity & materials

Ranking Values (identifying similarities in values
                  and beliefs)

when: two periods

what: questions to rank

how: 1) rank questions (1 for first choice, 2 for second
choice, 3 for third choice, and 4 for last choice)

1. When do you like to eat out?
_____breakfast, _____lunch, _____dinner, _____snack time

2. How many people do you like to be (play) with?
   _____alone, _____two people, _____small group or team, _____crowd

3. What is most important to you now?
   _____health, _____money, _____friendship, _____happiness

4. What do you think will be most important to you in the future?
   _____health, _____money, _____friendship, _____happiness

5. Where would you like to vacation?
   _____mountains, _____seashore, _____big city, _____ranch

6. Which would you prefer to do?
   _____read, _____watch TV, _____talk to a friend, _____go to a movie

> Students may want to make up own questions.
> Teacher may wish to make up questions on topic
> being studied or about to be studied. Questions
> may be used for discussion.

These two activities "Ranking Values" and "Personal Preference" are based upon the assumption that values determine choices between alternatives. To identify values it is sometimes important for students to identify their problems and also their needs and interests, for when a student identifies a problem, the problem leads back to a need or interest, and in turn needs and interests lead back to values. Simply, if you want to deal with values, you need to deal with those things about which people make choices.

> VALUES ――――――> NEEDS & INTERESTS ――――――> PROBLEMS

> 2) personal preference: have student place themselves
> on where they think they fit. Questions may be used
> for discussion. Teachers and students should make up
> preference questions. For example:

1. How do you feel about being with people?
   Solo Sam_____Crowd Seeking Chris

2. How do you like your music?
   "Rocking" Rita_____"Classical" Cloris

3. How do you like to settle an argument?
   Talk-it-out Tom_____Fighting Fred

4. What's your attitude about helping at home?
   Reluctant Rosie_____Helpful Hannah

4. Activity & materials

My Values and Yours[6] (identifying similarities
and differences in values and
beliefs)

when: one period
what: 3 X 5 file cards

how: give each student four file cards and have them

cut them in half so each student has eight cards.

Discuss values, those things that are most important

to you and that you like the best. List eight of the

classes' most important values on the board.

Have students write values on cards (one value from

board on one card, eight values--eight cards)

Have students stack cards in order of importance

(most important on top). Compare ranking with a

partner. Why do your values differ?

Value examples: making money   family
                  being a leader   friends
                  honesty   solo activities
                  getting good grades time
                  nice clothes   looking like friends
                                      (not being conspicuous)

5. Activity & materials

Expose--Disclose[7] (identifying similarities and
differences in values and beliefs,
also identifying a positive self
image)

when: one period

what:

how: use words to describe yourself that have a letter the

same as in your name.

```
                                     i                        p
                              t      n                        a
       M usic lover           h      t                 p      i
                              r      e                 l      n
       I maginative           i      l
                              f      l   i          M  A  T  T
thin K er                     T  I   M             u  n  e  a
                              y  g   p             s  n  r  l
  s E rious                      e   o             i  e  r  e
          capa B le              n   r             c  r     n
          pr E tty               t   t             i        t
           s T udious                a             a        e
              H appy                 n             n        d
                                     t
```

6. Activity & materials

   And Herrreees _____! (identifying a positive
                    student's name   self image

.when: recurring (one student at a time)

what: materials as needed

how: each student plans a day when he/she can experiment
       and try new things or activities. Preparation may be
       done in free time or spare time during the day.
       Students should make a collage of pictures that describes
       and shows things he/she likes.
       The student should collect and bring in photos of his/her
       life style (when little and now), family, home, etc.
       Fill in a personality sheet, make sure it is correct
       and copy it in best handwriting. Sheet should have:
         name, address, date, birthday, family members;
         favorite toys, TV shows, colors, school friends,
         school subject, season, outdoor sport or activity,
         indoor sport or activity, dessert.
       See teacher to set date for your special day on daily
       calendar. To the student:
       Fill in schedule for special day starting with checking
       in with teacher before school starts and at end of day.
       If activity involves another teacher or staff person,
       be sure to get that person's permission and initials on
       schedule.
       Prepare for your day by making a poster about yourself
       with your name, collage, photos, personality sheet.
       On your day place poster in hall where everyone can see
       it. Make sure you and teacher both have a copy of
       your schedule. Your day will be a success if you plan
       well.

IV. Purpose: Learning to apply knowledge through active participation in
society.

       Specific objective: Solving problems through organization.

   1. Activity & materials

       Responsibility (participation in rule making)

when: one or two periods

what: copy of school rules

how: have students recall that in their first three grades
        they may have had activities that examined school
        rules, advantages and disadvantages. Since students
        are now older it is time to take more responsibility
        in defining and possibly proposing changes in school
        rules.

        Have students examine series of school rules, discuss
        why each rule was made and whether it could be
        modified or changed to make it more effective. Is
        the rule practical and necessary?

> The following are school rules that fourth graders
> might be expected to comment on:
>
> Students are not allowed to ride bikes on school
> playground during school day._____
> _____
>
> Lunch periods are one hour and fifteen minutes;
> would you prefer to shorten the lunch period to
> an hour and be excused fifteen minutes earlier
> in the afternoon?_____
> _____
>
> Grades kindergarten through third are released
> five minutes earlier than grades four through six.
> _____

        Having examined the rules class should be encouraged
        to reach a consensus on those rules that need to be
        discussed with school authorities.

2. Activity & materials

        Getting Involved[8] (participation in rule making)

when: two or three weeks

what: interview cards

how: students should find out about organizations in the
        school and in the community. To teach students how
        to get involved in rule making whether it be in school
        or perhaps community organizations the following
        activities will help organize the effort.

Have students call members or officials of
organizations and set up an appointment for an
interview.

Interview Questionnaire

1. What is name of organization?
2. What is purpose of organization in community (or school)?
3. Suppose fourth graders became interested in your
   organizations might they be welcome?
4. Are there projects that fourth graders could do
   to help your organization?

Have class send memos, letters, or telegrams
to community or school organizations urging
some action:

WESTERN UNION

Date_____   I urge your committee/organization to:

_____

_____

_____

Sincerely_____

---

3. Activity & materials

   You Can Make a Difference

when: recurring

what:

how: 1) class members identify a service project on
       which they would like to work or with which they
       would like to become involved.
       One of the best ways to accomplish this is by field
       trips to service centers for the purpose of identifying
       needs of the organization and interests of the students.
       The following are the types of organizations that might
       be considered: community centers (working with young
       children); Red Cross; YWCA/YMCA; rest homes,

nursing homes, retirement villages, county farm
(working with senior citizens).

Example: Suppose the students decide to work with
senior citizens at a rest home they visited on a
field trip.

2) contact the rest home to clarity needs of the
organization and to obtain permission or approval
for your proposed project.

3) Students plan and decide on project to undertake
or way they may become involved with the senior
citizens.

--students might plan a play or party in order
  to meet senior citizens.

--adopt a senior citizen: groups of two or three
  students adopt one senior citizen to visit, write
  to, remember on holidays and birthdays.

--if senior citizens are well enough invite them to
  visit class. They might enjoy being a resource
  person or "gray angel".

V.   INTEREST FORM

You have just completed the Chapter Fourth Grade and in
an effort to have you identify activities and materials
that seem most promising at this grade level to you,
please fill out the following interest form.

Instructions:

Identify two activities from this chapter. Name the activities
and briefly describe why these particular activities are of
interest to you.

ACTIVITY 1

ACTIVITY 2

NOTES

CHAPTER FIFTH GRADE

ACTIVITIES AND MATERIALS FOR FIFTH GRADE

CHAPTER FIFTH GRADE

I.   Advanced Organizer

Each succeeding chapter represents a particular grade level,
in this case fifth grade. Each chapter consists of four parts and this is why
the introduction is called an "advanced organizer." In other words you ought
to know before reading this chapter how it is organized for such knowledge can
help you to remember the major parts. The four parts are: part I is a brief
discussion on courses, topics and national trends in teaching fifth grade
throughout the United States. The second part is an example of a state fifth
grade program. The third part is activities and materials for the fifth grade
categorized by the four purposes of teaching social studies: knowledge, processing, valuing, and participation. The fourth part of the chapter is an
interest form.

II.   Topics Taught and National Trends
in Teaching Fifth Grade[1]

Recall the fourth grade curriculum trends. Three different
course offerings were most frequently used. One approach emphasized historical
development of the state and nation. Another stressed state as a region with
comparison to other selected regions throughout the world. The third, communities around the world, centered on other cultures. It is useful to recall
these three approaches because the fifth grade social studies curriculum may
be keyed to the approach in the fourth grade. In fifth grade the three most
frequently offered courses are: United States History, United States History
and Geography, and Geography of North America. The fifth grade as distinct
from any other elementary grade seems to have been specifically reserved for
study of American history or the North American continent. There is a reason
for this, it did not just by accident happen. The recommendation that American
history be taught in the fifth, eighth, and eleventh grade cycle was purpose-
fully made in 1943 by the Committee on American History in the Schools and
Colleges, popularly known as the Wesley Report. The recommendation of this
committee has had significant influence on standardizing the teaching of
American history into the three cycles that are now almost universally taught
throughout the United States. Your attention is called to this report because
it not only identified the fifth grade as the proper place to begin a treatment of national history but also recommended appropriate content and the

amount of time devoted to certain periods of history. Recommendations of the
Wesley Report will periodically be mentioned throughout the remainder of the
chapter, for it does in fact set out a curriculum structure that is recognized
and followed by most school systems.

Courses, Topics, and Themes
most Frequently Covered in Fifth Grade
"United States History"

Objectives of the course: Intended to provide the first chronological survey
of American history. Emphasis is on (in accordance with the Wesley Report)
discovery, colonial, early national periods (Revolution, Constitution, establishment of the government) and growth of the United States (this is often
expressed as a unit on the movement west). The student is expected to understand the fundamental ideas that motivated Americans (democracy, freedom) also
to appreciate how the country expanded and incorporated territory.

Basic content of the course: Typically the course includes these topics:
European backgrounds; discovery and exploration; the colonial period, with
emphasis on the founding of the colonies and on colonial life; the winning of
independence and establishment of the nation; territorial expansion and the
westward movement; sectional differences leading to the Civil War; the war and
Reconstruction; the closing of the frontier; the growth of industry and of
cities; the U.S. becomes a world power, our nation today.

The following are illustrations of the type of topic headings
that are now found in some fifth grade American history books: The First
Arrivals, The Struggle to Build a Nation, How People Were Governed, How People
Made Their Living, How People Behaved, A Good Money System, Secession Tests
the Social System, The Chicago World's Fair of 1893, Immigration, The Staus of
Women, The Great Depression, Martin Luther King and the Bus Boycott, How
People are Governed Now, How People Behave Now, The Social System in the year
2000.

Comment: These chapter headings and the basic content look rather traditional
in the sense that the student is treated to a survey of Christopher Columbus
to the present. However, note carefully that a large portion of the time, at
least half, is devoted to the discovery, settlement, and the colonial period
up to the end of the American Revolution 1783. One quarter of the course is
given to the nation's growth in territory, settlement and transportation to
about 1850. The other quarter of the time is devoted to an overview survey of

American history to the present and in some cases speculation about the future.

Wesley Report: To clarify and summarize what has been difficult for fifth grade American history teachers to understand is that the American history course is to be an overview of the nation's history with special emphasis upon an indepth study of selected topics up to the Civil War. Why did the Wesley Report make such a recommendation? The reasoning was that the fifth grade would study in depth seventeenth and eighteenth century American history, eighth grade American history would study nineteenth century, and eleventh grade American history would cover the twentieth century. If this recommendation were followed, the teacher would not be put in the position of trying to cover all of American history in depth in one year. The key idea to understanding teaching of American history in school is to cover the entire national history but survey quickly some periods and study indepth on others.

Courses, Topics and Themes
most Frequently Covered in Fifth Grade
"United States History and Geography"

Objectives of the course: Developing the student's understanding of the physical, economic and cultural geography of the United States and the influence of geographic factors on the nation's development; providing the student with an overview of the nation's history with more detailed study of early explorations and the colonial period, continued growth in social studies skills, positive attitudes toward civic responsibilitites, and appreciation of the national heritage.

Content of the course: A typical arrangement of topics, according to several recent curriculum bulletins, is: geographic overview of North America; discovery and exploration; growth of English colonies, with some attention to the Spanish and French colonies; colonial life, the winning of independence and establishment of the new nation; an overview of United States history from about 1812 to the present; regional studies, heavily geographical but incorporating historical material--especially that dealing with territorial expansion and the westward movement.

This course United States History and Geography could just as well be called studies of the North American continent. In this course history and geography are integrated and some texts and teachers are quick to point out that geography modified the immigrant American to create a different people. This course also follows the Wesley Report, the difference, of course, is the geography of the North American content with the added dimension that Canada and sometimes Mexico are countries used to compare and contrast with the United States.

Courses, Topics and Themes
most Frequently Covered in Fifth Grade
"Geography of North America"

Objectives of the course: Developing the student's understanding of the physical, cultural and economic geography of the United States, Canada, and Mexico; continued growth in effective use of maps, globes, and charts. Students should identify the relationship between geographic factors and the development of particular regions and nations.

Basic content of the course: This course frequently consists of an introductory overview unit followed by regional studies. Each regional unit includes attention to: physical features and climates of the region; natural resources; ways of making a living in the region; cities; places of special interest.

The following topic headings are illustrative of the type of content normally covered in this geography course: Questions that Need Map Answers; Regional Maps; Regions Based on Variable and Culture; Regions Inside States; Regions that Cross State Lines; Natural Resources; Using and Conserving Resources; Jobs, Wages, and Production; Sights and Sounds of Cities; The Joys and Problems of Cities; Interesting Places to Visit.

Trends in Teaching Fifth Grade Social Studies
1. The fifth grade as distinct from all other grades was earmarked by the Wesley Report as the proper grade for teaching a course in American Studies. This recommendation has been accepted and adopted nationwide. The Report has generally been interpreted to mean the teaching of an in depth study of early American history and geography which leads by the end of the course to a study of "our neighbor" Canada.
2. The trend is to continue to follow the Wesley Report. As in the case of the preceding grades there is a strong attempt by historians and social scientists to base the course on key concepts. The course from their point of view should not be "just a wagon train west" but should emphasize such concepts as dependence and interdependence, cultural change, social control, conflict and values. The course, in other words, should be an integration of history and geography with emphasis upon key concepts which lend a real substantive body of historical knowledge.

3. There has been considerable criticism of the repetition of the three cycle study of American history in grades five, eight, and eleven. That criticism has not dislodged the cycles. They are firmly rooted in the social studies curriculum. Though many texts and other curriculum materials are designed to conform with the fifth grade concentration on the seventeenth and eighteenth centuries, the eighth grade on nineteenth century, and the eleventh grade on twentieth century, this is not well understood by most social studies teachers. Many continue to believe at all three levels that they must cover all periods of American history with equal depth. Of course, this has led to considerable criticism because students are required to cover approximately the same material three times. Efforts in the years ahead will probably be to educate teachers in their responsibility to teach in depth specific periods and survey others rather than trying to change the cycles.

4. American history was intended to be a capstone course. Recall for a moment the expanding spiral of themes and topics from self to family, to school, to neighborhood, to city or community, to state, and now in the fifth grade to nation. The fifth grade course is intended to tie together all of the above themes and topics. After all there were no guarantees that teachers from grade to grade would necessarily show the relationship between the themes. Fifth grade American history was assigned the task of showing how the individual, through the history of his nation, is related to all of the previous themes. In other words, the American history course was to integrate, clarify, summarize, and demonstrate the key concepts that have been taught through the first four grades.

Finally as a clarification and summary and perhaps the one clear idea you should take from this part on trends is that of the recommendations of the Wesley Report:that United States history should be taught in the fifth grade, about two-thirds of the time to be devoted to discovery, exploration, and the colonial period with emphasis on a social history overview to the present. Social history means the study of every day life, emphasis on national leaders and key dates and events.

III. Illustrations of a State
Fifth Grade Program

There is no one prescribed social studies program throughout the United States. However, one state's description of its fifth grade program will illustrate the content which the state expects to be taught. This illustration

is included so that you can identify how a state mandates the teaching of
social studies in the fifth grade.

> The United States is compared with other selected
> regions of the world. Students will examine how geography
> influenced the development of a area such as North America,
> and what impact technological development, trade, communication,
> transportation, economic, political and social systems had on the
> historical development of the regions studied. Knowledge, process,
> location, valuing, and social skills should have continued develop-
> ment.[2]

IV. Activities and Materials Categorized
by Knowledge, Processing, Valuing, and Participation

I realize a rather common practice is to skip purposes and
specific objectives which precede the activities, but in this case the objectives are extremely important for an objective in the fifth grade will be
found in proceeding grades. This is a developmental program with objectives,
activities and materials organized to build from one grade level to another.

FIFTH GRADE ACTIVITIES AND MATERIALS

I. Purpose: Gaining knowledge about the human condition which includes
past, present, and future.

> Specific objective: Identifying problems of exploration and
> colonization.
>
> 1. Activity & materials
>
> > Claiming the New World (practicing rule making)
>
> when: two or three weeks
>
> what: silver spray painted pebbles, solid spices such as cloves and
> cinnamon sticks cut in pieces.
> We know that the early explorers, the fifteenth and sixteenth
> centuries, were seeking among other things for precious metals
> and spices. When a new continent was discovered, disagreement
> between colonial powers arose over conflicting claims. This
> activity is intended to suggest how the conflicts arose over
> colonial claims.
>
> how: Suppose a new continent has been discovered and foreign
> countries are eager to claim land and mine its riches. Each
> student will represent a country and will make a claim on the
> new continent. Discuss with students the troubles that might
> arise in making claims. List the possible troubles on the

board. For example:

1) claims for the same area

2) lack of specific boundaries

3) how to know if land is already taken

4) what to stake claim with

5) etc.

Divide the class into groups and have each group establish
four to eight laws that they would use in claiming sections
of the new continent. Each group appoints one of its mem--
bers to list their laws on a chart on the board. When all
groups are done, a master list is compiled, similar laws
are combined.

The class now votes by ballot for four laws that
seem most important to them.

Example Ballot

_____1. Students may move another's claim if he wants his
own claim on another's spot.

_____2. Students may move boundaries of another person just
a little to squeeze his claim in.

_____3. All students must use same kind of boundary markers.

_____4. Claims must be registered with teacher.

_____5. There is a limit to how much can be claimed.

_____6. A claim must have a sign saying who it belongs to.

Teacher must stake out area on playground large enough
to accomdate a claim for each student with room to spare.
Seed (sprinkle) the ground with silver painted pebbles and
spices.

Students prepare to stake claim. They need a piece of
notebook paper 8½ X 11" (that represents size of claim they
can stake); boundary markers; claim sign; container for
pebbles and spices.

Teacher takes students out to area and allows them to
stake their claims following the laws they have selected.
When claims are established, they may search within their
area for precious metals (silver pebbles) and spices.
Return to class: Discuss with class what real countries

(Spain, France, England etc.) did with precious metals
and spices from their colonies. They used the wealth
to build armies and navies to gain world power.
Prepare a chart listing what can be bought by pebbles
and spices and a rate of exchange. For example:

1 boat----------1 pebble   1 pebble = 7 spices

3 cannons-------1 pebble   (whatever ratio
                                        you wish)
4 horses--------1 pebble

suit of armor---2 spices

sword----------1 spice

etc.

Have students decide what they can purchase with
what they found at their claim. They should be allowed to
trade pebbles for spices and vice versa at the ratio listed
above. See which student (country) can obtain the greatest
military strength.

2. Activity & materials

    Survival Island[3] (practice rule making and decision making)

when: 1 period

what: map of island

how: This activity is designed to encourage students to con-
       sider the problems of establishing a colony. What factors
       should be taken into consideration when establishing a
       colony? How do you survive in an alien environment? Students
       having first considered the problems of survival are more
       likely to identify with the problems of the early colonists
       at Jamestown, Plymouth, etc.
       You have been elected to lead a group of 500 people to begin
       a new society on an uninhabited island 2,000 miles from your
       nearest neighbor. You want to be isolated from the rest of
       the world. You will take with you livestock, seed, and
       building materials. Among your group are people who are
       skilled in almost every necessary trade. As the leader you
       must take all conditions into consideration and choose a
       location for your settlement.

SURVIVAL ISLAND

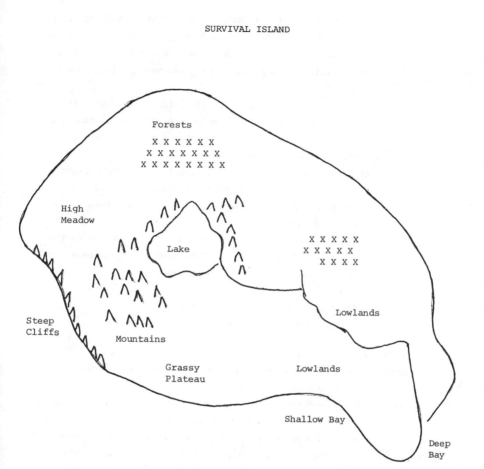

1) Each student or group of students is to play the
role of the leader of the settlement and as leader must make
a fundamental decision on where to place the island's one
settlement. This would seem to be a rather simple decision
but further consideration would suggest that a decision on
where to place the settlement involves a number of relatively
complex problems.

2) Encourage the students to identify all of the conditions
they can think of that will be important in choosing a
location for the settlement. Consider these: ecological

problems (disposal of waste, maintenance of water quality, power), other factors such as access to other parts of the island, protection from storms, and finally problems of population density and population growth, just to mention a few.

3) After students have selected their spot on the island, hold a class discussion in which the class identifies all the conditions that should be taken into consideration in choosing an appropriate site.

4) Locate where each member of the class placed his/her settlements and discuss whether the locations are or are not appropriate in terms of the considerations identified above.

Final note: Survival on an island at Jamestown or on the moon is not all that easy. Thoughtful decisions based on true knowledge is a must for survival.

3. Activity & materials

Who Gets to Go?[4] (practicing rule making and decision making)

when: 1 period

what: list of individuals requesting to go to domed city, on the moon (below)

how: This is a contemporary problem in selection for colonizing. This activity involves selecting appropriate people for a colony, and anticipating problems that might arise in the new colony. Students should be made aware that problems are much the same whether colonizing the new world or colonizing a new planet.

A domed city with controlled climate and life systems has been built on the moon to house a colony of settlers. A national selection committee has been established to determine what people may be transported to that city.

1) Divide the class into groups of four to six students.

2) Each group should imagine that it represents the national committee with the responsibility of choosing seven people from the list below.

3) The list of <u>seven</u> the group chooses must be approved
by a majority of the members of the group.

4) After the small groups have completed their lists,
the entire class should compare and discuss the different
groups' lists. Keep in mind that the very life (survival)
of the colony may well rest on the right choice of people.

Individuals Requesting to go to Domed City

1. 42 year old practicing surgeon whose fingers are
    becoming arthritic
2. 29 year old millionaire playboy
3. 45 year old male opera singer
4. 19 year old car mechanic who has been convicted of stealing.
5. 10 year old boy with learning difficulties
6. 25 year old nuclear physicist who has tried to kill himself.
7. 24 year old newleweds, both high school teachers.
    They have stated they will enter only if the other is
    accepted.
8. 35 year old lawyer who has been convicted of income
    tax evasion
9. 65 year old retired missionary
10. 39 year old architect with a history of emotional problems
11. 35 year old exconvict who runs a community center
12. 29 year old waitress who donates half of her income to
    research on cancer
13. 32 year old welfare mother with two children--will only
    enter with her children
14. 26 year old dentist who is also a black militant

4. Activity & materials
    <u>Seeking</u> <u>the</u> <u>New</u> <u>World</u> [5] (practicing rule making and decision-
                              making)

when: one period
what: copies of the following story:

The year is 1550. You along with your friends have
formed a company and have bought land in the new
world. On the way across the Atlantic from England

your ship is hit by a big storm. The captain of
the ship demands that you and your friends must
throw overboard all goods and equipment brought
to start the new colony, but that you and your
friends may retain only personal items (clothing,
money, etc.) and five other items of your company's
choice. You and your friends are faced with a decision--
what five items to keep.

how: 1) divide the class into groups. Assign each group
an identifying letter. A, B, C, D, E.

2) distribute the story to each group and ask
the students to read it.

3) ask the students to complete the activity in
the following way.

10 min.   groups compile original list of five items

 5 min.   groups rotate lists and make changes (see
            rotation plan below)

 5 min.   groups rotate lists and make changes
            groups continue to rotate lists and make
            changes every five minutes until lists
            return to original group.

4) discuss changes in lists, methods of making lists
and changes in lists, and reactions to changes.

5. Activity & materials

New World Bingo

when: two periods

what: blank BINGO cards large enough to write on
cards. Have students write a question
xploration of the new world or early
s in each square and a matching answer
r square B,1 What date did Columbus
ew world? answer chip B,1 1492:
Who led the Massachusettes Bay Co.?
7 John Winthrop.

Have teacher or student collect all the answer chips.
Students should exchange cards. Teacher or student calls
out square number and answer. If it fits student's card
he/she may cover that square. First student to complete
a row across, down, or diagonal wins.

B	I	N	G	O
1 What date did Columbus discover the new world?	6	11	16	21
2	7 Who led the Mass. Bay Co?	12	17	22
3	8	13 FREE	18	23
4	9	14	19	24
5	10	15	20	25

ANSWER CHIPS:

B, 1
1492

I, 7
John Winthrop

Specific objective: Identifying roles and contributions
of early colonists and events that led to changes in
their society: changes that may account for how we think today.

6. Activity & materials

Colonial Decision-Makers (identifying roles and
contributions of decision-
makers)

when: two weeks

what: materials as needed

how: students make reports on famous colonial leaders or
famous groups.

The following is a list of possibilities for reports.
The teacher should make up a list from which students
can choose or have students make their choice and have
it approved by teacher.

Puritans	Roger Williams
Sons of Liberty	Sam Adams
Minutemen	etc.
Mass. Bay Co.	
Salem "witches"	
etc.	

Chapter Fourth Grade has an activity that stresses what
information to put in a report, how to research for the
information, and how to write up a report. A fifth grader's
report, however, should be more detailed and more extensive
than that of a fourth grader. Reports should contain:

a cover (perhaps picture or outline of area person
was associated with)
table of contents
pictures of person or events
researched report
bibliography

7. Activity & materials

Colonial People, Places, and Things[6] (identifying historically
important events, people,
etc.)

when: three or four periods

what: materials as needed

how: students write a statement of several sentences describing an early American without naming the person (statements should be checked for accuracy by teacher).

Put statment on an index card along with answer. Examples:

-I am the Puritan who organized the Mass. Bay Co. I am the first governor of that settlement and I do not like democracy.(John Winthrop)

-I am a person who is opposed to tax laws and I make speeches in the Mass. House of Representatives to unite the people who feel the British are not ruling us fairly. (Samuel Adams)

-I was a Puritan minister who felt that the church and state should be separated. I was forced to leave the Mass. Bay Colony so I started my own colony. (Roger Williams)

-I am a small town in New England where the Minutemen and British exchanged shots. It was known for "the shot heard round the world." (Concord)

-I am a product imported to New England. There is an import duty tax on me. The king has granted a monopoly on shipping me to one English company. I was dumped in the Boston harbor as a protest. (tea)

This activity can be done by two students, small groups, or the entire class. The basic procedure is for all the cards to be placed in a box. The first student or group picks a card and reads the statement to his/her opponent or opposing group. If they can tell who is described, they get one point. The opponent reads a statement to the first student or group, and if they guess correctly they get one point. The students or groups take turns reading statements and guessing answers and the one who ends up with the highest score wins.

Alternative: students or groups get to mark a tic-tac-toe game (X-O) when they get a correct answer.

8. Activity & materials

   <u>Historical</u> <u>Dioramas</u>   (identifying historically
                                           important events, people, etc.)

when: two or three periods

what: boxes and art supplies

how: students should make dioramas depicting events connected
        with early American history, i.e., first Thanksgiving,
        Battle of Lexington and Concord, Paul Revere's ride, Salem
        witch trials.

        Practice questioning by having one open and one closed
        question for each diorama. Example:

        How did Paul Revere know which way the British were
        coming? (closed)

        Suppose you were Paul Revere, what might have happened
        to you if you had not been caught by the British? (open)

9. Activity & materials

   <u>Private</u> <u>Papers</u>   (identifying historically important
                                        events, people, etc.)

when: one week

what: paper (made to look old by wetting it with weak tea and
        allowing it to dry in sun), pen and ink.

how: divide students into groups and have them research early
        Americans. The group then uses the paper to write:

        -a letter a member of the Continental Congress might
        write home telling what is happening.
        -diary of one of the Sons of Liberty telling of feelings
        on growing rebellion of patriots.
        -report of British officer to his superiors in England.
        -a New Encland farmer writes to a relative in England
        explaining what freedom means to him.

10. Activity & materials

    <u>Decisions</u> <u>Cause</u> <u>Change</u>   (identifying historically important
                                                   events, people, etc.)

when: three or four periods

what: interview sheet below

how: after students have studied leaders who make decisions
        that changed early American life, the class must decide
        what questions should be asked to study the idea of "change".

See interview sheet below for sample questions.
Have students pick an example of change in early American
life. Pair students so everyone has a partner. Give each
student an interview sheet and have him/her interview
partner and write down reply.

Interview Sheet

name _____ date _____ interviewer_____

1. Who brought about the change? Reply_____

2. What was the reason for the   Reply_____
    change?   _____

3a. What was the decision?   Reply_____

b. Suppose you had been this   Reply_____
    person, would you have made   _____
    the same decision?

4a. What was the effect of the   Reply_____
    person's decision?   _____

b. What do you think the effect   Reply_____
    would have been if he/she had   _____
    not made the decision?   _____

After students have completed interviews, compile
replies on board under heading representing each.
Discuss change and how it affects our life today:
free speech, religion, self-government, etc.

Specific objective: Identifying and examining the ideas
of separation of powers, democracy, republic, and federalism.

11. Activity & materials

Separation of Powers (identifying the structure of government)

when: one period

what: newspapers, TV news

how: discuss separation of powers with class. Have students
bring in newspaper stories (or use old newspapers at
school) or TV news stories of separation of powers in
action such as Supreme Court declaring law unconstitutional,
Presidential veto, or Congress overriding the veto.
Pick a branch of government and list powers granted it

by the Constitution. Discuss what additional powers
it has acquired over the years.

12. Activity & materials
       Federalism[7] (identifying the structure of government)
when: one period
what: list of topics that are government responsibility.
       for example:
              regulating manufacturing of medicines
              inspecting hospitals, nursing homes, etc.
              regulating banks
              granting driver's license
              income tax
              building schools
              building highways
              etc.
how: have students establish which are functions of the
       state government, which are functions of the federal
       government, and which may be shared.
       Discuss students' findings.

13. Activity & materials
       Democracy or Republic [8] (identifying the structure of
                                    government)
when: one period
what:
how: have students agree on a definition of republic and
       a definition of democracy. For example:
          "Republic is a system where representatives of
           the people make decisions, democracy is a system
           where people make decisions."
       Make a scale and place on the scale where certain
       government activities fit. Is the activity closer to
       democracy or republic or somewhere in between?

	Supreme Court	War is declared	School Taxes	Senators are elected	
republic	____l____	____l____	____l____	____l____	democracy

Examples of what to place on scale:

School taxes go up (as voted by the people)

Supreme Court judge is appointed (by the President)

War is declared (by Congress and President)

Senators are elected (elected by the people)

Treaty is negotiated between nations (by the President)

55 mile speed limit (set by the Congress)

Car inspection (set by the state)

House of Representatives are elected (by the people)

The President is elected (by the electorial College)

14. Activity & materials

Fill in the Capital   (identifying the structure of
                        government)

when: one period

what: drawing of capital

how: fill in drawing using definitions listed below.

1. A part of Congress, House of _____

2. Highest court in the land _____

3. The part of the government that makes the laws _____

4. The head of our country _____

5. The part of our government that carries out justice_____

6. The part of our government that caries out the law _____

7. Washington is in the District of _____

8. The House of Representatives and the Senate make up _____

9. The President's assistants are his _____

10. Washington is located on the _____ river.

11. A part of Congress _____

Specific objective: Identifying some of the ways
transportation and communication helped the westward
movement and the growth of the country.

15. Activity & materials

   Transportation

when: several weeks

what: boxes, cardboard, materials as needed

how: divide the class into two groups. One group will
      research ways pioneers traveled over land and the other
      group will research ways pioneers traveled over water.

Students should use whatever resources are available.
Each group should list the ways:

water: canoe, flatboat, raft, keelboat,
        steamboat, ferryboat, sailing ship, etc.

land: walk, horseback, conestoga wagon,
        stage coach, train, etc.

Each group should make a mobile using models of the
types of transportation they have listed. Have students
use imagination and whatever supplies they need to
model the parts of their mobiles.

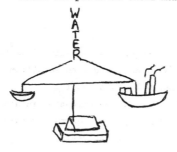 

Alternative: have students make a collage of pictures
depicting water travel or land travel.

On a large map of the U.S. have students trace some of
the famous routes west. Discuss what means of transportation were used along each route and what present
day states the routes passed through.

16. Activity & materials

The Covered Wagon

when: one week

what: table, cloth materials or paper, cardboard

how: 1) turn a table into a covered wagon by covering it
       with material or paper draped down the sides. Add big
       wheels made out of cardboard to fasten on the legs.
       Students could get under the table for quiet work such
       as reading.

       2) pretend the covered wagon has stopped for the night.

This is a good time to read stories and sing songs
about pioneers, wild west heroes/heroines.

3) if some students would like to they could bring
in foods to share that are typical of what people on
the trail might have eaten. (beef jerky or dry beef
sticks are available in super markets) Teacher must
approve of foods suggested and set up a schedule.

17. Activity & materials
    Communication[9]

when: one week

what: materials as needed

how: have students list means of communication from talking
       through letters, telephones, etc., to satellite
       communication. Compile lists on board.
       Have students list means of communication in historical
       chronological order the way they personally think
       communication developed over the years.
       Have class research dates and make a time line of
       means of communication. How does this time line
       compare with their personal individual chronological
       lists?

       Other suggestions:

            Students could pantomine means of communication
              for class to guess. (telephone, pony express,
              telegraph key)

            Students could describe a type of communication
              without mentioning name and others would have
              to guess. For example: "I carried letters very
              quickly in leather pouches on horseback in the
              west." (Pony Express)

            Students could design a future means of communication,
              draw or model it, and write short explanation of
              how it would work.

Specific objective: Identifying factors in continental
expansion and how populations move.

18. Activity & materials
    How We Grow

when: one week

what: make a large outline of U.S. either by tracing wall
        map or projecting transparency on paper. Cut out map.

how: have students trace outline of the following:

        U.S. of 1783

        Louisiana Purchase   1803

        Texas Annexation   1845

        Oregon Territory   1846

        Mexican Cession   1848

        Gadsden Purchase   1853

Divide students into groups and give each group a
territory cutting that section out of map and giving
it to them. Have each group research their section:
reasons it was acquired, size, states contained in it,
major cities, natural characteristics (land forms,
weather), resources, etc.

Each group will decorate their section using as
much of their research information as possible.
Starting with U.S. of 1783 each group will present
their section and describe it to class. As each
section is discussed it will be attached to the ones
before it, eventually making a complete map and large
wall display.

Note: We know that in the U.S. citizens often move. The average present day
family moves up to six times on the average. The expansion of the U.S. and
the concept of movement are linked together in the notion of manifest destiny.
In the following activity "Moving" students' attention is directed to the
reasons families move.

19. Activity & materials

    Moving

when: three or four periods

what: Questionnaire on moving below

how: pass out questionnaire to students and have them fill
        out as much of it as they can, then take it home to complete
        it with help from parent, grandparent, etc. Hold class
        discussion on answers and reactions.

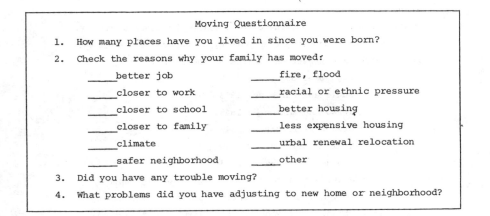

Moving Questionnaire

1. How many places have you lived in since you were born?

2. Check the reasons why your family has moved:

_____better job   _____fire, flood

_____closer to work   _____racial or ethnic pressure

_____closer to school   _____better housing

_____closer to family   _____less expensive housing

_____climate   _____urbal renewal relocation

_____safer neighborhood   _____other

3. Did you have any trouble moving?

4. What problems did you have adjusting to new home or neighborhood?

Specific objective: Identifying people and events surrounding the Civil War.

20. Activity & materials

   Your Title Is Your Point of View

when: one or two periods

what: list of titles for Civil War:

   War Between the States   The War for States' Rights

   Mr. Lincoln's War   The Lost Cause

   The Great Rebellion   The Yankee Invasion

   The Brother's War   American Civil War

   The War for Southern Independence

   The Second American Revolution

how: give list to students. Have students write several reasons why each of these titles applied to the Civil War. Have class discussion on possible reasons.

21. Activity & materials

   Who Am I?

when: two periods

what:

how: 1) Have students write a paragraph describing someone connected with the Civil War without revealing name. Have student read paragraph, other students must try to guess

identity. For example: "I planned a march across
the south towards the end of the Civil War. Railroads
and supplies were destroyed as were crops and farms.
Houses and barns were burned and Atlanta burned to the
ground in my march to the sea." (General Sherman)
2) Have students pick a person to represent. Class asks
yes/no questions of "person" until they guess his/her
identity.

22. Activity & materials

Letters

when: one or two periods

what: writing materials (aged paper may be made by dipping paper
in weak tea solution and allowing it to dry)

how: Pair students and have them pretend to be related or
close friends who are on opposite sides in the Civil War.
Have them write several letters expressing to each other
their reasons for the choices they have made. For example:

Sisters: The one from the north would write about:

married to northern merchant

joined Quaker faith and therefore does
not believe in slavery or war.

The one from the south would write about:

married to plantation owner

house slaves are treated well

field slaves do not want more than their
primitive lives

slavery is a necessary evil both for the
slave and the economic well being of the
plantation

slavery permits her to live a highly civilized
life.

her religion recognizes slavery as a way of life.

II. Purpose: Develop skills necessary to process information.

Specific objective: Students will process questions by
differentiating between open and closed.

1. Activity & materials

Questioning Skills (practicing the skill of asking and
answering open and closed questions)

when: two class periods

what: check sheet

how: this is a continuation of the questioning skills introduced
in Chapter Fourth Grade. . Refer back to the previous chapter,
Activity 1 under II. It may be necessary to review with
students the definitions of open and closed questions. The
following exercises is a pre-test that should help students
differentiate between open and closed questions. After
marking, be sure to go over pre-test with students. Use
this as technique for opening discussion.

Mark the following questions either O for open or C for
closed.

C 1. Was John Adams President?

C 2. When was the War of 1812 Fought?

O 3. Suppose you were from New England what might be your
religion?

C 4. Why did the South support slavery?

O 5. How might you have felt about slavery in 1850?

C 6. What state was Henry Clay from?

O 7. How do you feel about Daniel Webster's stand on slavery?

C 8. Was John Q. Adams ever a member of the House of
Representatives?

Test student skill completion exercise: turn the following topics into
one open and one closed question.

1. Leif Ericson
   (example)

   open: Suppose you were Leif Ericson, what
   might your reasons be for exploring
   North America?

   closed: What is the name of the man who some
   believe discovered America before
   Columbus?

2. Pilgrims

   open: _____

   closed: _____

3. Lexington & Concord

   open: _____

   closed: _____

4. Declaration of
   Independence

   open: _____

   closed: _____

> Check textbooks for study and end of chapter
> questions. Go over some of the questions with class
> and classify them as either open or closed.
> Assignment: have students read headings of both
> chapters and sections of chapters, turning the headings
> into open and closed questions. For example:
>
> Heading "Indian Skills"--questions might be:
>   What skills did Indians have?
>   Do you feel that Indian skills were useful to
>   the colonists?
>
> Heading "Jamestown Is Founded"--questions might be:
>   What country founded Jamestown?
>   In your opinion why did the English settle a
>   colony at Jamestown?

Why do this, why teach students the skill of questioning? There is a relationship between questioning and ability to learn. The two levels of thought,
lower which refers to closed questions often associated with recall, repeat,
recite, or higher which refers to open questions often associated with opinion,
judgment, evaluation, predicting, are both necessary for learning. As much as
thirty percent of instruction in social studies is in the form of questions
from the teacher and the text. Common sense alone suggest that to know how to
ask and answer questions would be a useful skill. The examples of questions
in this chapter are designed to illustrate open and closed type questions. If
you believe in stimulating creative behavior then practice using both types.

> Specific objective: Learning to differentiate between fact,
> and opinion.
> 2. Activity & materials
>   Facts and Opinions
> when: two or three periods
> what: fact and opinion list below
>   example story with questions
> how: discuss with students the terms "fact" and "opinion".
>   To check how well students can identify differences,

teacher may want to give fact and opinion checklist
(as a pre-test) below to students.

Facts and Opinion Checklist

Mark each statement either F for fact or O for opinion.

F 1. George Washington was the first President of U.S.

F 2. The ship the Pilgrims came to New England on was
called the Mayflower.

F 3. The Pilgrims learned how to grow corn from the Indians.

O 4. The British were hated by all of the colonists.

O 5. The Puritans spoke "Old English" so you would have no
trouble understanding them if we could talk to them today.

O 6. The pioneers had an easy trip west after they crossed the
Appalachian Mountains.

O 7. Man is basically good.

O 8. All men have natural rights of life, liberty, and property.

O 9. Alexander Hamilton was a "good" Secretary of the Treasury.

O 10. Thomas Jefferson was a "good" president.

O 11. The Boston Massacre was not a massacre.

F 12. Real American Indians did not throw tea in the "Boston
Tea Party."

O 13. All Minutemen believed "Give me liberty or give me death."

F 14. The Declaration of Independence contains these words
"That all men are created equal."

O 15. Fifth graders are always good social studies students.

Teachers are encouraged to make up their own
checklist as a pre-test to some of the major historical
divisions, i.e., Discovery, Colonization, American
Revolution.

After each child has marked his/her list, go over the
fifteen items with the entire class so that each understands that there are facts and opinions. For example
teacher might ask class these questions:

a) Can all communication be separated into either
fact or opinion?

b) Can something be partly true and partly opinion?

c) Were you able on the checklist to identify the
difference between fact and opinion?

d) Is everything printed in your social studies

text fact?

Test their skill - have students mark fact (F) and opinion(O) statements at end of following story:

Pioneer Schools

You might think that pioneer children were lucky for many pioneer children did not ever go to school. Often there was no school to attend. Schools were built by parents who wanted their children to have an education, but even when there was a school most children had important chores that came before attending school. The school was usually a one room log cabin holding up to twenty children of all ages and grades. The children sat on benches, for they had no desks, in front of a schoolmaster. The schoolmaster would call each child in turn to read outloud.

_O_ 1. Pioneer children enjoyed attending the one room school.

_F_ 2. The school house was built by parents of the students.

_O_ 3. The one room school offered each child a good education.

_F_ 4. The schoolmaster gave individual attention to each child.

_F_ 5. All ages and classes were in the same room together.

_O_ 6. Probably all pioneer children had a chance to attend school.

---

3. Activity & materials

What Really Happened?

when: one period

what: materials as needed

how: have two students create an altercation. This can be any type of situation where there is conflict. For example: two children run into each other, each blaming the other for carelessness; two children working on the board fight over the use of an eraser; children in a dispute over a book they are both reading together; two children in a dispute over a game.

1) have each student in class write a paragraph describing what happened.

2) divide the students into groups. Have the
members of each group read each other's paragraphs.
3) groups must decide what was fact and what was
opinion and make a list.

For example:

Altercation: Sally and Trudy were reading the same
book together. Sally turned the page. Trudy grabbed
the book and turned the page back. Sally shoved
Trudy off her seat.

FACT	OPINION
Sally and Trudy were involved	Sally and Trudy were angry
Trudy took the book	Sally was wrong to turn the page
Sally pushed Trudy	Trudy was wrong to take the book

Altercation: Randy and Jack ran into each other
coming from right angles. Randy fell down and
bumped his head and appeared unconscious for a
few seconds, then he tripped Jack.

FACT	OPINION
Randy and Jack were coming from right angles	Neither boy was playing safely
They ran into each other	They were not looking where they were going
Randy tripped Jack	Randy was mad at Jack

The point of activity is to demonstrate the difficulty
of knowing what really happened. Would the students
suppose that story tellers and historians might
have the same problems of knowing what really
happened in the past? Are history texts facts or
opinions about history? If students were to write
their own history, would they write facts, opinions,
perhaps both. Be sure students know the difference.

4. Activity & materials

Cartoon Study

when: one period

what: cartoons

how: teacher or students bring cartoons to class. Show
cartoon to entire class and have them decide what they
think happened. Discuss what are facts and what are
opinions and list on board.

FACT	OPINION
Tea in water	Colonist accuses Indian
Boston Harbor	Indian fearful
American Indian denies participation in tea party	Colonist angry

Specific Objective: Learning to recognize propaganda, bias
and stereotypes.

5. Activity & materials

     Propaganda

when: four or five periods

what: definition of propaganda techniques listed below

how: Given the amount of advertisement that is now aimed
directly at pre-teens and teenagers it is important
that the techniques used in these advertisements be
identified so that the students can learn to be a
bit more discriminating about what they are told to
believe. The fifth grade is not too early for

students to become aware of propaganda.

1)   Hand out definitions to class and discuss with students these most common forms of propaganda.

2)   Have students think of examples from TV, etc., and put them on the board.

3)   Have each student bring to class at least three different propaganda techniques to share with class. May display these on bulletin board.

4)   Have each student prepare own original propaganda example using any one of the seven techniques: a TV commercial, a magazine ad.

Propaganda techniques can easily be related to the various war efforts in the U.S. and abroad. Often featured in American history textbooks are posters from the Spanish-American War and the First and Second World Wars that demonstrate how feelings were generated against the "enemy".

Techniques

1.   Testimonial: a famous person endorses product. Credit card advertisements on TV by well known personalities.

2.   Transfer: connecting a popular or unpopular symbol or feeling to a person, event, etc. Successful general or U.S. astronaut running for political office.

3.   Plain folks: appealing to the common man as "just one of the folks." Showing presidential candidate fixing his own breakfast.

4.   Glittering generalities: general ideas that promise much. Glowing ads for land sales in distant states or vacation locations.

5.   Name calling: putting a negative label on something. Often used by politicians.

6.   Card stacking: offering only favorable facts or exaggerating good facts. Car selling--only mentioning favorable aspects of the car you are selling.

7.   Bandwagon: urged to go along with the majority. Pressuring your parents to let you stay up later because "all the kids are doing it."

6.   Activity & materials

Understanding Bias

when: one or two periods

what:

how: along with studying the propaganda techniques by
        which we are persuaded the teacher should also
        introduce the notion of bias. People who wish
        to persuade us have a bias, a preference for some
        product or value, or action. Most written material,
        movies, advertisements, and other forms of media,
        are written and produced with a bias. The fifth
        grade is not too early to begin suggesting that
        students identify what bias is and the effect of
        bias.

1) Discuss bias with students:

        What is bias?

        Do you suppose that most people are biased?

            Are you biased?

        Should we be able to recognize bias?

        How does bias affect you?

2) Have students as a class or in groups establish
ways to check for bias. Students should prepare a
checklist or test that can be applied to items to
check for bias.

        How is item reported?

        Is emotion involved?

        Does the reporter have a person interest in item?

3) Make sure each student has a copy of checklist
to test for bias. Students should begin by checking
their social studies book for bias.

Sources for bias	What biases to look for
newspapers: editorials	sex (male, female)
letters to editor	age (too young, too old)
movie adds	
want ads (best place to look)	size (too small, too fat, too tall)
some comics	handicapped (blind, deaf, disabled)
TV: Bias toward certain audience	experience (must have extensive
or product	experience or no experience
	needed--will train on job)

7. Activity & materials

    <u>Stereotypes</u>

when: one or two periods

what: materials as needed

how: 1) Divide class into two groups based on some simple
difference, i.e., boys vs. girls, those who are
bused to school vs. those who walk or get car-pooled,
those who wear glasses vs. thoses who do not. The
groups do not necessarily need to be evenly divided.
2) Give each group the same task to do. However, the
task should be made easier for one group than for the
other. For example give a small test with difficult
questions. On the test for one group just have the
questions. For the other group give the questions
and responses to choose from. Separate the two
groups. Be sure the two groups do not talk to each
other, but let the group with responses talk among
themselves.

<u>Sample test</u>:

Questions: 1. What exact date did Christopher
Columbus sight the new world?_____

                2. John Cabot sailing under an English
flag reached the coast of North
America in what year?_____

                3. What did Sir Walter Raleigh establish
on Roanoke Island in 1585?_____

                4. What date did La Salle explore the
lower Mississippi?_____

Responses: Oct. 12, 1492
(given to
only one   English reached North America in 1497
group)
        first English colony

        Mississippi explored in 1682

3) The group with the answers will finish earlier than
the other group, allow them some extra privileges.
When the other group complains, tell them to keep working.
4) After a short while call a halt and start a class
discussion. For example:
What were the feelings of each group?

(pleasure vs. frustration)

What did one group feel about the other?
(lucky vs. unlucky)

Was it easy to think of all members of one group as
being fortunate or unfortunate?

This is stereotyping: thinking about a person in a
particular way because he/she is part of a certain
group.

4) Can the class come up with its own definition of
stereotyping? Are there examples of stereotyping that
the class could identify within the school, the community, the nation, the world? For example:

<u>Stereotypes in school</u>

athletes are dumb

prettiest girl is brainless

those who play musical
instruments are brainy

<u>Stereotypes in community</u>

all those living in a certain
part of town are...(poor,
wealthy)

all those going to a competing
elementary school are jerks

<u>Stereotypes nationwide</u>

all politicians are thieves

all southern Californians are
crazy

all Texans are either rich or
poor

all Easterners are snobs

<u>Stereotypes worldwide</u>

all Africans live in the jungle

all Asians eat rice

all Scandinarians are blond

5) Having identified stereotypes both near and far
the following questions might be appropriate.

    a) Are stereotypes useful in thinking about
       other people?

    b) Can stereotypes be harmful because they
       may mislead?

    c) Do you have any personal stereotypes of others
       that you might now want to examine?

III. Purpose: Develop the skill to examine values and beliefs.

      Specific purpose: Identifying values and cultural
characteristics in history and contemporary society.

      1. Activity & materials

          <u>My</u> <u>Values</u>, <u>Your</u> <u>Values</u>

when: three or four periods

what: materials as needed

how: 1) Discuss the idea of values and beliefs with students.
Have students examine the following list of people
to decide what values motivated them to carry out the
activity for which they are noted.

> Columbus discovered America. (wealth, prestige,
> discovery)

> John Wilkes Booth shot Lincoln. (The cause of the
> south)

> Paul Revere rode to alert the people that the
> British were coming. (The cause of American patriots)

> John Glen orbited the earth. (discovery, adventure)

> Charles Lindbergh flew the Atlantic alone. (adventure,
> money)

> Susan B. Anthony fought for women's rights. (cause of
> womens
> rights)

> Harriet Tubman freed the slaves. (Freedom)

2) After students have discussed what values these people
had, help students arrive at a definition of "value".
Discuss with student what values are important to them
and list them on the blackboard: fairness, education, money,
"the future", things. Each student should list the five
most important values to him/her from those written on the
board.

3) Some people say Americans share in part the following
values: justice, liberty, worth of the individual, equality
of opportunity, individual responsibility, brotherhood,
limited government.

Have students examine the Mayflower Compact, the Declaration
of Independence, and the Constitution of the United States
(found in almost every American history text) to see if the
above values are found in these three documents.

Fill in the following chart by writing yes if that value
is found in document and no if it is not. If yes, then
tell what line of document value is found on. Do this for
all three documents.

(values)	Mayflower Compact		Declaration of Ind.		Constitution	
	yes/no	line	yes/no	line	yes/no	line
Justice						
Liberty						
worth of individ.						
equal opportuntiy						
individ. respons.						
brotherhood						
limited gov't						

Have students list the five most important values from
the combined three documents.

2. Activity & materials

It Was Like This...

when: two or three periods

what:

how: 1) divide students into three groups. Each group will
role play the making of a document; Mayflower Compact,
Declaration of Independence, or Constitution of the U.S.
Give them time to plan out their actions, and then they
can role play their parts.

2) Have several students act as secretaries. Their job
will be to write down all the values and beliefs they
see displayed as the others are role playing.

3) When the three groups are finished the secretaries
will list the values and beliefs on the board.

4) Hold a class discussion on the values. For example
these questions are appropriate:

    a) Do most of the people in U.S. hold the
       values found in the three documents?

    b) If we believe in the values expressed in
       these three documents, then are those beliefs
       carried out in your personal life?

    c) Are there instances when we do not follow our
       beliefs? Do we ever say one thing and do
       another? Wonder why that is!

3. Activity & materials

Decisions in the Past[10]

when: two periods

what: list of historic decisions

how: have students examine list of decisions made by leaders
in early American history. For example:

> crossing Atlantic to form first colonies
>
> dumping tea in Boston Harbor
>
> declaring independence to free colonists from
> England
>
> moving west for land
>
> moving west for gold
>
> leaving Mass. Bay Co. and separating church from
> state
>
> resisting the British at Lexington and Concord

Have students list values that must have motivated
the people who took the actions listed above.
Discuss what alternatives were open to the people
involved in the actions above. If they had chosen
an alternative, what values would they have held then?

4. Activity & materials

Suspicion on Trial

when: two or three periods

what:

how: 1) Some students always show a particular interest in
the stories of witches and witch trials in early New
England. Have those students research the trials to
gather information and notes that could be used for
role playing a classroom trial. Have students decide
on a situation. For example:

> "Christina likes to take a walk (on the beach,
> in woods, etc.) early in the morning before she
> starts the work for the day. When something
> strange happens or goes wrong during the day,
> people in the town say Christina had planned on
> those early walks with the devil for it to
> happen".

2) Students must prepare for trial by selecting a
judge, clerks, and secretaries, etc. The class can
act as a jury. From their research the students will
learn (and should include in their role play) that
accusations against witches were much stronger than
protestations that they were innocent. A person who
supported a suspected witch often ended up being
suspected himself/herself. Emotionalism also ran
high in the trials and this too should be brought
out in the mock trial.

Have students role play the trial.

3) When the trial is over the class can discuss the
values and beliefs that made the participants act
the way they did, and what effect values and beliefs
had on the outcome of the trial.

4) A culminating discussion should follow that relates
the witch trials to contemporary events. Are there
still "witch trials", that is people who accuse others
on the suspicion that the other person might be
subversive, i.e., The McCarthy era, minority rights
groups, ecology groups, anti-war groups, in general
protestors? Would there be anything in the newspaper,
radio, TV newscast or in the community that would
suggest suspicion on trial?

5. Activity & materials

What Is an American?

when: two periods

what: art supplies

how: 1) Discuss with class the question, Are Americans unique,
that is different from all other people? If so how are
they different? If not, how are they similar? Are there
certain ideas, symbols, etc. that characterize or represent an American?

2) Have each student produce either a collage or a mobile,
filmstrip or transparency that expresses what he/she

thinks Americans look like.

3) Let students share their projects with the class.
Be sure in summarizing that notice is taken of the
likenesses and differences between the visual portrayals
of Americans.

4) Discuss whether or not the class feels that values
held by Americans are different than those held by most
people around the world. Do Americans look different,
sound different, think different, feel different than
other people from other countries or cultures? What is
an American?

6. Activity & materials
    Stairway to the Stars[11]

when: one or two days

what: copies of "Stairway to the Stars"

how: c 1) Give each student a copy of "Stairway to the Stars".
        Explain that stars are rewards valued by students and
        that stairs are the way to obtain rewards. Let each
        student fill out his own copy. Let some students fill
        out transparency for Stairway for use with the overhead
        projector. Discuss values students have marked in their
        stars. How do the students' values compare with the
        values of early Americans as listed in activity number
        2 under this section above called "It Was Like This..."
        See next page for illustration.

Stairway	Stars
love	good looks
honesty	money
work hard	good family
set high goals	go places
work with others	do things
develop my talent	a nice car
	good grades

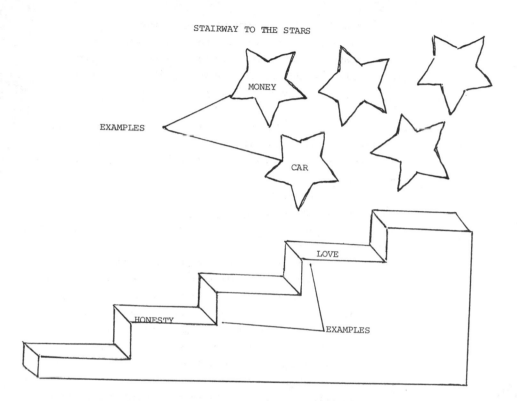

STAIRWAY TO THE STARS

7. Activity & materials

2001 Years from Now (identifying values and cultural
characteristics of contemporary
society)

when: one week

what: waterproof container (time capsule)

how: 1) Discuss with students what people 2001 years from
now would be interested in learning about our civilization.
Have student suggest everyday items that could tell someone in the future something about how we live. Establish
categories such as food, clothing, etc.
2) Divide students into groups and give each group
a category. Group members should discuss and decide on
objects to bring in that fit their category and small

enough to put in a waterproof container.

3) Get permission to bury the capsule (waterproof container) somewhere on school grounds or in a park. Make a map of location. Have a small ceremony to bury capsule and preserve map.

IV. Purpose: The application of knowledge through active participation.
Specific objective: Identifying the process of consensus and the skills and attitudes necessary for participation in community problem solving.

1. Activity & materials

Reaching Consensus on a Problem

when: three weeks

what: materials as needed

how: 1) Have each child identify a problem in the school or neighborhood community that should be solved. For example: problems of ecology, problems of safety, problems having to do with senior citizens, problems in school, problems a student in the class might face (illness, special treatment, needs of a family.)

2) Discuss these problems with the class and have the class reach a consensus on one problem that interests the class as a whole. (Take note of next activity which stresses reaching a consensus.)

3) Discuss and list on board:

a) What values caused them to pick this problem to work on? (worth of individual, brotherhood)

b) what attitudes will help them focus on the problem? (openmindedness, positive participation, cooperation)

c) What information will they need to gather to reach a solution to the problem?

d) What skills will be needed to process the information? (gathering information, interviewing, presentation)

3) Are there certain talents among class members that might help in working on the problem? (conservation

skills, relatives in senior center, might
have been involved in paper drives, fund
raising drives)

4) Set out tasks based on discussion above that class
must undertake to solve problem stressing the attitudes,
values, information, and skills needed to successfully
undertake the tasks. Divide class into groups and
assign tasks. Each group should keep a list of tasks
performed and the amount of time involved.

5) After a reasonable time a solution should be
reached or it should be agreed that no solution is
possible at this particular time.

6) It would be helpful to review how the students
proceeded and to summarize the activity. Keep in
mind that the central purpose is to encourage students
to identify problems and to believe that through
planning and organization they can do something about
the problem, they can be effective. Participation in
problem-solving is not a guarantee to success. We want
students to know they can participate. Both success and
failure are valuable learning experiences.

2. Activity & materials

What Is Our Consensus?

when: one period

what: list of statements

how: 1) Divide the students in groups of five or six and give
each group a copy of the list of statements.

List of Statements

Mark each statement with the
number that represents your
group's response to each
statement:

(1) agree strongly
(2) agree
(3) no opinion
(4) disagree
(5) disagree strongly

_____ 1. The American Revolution solved the problem of British domination
by freeing Americans to do what they want.

_____ 2. Without the Civil War America would still be suffering with
slavery.

_____ 3. Protesting over the use of nuclear power and women's rights
is un-American and should not be allowed.

_____ 4. Americans should be free to do absolutely anything they want.
_____ 5. Violence is necessary sometimes to achieve a citizen's rights.
_____ 6. Some citizens should have more rights than others because they contribute more.

2) Explain to groups that they must reach a consensus on how they feel about each statement. Make sure students understand that consensus is not a majority. Consensus means that <u>every member of the group must agree</u> to the strength of feeling they record on their list. Tell groups they have fifteen minutes to get agreement on the list.

3) After groups have worked only seven or eight of the fifteen minutes stop them and tell them to leave the task. Discuss the following:

    a) Would it help to have a group leader? If you had a leader, how did that person get the position?

    b) Is each member of the group allowed to express his/her opinion or are some members ignored?

    c) Did your group work out a plan on how to respond to the statements before you began?

    d) How could the group members work together more effectively?

4) Have the groups go back to reaching a consensus on the statements. After seven or eight minutes again stop the groups.

5) Discuss how each group worked and whether they were more efficient after they had considered their structure and procedure. What did the class learn about working in a group? For example these questions might be appropriate:

    a) What attitudes does one need to make a contribution to the group? (cooperation)

    b) What skills are important to group work? (leadership, recording)

    c) Is it always possible to arrive at consensus in a

small group?

d) Does consensus require compromise? Should you
always be expected to compromise? Is compromise
always good?

The following is a Pupil Evaluation of Self and
Group form. Students can evaluate their own
participation with the group and the group's
participation as a whole.

PUPIL EVALUATION OF SELF AND GROUP					
date_____	most all the time	frequently	about average	not often	did not do
SELF 1. I participated by making suggestions, arguing, discussing.					
2. I cooperated by listening to others and tried to work out difficulties (compromises)					
3. I am satisfied that I did my best to accomplish the group task.					
GROUP 4. The group made a real effort to accomplish the group task.					
5. The group worked together well by cooperating with each other.					
6. The group shared the responsibilities, no one was left out.					

V.   INTEREST FORM

You have just completed the Chapter Fifth Grade and in
an effort to have you identify activities and materials
that seem most promising at this grade level to you,
please fill out the following interest form.

Instructions:

Identify two activities from this chapter. Name the
activities and briefly describe why these particular
activities are of interest to you.

ACTIVITY 1

'ACTIVITY 2

CHAPTER SIXTH GRADE

ACTIVITIES AND MATERIALS FOR SIXTH GRADE

CHAPTER SIXTH GRADE

I. Advanced Organizer

Each succeeding chapter represents a particular grade level, in this case sixth grade. Each chapter consists of four parts and this is why the introduction is called an "advanced organizer." In other words you ought to know before reading this chapter how it is organized for such knowledge can help you to remember the major parts. The four parts are: part I is a brief discussion on courses, topics, and national trends in teaching sixth grade throughout the United States. The second part is an example of a state sixth grade program. The third part is activities and materials for the sixth grade categorized by the four purposes of teaching social studies: knowledge, processing, valuing, and participation. The fourth part of the chapter is an interest form.

II. Topics Taught and National Trends
in Teaching Sixth Grade[1]

To understand the course offerings in the sixth grade it is useful to recall the most frequently offered courses in the fifth grade: United States History, United States History and Geography, and Geography of North America. It is useful to recall these three approaches because the sixth grade social studies curriculum may be keyed to the course offerings in the fifth grade. In the sixth grade the three most frequently given courses are: American Neighbors, Western Europe and Latin America, and Eastern Hemisphere Geography and History.

Courses, Topics and Themes
most Frequently Covered in Sixth Grade
"American Neighbors"

Objectives of the course: Acquainting students with basic information about the geography and history of Canada and Latin America, or just in some cases Latin America; to extend the global view and help them develop an interest in world affairs; continuing their growth in command of basic social studies skills (processing information and valuing) and geographic concepts.

Basic content of the course: The course frequently opens with an overview of world geographic patterns--continents and their physical features, oceans, climates, etc., then moves into closer study of "American neighbors." If

Canada is treated the topics dealt with usually include, though not necessarily in this sequence; geographic overview of physical features and climates; historical development, with comparisons to United States history; resources and industries--i.e., ways of making a living in the various regions; relationships between United States and other nations.

Latin America is usually treated in a similar fashion: geographic overview; historical development, with special attention to the struggle for independence; study of selected individual countries or groups of countries, with attention to natural resources, industries and products, and daily life, changes that are under way and current problems. Nations or groups of nations that are frequently studied are Mexico; Central America; the Caribbean lands; northern South America (Venezuela, Colombia, Equador); the Andean republics (Peru, Bolivia, Chile); the Pampas countries (Argentina, Uraguay, Paraguay); and Brazil. A final block of study treats Latin American countries in world affairs, including their participation in the Organization of American States and the United Nations.

Courses, Topics, and Themes
most Frequently Covered in Sixth Grade
"Western Europe and Latin America"

Objectives of the course: Acquaint students with the relationship between European origins and American institutions. Though geographic concepts are stressed, the course is heavily oriented toward the history of the old western world. Students should identify and appreciate the basic foundational ideas of western civilization, and finally to identify the differences and similarities between the settlement and growth of Latin America and the North American continent.

Basic content of the course: The course places emphasis upon the geographic setting of western Europe, a brief examination of the foundations of western civilization which may include Greek, Roman, Renaissance, Reformation, Age of Reason, the Modern State and Nation. Emphasis is placed upon Europe's contribution to American heritage with particular stress on contemporary development of western Europe.

The course also places emphasis on the geographic setting of Latin America, the European role in exploration and discovery with special notice of Indian civilizations and their eventual conquest. Most time,

however, is spent on specific Latin American countries since their independence
concentrating on their political, social, and economic problems. The popularity
of this course is increasing because it does offer considerable flexibility.
Teachers can point out that the American continent, though settled by Europeans,
has contrasting cultures. American history in the fifth grade should provide a
foundation for studying western civilization with a comparison and contrast of
Latin American cultures with those of western Europe.

Courses, Topics and Themes
most Frequently Covered in Sixth Grade
"Eastern Hemisphere Geography and History"

<u>Objectives</u> <u>of</u> <u>the</u> <u>course</u>: Extending students' global education by acquainting
them with eastern hemisphere lands; continuing growth in command of geographic
concepts; developing appreciation of the contributions of great civilizations
of the past.

<u>Basic</u> <u>content</u> <u>of</u> <u>the</u> <u>course</u>: This course frequently devotes one-third to one-
half of the year to "old world backgrounds"--i.e., ancient civilizations, in-
cluding early civilizations in India, China and Egypt; through ancient
civilizations Greek and Roman up past the medieval period to the Age of Reason.
The other two-thirds of the year is spent in study of Europe, Asia, and Africa,
with emphasis on geography, economic life, ways of life, and modern problems
of the peoples of these lands. Fairly typical are the following units:
Geographic Overview (review of latitude, longitude, different types of maps,
continents, oceans, important cities, general land formations); Prehistoric
Times; Beginning of Civilization (Egypt, Babylonian, Greek, Roman); Western
Europe (Austria, Belgium, France, Germany, Great Britain, Greece, Ireland,
Italy, Netherlands, Scandinavian countries, Switzerland); Eastern Europe
(USSR and satellites); China, Japan, Southeast Asia and Australia; India,
Middle East and North Africa; Emerging Africa.

Trends in Teaching Sixth Grade Social Studies
1. The trend continues to be toward a combined geographic and historic
treatment of Europe and Latin America.
2. The trend is away from treating all countries in the hemisphere towards
the selection of a few representative countries in specific regions. The
effort is to get away from ground covering, hurrying from one state to another,

towards indepth studies that focus on economic and cultural life. Textbooks
for the sixth grade focused on studies of population, land form, exports,
and the countries geographic location in relation to other states. Contemporary texts place much more emphasis on life processes, that is how the
economic, social, and political systems people work under function to meet
their needs and interests.

3. A growing trend is that of treating the Soviet Union and its
satellite nations with considerable more attention than was true a decade
ago. What traditionally used to be the study of separate nations is now
becoming the study of certain world power blocks (Atlantic Treaty Organization
versus Warsaw Pact).

III. Illustration of a State
Sixth Grade Program

There is no one prescribed social studies program throughout
the United States. However, one state's description of its sixth grade program
will illustrate the content which the state expects to be taught. This illustration is included so that you can identify how a state mandates the
teaching of social studies in the sixth grade.

> In further developing the examination of regions of
> the world, a focus on either the western or eastern hemispheres
> may be chosen. Students should recognize links between the
> geography of the regions and the subsequent economic and social
> development which has occured. The Indian cultures of the western
> hemisphere or European cultures of the eastern hemisphere provide
> unique links with early and modern world civilizations and a
> focus for the study of cultural influences on American heritage.
> Examine how these regions are interdependent and how technological
> development has influenced them.[2]

IV. Activities and Materials Categorized
by Knowledge, Processing, Valuing, and Participation

I realize a rather common practice is to skip purposes and
specific objectives which precede the activities, but in this case the
objectives are extremely important for an objective in the sixth grade will
be found in proceeding grades. This is a developmental program with objectives, activities, and materials organized to build from one grade level to
another.

SIXTH GRADE ACTIVITIES AND MATERIALS

I. Purpose: Gaining knowledge about the human condition which includes past, present, and future.

Specific objective: Identifying the explorers of the western hemisphere and the countries they explored.

1. Activity & materials

Mapping Explorations

when: three periods

what: map of western hemisphere stressing Central and South America, colored pencils or magic markers

how: have students use different colors to trace on map the exploration routes of early world explorers (Columbus, Magellan, DeGamma, Vespucci, etc.) stressing those that reached South America. Discuss each explorer covering the following topics:

1) Name of explorer and country he represented.

2) What did the explorer find?

3) What were the results of the exploration?

4) Suppose you could have joined any of the explorers of South America, which would you have joined and why?

2. Activity & materials

Latin Lexicon

when: one period

what: list of definitions

how: have students match up names of countries with the definitions. It will help students become familiar with the names of Latin American countries.

Argentia	El Salvador	Colombia
Brazil	Nicaragua	Bolivia
Venezuela	Costa Rica	Trinidad
Uraguay	Peru	Tobago
Mexico	Honduras	Panama
Haiti	Guyana	Guatamala
Cuba	Barbados	Equador
Dominican Republic		Chili
Paraguay		Jamaica

Definitions

1. (R) + (slang term for male) + (INA) = (Argentina)

2. (what is mined for fuel) + (bump on the head) + (IA) = (Colombia)

3. (what you tie with a ribbon) + (what you do with life) + (IA) = (Bolivia)

4. (cut something just a little) + (AR) + (Spanish name for water) = (Nicaragua)

5. (L) + (nickname for Sally) + (VA) + (what you open to go from one room to another) = (El Salvador)

6. (what you say when you're cold) + (Wizard of _____) + (L) = (Brazil)

7. (what you say when it's cold in a room. "It's _____) = (Chili)

8. (opposite of smart) + (INI) + (what food is packaged in) + (RE) + (name for English drinking place) + (what you do to an ice cream cone) = (Dominican Republic)

9. (equal minus the 1) + (what you open to get in the house) = (Equador)

10. (nickname for Barbara) + (A) + (what you do when you take a nap) = (Barbados)

11. (box with equal sides) + (A) = (Cuba)

12. (GUA) + (favorite English drink) + (what you call your mother) = (Guatamala)

13. (boy) + (girl's name) = (Guyana)

14. (opposite of love) = (I) = (Haiti)

15. (what you spread on bread) + (pain) + (A) ▬ (Jamaica)

16. (motorcycle name minus A) + (UR) + (we) = (Honduras)

17. (rhymes with Texaco) = (Mexico)

18. (what you cook in) + (A) + (name for mother) = (Panama)

19. (name for two matching things) + (A) + (waterside dock) = (Paraguay)

20. (cat sound) + (R) = (Peru)

21. (your) + (A) + (waterside dock) = (Uraguay)

22. (name of Italian city with canals) + (highway minus high) + (musical sound) = (Venzuela)

23. (price) + (A)   (R) + (what you say when you see a mouse) + (A) = (Costa Rica)

24. (TR) + (not out) + (I) + (name for father) = (Trinidad)

25. (end of foot) + (sheep sound) + (opposite of come) = (Tobago)

3. Activity & materials

Researching South American States

when: two weeks

what: resource materials, list of names from previous
        activity (or teacher can make up list from what
        class is studying)

how: 1) Divide class into groups and give each group
        a different portion of names from the list.
        2) Each group will research its own list of
        names using the following questions:

      a) Where on map is country found?

      b) Why is country important to study?

      c) Suppose you could visit this country what would
         you want to see?

      d) How would you feel about living in this country?

        3) Each group may be requested to turn in a written
        report of its findings.
        4) When all groups have finished they can share findings
        with entire class.

Specific objective: Identifying the effect of environment
on developing societies and cultures.

4. Activity & materials

    Investigating a Society

when: two weeks

what: materials as needed

how: Divide the class into groups. Each group must choose
        a society or culture to study. Students research to
        learn about the land, people, customs, government, food,
        housing, religion, arts, etc. Each group must decide
        how to present their information to the rest of the
        class. For example:
        1) mobile: Each thing hanging from the mobile must
        represent something in the certain society being
        reported on. Each member of the group will have
        several things hanging on the mobile to explain and
        perhaps elaborate on to the class.
        2) float: Make a float (as in parade) using any means
        for wheels (skate boards, wagons, etc.). Group will need
        to decorate float to represent the society researched.

The float can be divided into sections and each member
of the group can explain his/her section to the class.
3) skit: Prepare a skit that includes costumes, scenery,
props, singing, dancing, food, etc., that is representative
of the culture or society being studied.

5. Activity & materials
   Comparing Cultures

when: one week

what: large paper or bulletin board

how: (this can be a follow-up activity to the previous one
which studied characteristics of various cultures) Make
a chart. Name the countries or civilizations being studied
down the side. Across the top make columns for such items
as climate, land forms, food, housing, clothing, religion,
the arts, etc. Groups will fill in the columns according
to the civilization they researched.

	climate	land forms	food	clothing	etc.
Ancient Greece					
Roman					
Asia					
Ancient Egypt					
etc.					

Have class discussion comparing and contrasting
the societies using the following questions:
   a) How did climate and land effect what
      people wore, what they ate, and the type of
      house they lived in?
   b) What customs arose from everyday life?
   c) Did religion effect or give rise to any
      customs?
   d) Suppose you had lived in that society, what

part of living in that time would you have
liked best? Liked least?

6. Activity & materials

"A Picture is Worth 1000 Words"[3]

when: one period

what: paper, pencil or crayons

how: In ancient Greece tombs were decorated with friezes
of figures and drawings depicting the life and activities
that surrounded the person whose tomb it was.
Have students draw small frieze using stick figures
depicting some everyday activity or holiday.
Have students exchange drawings to see if they can
understand each others.
Alternative: have groups draw frieze of culture
or society being studied.

Specific objective: Identifying the ideas of domination and
freedom as they are applied to people in the past and present.

7. Activity & materials

Are We Controlled?

when: one period

what: chart

how: 1) Have students list ten specific things they have done
within the past twenty-four hours. Next to the activities

have them list any rules, regulations, or laws or other
controls that might relate to the activities. Did they
do anything that had no control related to it. For example:

    played baseball - rules of the game.

    watched TV - stations regulated by FCC

    ate apples from own tree - no controls

    etc.

Alternative: set up chart of different areas of
students lives and have them fill in laws, rules, or
regulations that affect them in everyday life.
For example:

SCHOOL	HOME	COMMUNITY	SPORTS	ETC.
tardy bell	make bed pick up clothes	traffic light	baseball (game rules)	

8. Activity & materials

    Do We Need Rules?

when: one period

what: chart

NECESSARY RULES	UNNECESSARY RULES
_____	_____
_____	_____
_____	_____

how: Have each student think of a series of rules that
control his/her life. Have each student list those
they think are necessary in one column and those
they think are unnecessary in another column. Students
should be ready to defend their positions. Hold class
discussion to see if students can come to a consensus
on necessary rules.

9. Activity & materials

    Government Controls

when: one week

what:

how: Have each student pick a country to study. Students
        should concentrate on the country's government and
        the amount of control in the country.
        Questions for consideration:
        a) Does the country have one set of beliefs that
           must be believed and followed?
        b) Are people free to contradict beliefs of the
           country?
        c) Are people jailed for holding contradictory
           beliefs?
        d) Are people free to hold whatever job they want?
        e) Must people join a workers' organization?
        f) Are people free to criticize political leaders?
        g) Is education compulsory?
        h) Can people own property?
        After doing research on the above questions students
        should write a report on the amount of freedom allowed
        in the country he/she studied. A class discussion may
        be held using the reports.

10. Activity & materials

     Domination and Freedom

when: three periods

what:

how: 1) Discuss with students the ideas of domination or
        control of people and freedom or what kind of freedom
        can be allowed by a society.
        2) Examine each of the following societies on the
        following questions:

	Egyptian	Greek/Athens	Roman Empire	Modern Amer. Soc.
Who has freedom?				
Who is controlled?				
Who is doing the controlling?				
How is freedom defined?				

II. Purpose: Develop skills necessary to process information.

> Specific objective: Identify the four levels of questions: memory, description, speculation, and evaluation.

> 1. Activity & materials

>> Questioning Skills--Sixth Grade

> when: two periods

> what: Questioning Skills Self-Test

> how: Questioning skills identifying and classifying were introduced in the fourth and fifth grades. Questions were classified into two broad categories, open and closed. Why is knowing about the differences between questions important? The argument is that the teacher and the students spend a large portion of their time either asking or answering questions. We know that good questions may produce effective learning. Also we know that children ask and are asked both open and closed questions in, as well as out of school, and that open questions are related to the act of creativity. Because questions are such an integral part of the teaching-learning act it just seems to be common sense to train students in the skill of asking and answering questions. In the fourth and fifth grades questioning skill activities classified questions into two categories, open and closed. This sixth grade activity will identify two levels of open and two levels of closed type questions. Open is specu-lation and evaluation questions, closed is memory and description questions.

Open Questions:

In brief open questions are those that do not
have answers. Open questions require speculation
such as suppose and evaluation such as opinion.
Speculation questions allow for a variety of answers.
This type question is often considered to be one that
is thought-provoking. Teachers who ask speculative
questions are seeking original or creative responses.
This question often confronts students with problem
situations which ask them to combine facts and ideas
in new ways in order to construct a viable solution.
Examples of speculation questions are:

a) Suppose you had been born as a citizen of Panama
rather than the U.S., how might you feel about
the Panama Canal?

b) Who would you predict will be the Republican
candidate for the presidency in the next election?

c) How might your community be improved?

d) What would you hypothesize about the chances for
a Third World War?

The second type of open question is evaluation which calls
for judgment, values, and choices. Evaluation questions
require students to reach a decision to take a position.
For example:

a) What is your opinion of the President?

b) Why do you think the football team will win?

c) What do you think about the weather?

Test your skill at identifying the difference between
speculation and evaluation type questions. Mark S for
speculation and E for evaluation.

_(E)_ 1) What do you think about living on the moon?

_(S)_ 2) Suppose you lived on the moon how would that be
different from the way you are now living?

_(E)_ 3) Do you believe we will ever live in another galaxy?

_(S)_ 4) What would you predict would happen if the earth
acquired a second moon?

Closed Questions

In brief two closed type questions, memory and
description, have answers. Memory type questions call for
the lowest level of thinking. This type seeks answers
which require students to recall factual information.
Students respond to memory questions by recalling a
fact, defining a term, noting something they observe,
or simply giving an answer based on rote memory.
For example:

    a) What is the name of your school?

    b) Are you a boy or a girl?

    c) Were you sick last year?

    d) According to the weather report, what will the
       weather be today?

Description type questions require students to
establish a relationship between facts. They are
aimed at getting students to recall one right or
best answer to be put in their own words. Description
type questions are different from memory type because
they call for the student to explain, compare and
contrast, relate or associate whereas memory only calls
for recall of a specific fact. Description type
questions for example:

    a) Why was the bus late today?

    b) How does the pencil sharpener work?

    c) Compare your elementary school to another?

    d) Why are you in the sixth grade?

Test your skill at identifying the difference between
memory and description type questions. Mark M for
memory and D for description.

 (M) 1) Name the school principal?

 (D) 2) Compare the fall weather last year with the
       fall weather this year?

 (D) 3) How are you different from a ninth grader?

 (M) 4) What is your zipcode?

The following is a check on how well you can classify
questions using the four levels of questions you have
just learned.

QUESTIONING SKILLS SELF-TEST

Use the letters E (evaluation), S (speculation), M (memory),
D (description).

 M 1. How many states make up the U.S.?

 D 2. What is a peninsula?

 S 3. Predict what would happen if there were heavy rains
       in the Mississippi Valley?

 E 4. What is your opinion of moving the U.S. capital
       from Washington D.C. to a more central location
       in the nation?

 E 5. In your judgment who has made the greater contributions
       to space travel, the U.S. or Russia?

 D 6. What are the similarities and differences between
       the states of Maine and Florida?

 M 7. Was Texas one of the thirteen original colonies?

 E 8. Why do you feel that the summer is the best season of
       the year?

 S 9. Suppose we could control the weather how might this
       effect your life?

 D 10. Why does time start at Greenwich, England?

        Follow through activities

            a) As a follow-up activity students should examine their
               social studies texts for examples of the four levels
               of questions. Questions are usually found at the
               end of each chapter.

            b) Be sure that evaluations (tests) written and oral,
               reflect all four levels of questions. Test questions
               reflect the real priorities of the class.

Specific objective: Learning to measure chronologically using
the correct terms.

2. Activity & materials

    Understanding Time

when: three periods

what: materials as needed

how: 1) Prepare a chart of days spanning two weeks.
Combine Saturday and Sunday and call it "Weekend"
between the first week and the second week. Do
first week in red ink and second week in black ink.

Mon	Tue	Wed	Thu	Fri	Weekend	Mon	Tue	Wed	Thu	Fri

Explain that each day represents a century, that
"red week" will represent BW (before weekend) and
that the "black week" will represent AW (after
weekend). Help students to understand the concept.
For example:

red Tuesday is the fourth century BW.

black Wednesday is the third century AW.

2) Divide each day of chart into ten sections. Each
section represents ten years or a decade. Explain
to students that you count back from BW and count
forward from AW. Check students' understanding.
For example put an X on Red Friday (see below)
that is thirty years BW. Place an X on Black Monday
(see below) that is sixty years AW. Point to other
sections and see if students can tell decade and
century.

M T W T |||||||||| Friday || | Weekend | | Monday |||||| T W T F

3) Explain terms BC (before Christ) and AD (anno
Domini). Draw a chart of centuries and have students
mark centuries spanned by cultures or civilizations
that have been studied.

3. Activity & materials

Personal Time Line

when: one period

what: personal time line chart

how: Have each child create a personal time line.

See examples below:

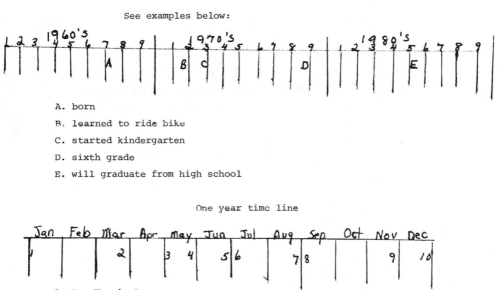

A. born

B. learned to ride bike

C. started kindergarten

D. sixth grade

E. will graduate from high school

One year time line

1. New Year's Day

2. spring starts

3. birthday

4. Memorial Day

5. summer vacation starts

6. Fourth of July

7. summer vacation ends

8. Labor day

9. Thanksgiving

10. Christmas

    4. Activity & materials

        <u>Western</u> <u>Civilizations</u> <u>Time</u> <u>Lines</u>

when: recurring

what: paper, yarn, markers

how: 1) Long sheets of butcher paper or news print are
fastened to the wall. Decide on number of time
lines desired (you may want only one or you may
want several to show the relationship between the
political, social, economic events in world history).

Draw the line or lines on paper using a different
color for each line.
2) As major events are studied the students should
put them on construction paper and fasten them
to the appropriate line at the appropriate time.
(lines could have century or even half century
markings).
As different lines are completed yarn matching color
of lines can be fastened from one event to another
that may have influenced it.

5. Activity & materials
    Time Line Rollers [4]
when: three periods
what: cardboard rolls from toilet tissue or paper towels.
       Teacher should label series of rollers with a date:
       decade, year, century, etc.
how: Rollers are handed out to students at random. Students
       write a report or draw a picture of a preselected topic,
       i.e., government, machines, housing, etc. that fits the
       date of their rollers.
       Reports are rolled and placed in rollers, rollers may
       be decorated.
       Students line up rollers in chronological order.
       A long rope is attached to one wall. Each student in
       order of dates on rollers reads his report or shows his
       picture, rerolls, it, and places it in roller and hangs it
       on the rope making a time line.

Specific objective: Identifying the culture and values
of people from items that they have lost, buried or left behind.

6. Activity & materials
    To Artifact or Not. That is the Question!
when: one period
what: paper bag, small objects

how: 1) Hold a class discussion on artifacts. Define
term and discuss importance of finding artifacts from
past cultures and civilizations. Definition: "Artifacts
are objects such as tools, pottery or ornaments discovered
in ancient ruins and known to be man-made."
2) Teacher fills a bag with small objects such as <u>flower</u>,
<u>stone</u> crayon, paper clip, <u>apple</u>, nail file, penny, bottle
cap, thimble, etc. Make sure bag has enough items so
each student can have one. The underlined items are not
artifacts because they are not man-made.
3) Students reach into bag and pick one item without
looking. Student then places object on table in either
an area marked "artifacts" or an area marked "not artifacts."
Students must give reason for placement.

7. Activity & materials
    Uncovering a Lost Civilization
when: four periods
what: materials as needed
how: 1) Divide class into groups. The students are going to
be archaeologists and uncover a "lost civilization."
Have each group choose a civilization or culture that they
would like to study. Groups must keep their culture a
secret.
2) Groups should use the following form for their reports:
    a) name of civilization
    b) names of artifacts that would be found in that
       civilization
    c) bibliography of references that were used
    d) pictures of artifacts (if possible) or careful
       drawings.
    e) model of one artifact (use art supplies, clay, etc.)
    f) make a diaorama of a cross section of an archaeological
       dig showing how at least three of the named artifacts
       might be found.
3) Groups should set up displays of their models

and dioramas. Other groups will try to determine
what culture was being studied.

Examples of Artifacts

Classical Rome	Medieval Europe	?
water wheel	water mill	
treadmill	stamping mill	
chariot	saddle, harness	
aquaduct	wooden plow	
stone paved roads	hand sickle	
stone bridge	wind mill	
arch	castle	
stylus	lance	
	battle ax	
	armour	

8. Activity & materials

School Artifacts Box [5]

when: one period

what: grocery bag or box, articles from school's lost and
found.

how: 1) teacher should go to school's lost and found and
fill bag or box with a variety of items children have
lost at school. For example: scarves, pencils (thin
ones, big kindergarten ones, stubs, chewed ones),
gloves or mittens (all sizes), boots, books, papers,
T-shirts, gym shoes (different sizes). If possible
fill box in layers according to the seasons.

2) The objective of this activity is to prepare
students to make accurate inferences about their
culture by observing what students in their school
have either thrown away or lost.

3) Either teacher or designated student in front of
class will select items one by one from box.
As each item is selected it should be recorded on the
board. For example: one layer might contain boot,
scarf, glove, hanky, and heel broken off of a shoe.

These things were touching each other, is there a
relationship between these items? Yes, these are all
items used in winter. Students might hypothesize that
heel was broken off when attempting to pull off boot.
Consider the following questions:

    a) Do the items tell you anything about the
       season of the year?

    b) Can you infer anything about the age and
       size of people who lost items?

    c) Do the different layers of lost and found
       items tell you anything about the change
       in seasons?

    d) Does the specific item tell you anything
       about who lost it, i.e., boy or girl, rich or
       poor, race, religion or beliefs?

This is really an exercise in observation and
inference. We can learn a great deal about people,
a culture by just observing what they leave behind.
This is as true for finds in Egypt as it is for the
school's lost and found.

9. Activity & materials

    What Culture Is This?

when: one period

what: foam plastic container that "Big Mac," "Super Chef,"
      etc. come in.

how: 1) Collect trash along road, in fields, around the
     neighborhood, i.e., paper, cans, etc. A civilization
     is known by the "things" it throws away. What can you
     infer about a civilization from the throw aways?
     Discuss above with class.
     2) Students pretend they are explorers from another
     planet and have landed on a dead earth which is
     covered by dust and nothing else. Only one item can
     be found by the explorers--the "Big Mac" container.
     3) The class must now decide what it can infer about

the civilization from just this one item. Have class
describe item. For example:

    a) it has color

    b) it has symbols or writing

    c) it has two sections that fasten together to
       make a container.

4) Discuss how this item might have been used and
what the culture might have been like that used it.

Specific objective: Using maps, charts, and tables for
comparison and decision-making.

10.   Activity & materials

      Buried Treasure

when: four periods

what: teacher prepared maps, charts, and tables (see example)

how: Teacher announces that there are three buried treasures
and the students must decide which treasure they want to
go for after studying the available information.
Divide class into groups for this activity.
Materials provided for study:

    a) Maps of three different countries where the
       treasures are buried. Maps of any countries
       will do as long as the maps have a scale of
       miles and physical features. The students will
       need to seek the treasure by land or water so the
       more rivers and mountains on the maps the better.
       Mark an X where the treasure is buried, and mark
       one port as the entry for the treasure seekers.

    b) Charts of monthly climate, population, and crime
       rate. For example:

CLIMATE		Jan.	Feb.	March	April	May	etc.
Country One	average temp.	10°	20°	35°	70°	75°	
	rain fall	11"	15"	6"	0"	0"	
Country Two	average temp.	95°	105°	95°	75°	70°	
	rain fall	0"	0"	0"	25"	32"	
Country Three	average temp.	65°	42°	20°	0°	-20°	
	rain fall	5"	7"	6"	0"	0"	

	POPULATION PER SQ. MILE	CRIME RATE
Country One	245	25%
Country Two	473	18%
Country Three	6	2%

c) Tables which show what the treasure consists
of (money, precious stones) and the amount
in each treasure. For example:

	money	gold	silver	jewels
Country One	$1,000,000	32 bars	none	none
Country Two	50,000	none	none	$2,000,000 worth
Country Three	none	300 bars	564 bars	none

gold bar = set a price
silver bar = set a price

Using materials provided groups must determine:

a) distance to each treasure

b) routes and transportation

c) what physical features must be passed

d) climate, what time of year would be best to go

e) where to get workers to help on the trip

f) crime rate--where treasure might be stolen

g) worth of treasure

After having considered all the above factors groups must decide what treasure they would go after.

Specific objective: Learning to identify differences between fact and opinion and primary and secondary sources.

11. Activity & materials

Primary and Secondary Sources of Information

when: one period

what: list of sources and secondary reports. The best place to find evidence of primary and secondary sources are newspapers, popular news weeklies, textbooks.

how: 1) Discuss with class the terms source or primary source and secondary source or secondary report. Primary sources are actual objects or records that tell us about the past. Since we cannot study all primary sources we rely often on secondary sources. These are usually reports from someone who has examined a source or other accounts and has put his/her own interpretation in the report. Secondary sources can be of great help, but they can also be misleading.

2) The following is a list of primary and secondary sources. Pass out list to students. Have them put P before those they believe are primary sources and S before those they believe are secondary sources.

Sources

P	1.	Watching Monday night football broadcast.
S	2.	Listening to sportscaster description of Monday night football game.
P	3.	Dead Sea Scrolls.
S	4.	History text.
S	5.	The Sword in the Stone -- story of King Arthur.
P	6.	President's televised State of the Union address to Congress.
P	7.	Satellite photo of weather condition on TV weather report.
P	8.	Sam Adams letters to his wife Abigail before American Revolution.

 P 9. Photo of the moon taken by Gemini space crew.

 S 10. News report on interview with astronauts.

 S 11. Painting of the Mayflower arriving in New England.

 S 12. A Thousand Days, report of President Kennedy's days in office by A. Schlesinger, Jr.

 P 13. Selected TV coverage of Olympic events.

 S 14. The TV showing of Roots.

12. Activity & materials

Fact or Opinion[6]

when: two periods

what: newspapers

how: Teacher should find-editorials from two papers on the same subject. Students should see if they can separate fact from opinion and give the reasons for their choices.

Find a report on a speech or event from two newspapers. Have students decide what is fact and what is opinion. Compare the two accounts. This is particularly good with a speech if you can obtain the actual text of the speech. For example:

Washington, D.C.: President's News Conference. The President held his monthly news conference this week. At the conference he spoke about inflation. "For the past ten years inflation has eaten away at the dollar to the point where America's money is in trouble around the world. American money is still respected and will remain the base for world trade."

Editorial Comment: The President held another rather useless, mostly ineffective news conference this week. As usual the President started the conference with an oft repeated, dull and uninspiring lecture on inflation. In his lecture he said that America's money is no longer respected anywhere in the world and is losing its value as the base of world trade.

13. Activity & materials

Bias in Media Reports

when: two periods

what: newspapers or school paper

how: 1) Have students select an article about a person

or event from any paper and pick out all the
descriptive words. Do the words suggest approval
or disapproval of the person or event?

2) Have students select articles that have a lot of
descriptive words (sports reports are good for this)
and for each positive word substitute a negative word
and for each negative word substitute a positive word.
How does this change the article. For example take the
Editorial Comment from the above activity. The article
below is the same editorial with positive words substituted
for negative words and vice versa. The words substituted
are underlined.

Editorial Comment:

The President held another rather
helpful, mostly effective news
conference this week. As usual
the President started the conference with an oft repeated, stimulating
and inspiring lecture on inflation.
In his lecture he said that America's
money is still respected anywhere in
the world and has not lost its value
as the base of world trade.

3) Have each student write his/her own two news reports of
something that happened in school. Use positive descriptive
words in one report and negative descriptive words in the
other report. How does this change the character of the
report?

14. Activity & materials

Point of View

when: one period

what: materials included below

how: 1) Hold class discussion on patriotism. Everyone has some
idea of what is right and what is wrong for the country.
Most everyone thinks he/she is patriotic.

2) Have students write brief paragraphs giving their
definition of patriotism.

3) Have students read the excerpts from a speech

on patriotism given by Mr. Rafferty and excerpts from
Thomas Jefferson's writings. (see below)

4) Discuss whether or not there is much difference
between Mr. Rafferty's and Thomas Jefferson's feelings
about patriotism. How do the students' definitions compare
with those of Mr. Rafferty and Thomas Jefferson?

Excerpts from a speech "The
Passing of the Patriot" by Mr.
Max Rafferty, former Super-
intendent of Schools, La Canada,
Calif.
"...teach /_children_/ every day in
every neccessary way to memorize and
to believe and to live Decatur's
great toast: 'Our country! In her
intercourse with foreign nations,
may she always be in the right,
but our country, right or wrong!'"

"Had they been taught to love their
country with the same passion that
inspired other generations of American
youth, they would not now be wondering
what all the fuss /_Viet Nam War and
civils rights_/ is about. They would
know that their country was in danger,
and that would be enough today. Too
many of them neither know nor care."

Excerpts from Thomas Jefferson's
letters.

"A little rebellion, now and then,
is a good thing, and as necessary
in the political world as storms
in the physical...It is a medicine
necessary for the sound health of
government" (To Madison, 1787)
"The tree of liberty must be re-
freshed from time to time with
the blood of patriots and tyrants.
It is its natural manure." (To
Colonel Smith, 1787)
"What country can preserve its
liberties, if its rulers are not
warned from time to time that this
people preserve the spirit of re-
sistance? Let them take arms."
(To Colonel Smith, 1787)

15. Activity & materials

   Modifying a Stereotype

when: recurring

what: magazines and newspapers

how: 1) Discuss meaning of stereotypes and have students think
of examples, i.e., minorities, old people, teenagers,
women, foreigners, the poor, welfare.

2) Have students bring in pictures of stereotypes or cut
them from magazines or newspapers in class. Display them
on bulletin board.

3) Teacher picks one example from the display. Each
student must obtain one example contrary to the stereotype.
For example: Teacher picks stereotype picture of old
person sitting in a rocking chair. Students must get

pictures of active or involved senior citizens.

Alternative: Have students bring in only pictures that
show stereotypes giving way--pictures contrary to stereotypes, i.e., Black executive, woman telephone repairperson

16. Activity & materials

I Am Pretending to be a.....Stereotype

when: one period

what: index cards with name of occupation or person that
is often stereotyped. For example: housewife, absent
minded professor, dentist, hippie, etc.

how: Have each student draw a card and role play the
stereotype. Can class guess who or what occupation
is being portrayed? Discuss characteristics commonly
used to stereotype each specific occupation.

For example: a) Are the characteristics true to life?
b) What are other characteristics common to
this occupation?
c) Suppose you worked at this occupation
would you try to practice a different set
of characteristics?
d) Are stereotypes of occupations helpful or
harmful when trying to understand the
world of work?

17. Activity & materials

Propaganda: the Art of Persuasion

when: two days

what: definitions

how: An introductory unit on propaganda was suggested for use
in the fifth grade. Propaganda techniques are now so
skillfully and persistently aimed at the general public
that it is not too early to start identifying and examining the different types of techniques at the fifth,
sixth, and seventh grade levels. Studying propaganda
techniques is an attempt to help students gain control
over a method of influencing them to believe and act in a
particular way. Propaganda is properly used to disseminate
information. However, it is important that children begin

to understand that propaganda can be used to get them to accept questionable points of view.

1) Hand out definitions to class and discuss with students these most common forms of propaganda.

2) Have students think of examples from TV, etc. and put them on board.

3) Have each student bring to class at least three different examples of propaganda techniques selected from the list of six below to share with class.

4) Have each student prepare one original propaganda example using any technique they wish, TV, magazine articles, etc.

Propaganda Techniques

1. Wishful thinking: assuming something to be true just by wishing that it were true.
   "I could knockout the heavyweight champion of the world, just let me get at him." "I know I can win, after all I'm from Texas."
2. Oversimplification: a simple or single cause explanation for a complex event that was the result of many causes. "The reason the school burned down was because it was Friday, the thirteenth."
3. Slogans: a snappy, short, catchy phrase calculated to stimulate and promote a particular point of view. "Coke adds life." "A and W rootbeer's got that frosty mug taste." "Tippecanoe and Tyler Too." "Go, fight, win, Wildcats."
4. Prejudice: reluctance to consider evidence or reasoning which is contrary to one's belief. A prejudgment about an event before the situation and facts are known. "All those kids over in Westside Elementary are snobs." "Look at him, he's just like his older brother."
5. Vagueness: the person uses a word that leaves an undefined, uncertain meaning.
   "Eat this, it's good for you." "The best things in life are free." "This movie is the worst." "This movie is far-out, cool, tough, bad, and not quite with it."
6. Out of context: statement or idea taken out of its original context for the purpose of distorting the meaning of the statement.
   Suppose you said, "All fourth graders at Lincoln Elementary are brats." but were later quoted as having said, "All fourth graders are brats." Suppose you said, "The book I read is boring, tasteless, surprising, and occasionally mildly humorous." and were later quoted as saying, "The book was surprising and humorous."

III. Purpose: Develop the skill to examine values and beliefs.

Specific objective: Identifying values of other cultures and comparing them to each other and to one's own values and beliefs.

1. Activity & materials

Values in the Past

when: recurring

what:

how: As each country, region, or culture is studied have students compile list of values and beliefs important to those people. Students should have research to support their lists. Alternative: Develop a master list of values and rank importance of values for each country, region, or culture being studied. For example:

Values   Countries

Values	Brazil	Other Latin Countries	Ancient Greece	Ancient Rome or European nations during monarchies or ? whatever is being studied.
Education			1	
Future			3	
Authority			2	
Past heritage			5	
State-supported Religion			4	
Developing natural resources			6	
Etc.			7	

Discuss with class that these are generalizations, that there are always some people who may disagree with their society's values. (Students should discover this in their research).

2. Activity & materials

Fly Your Own Flag

when: three periods

what: dowel rods, construction paper, art supplies

how: 1) Hold class discussion on beliefs valued by ourselves and our ancestors. Some students may have family crests they would like to bring in and explain to the class.

2) Students are now ready to construct their own pennant. Cut a large pennant from construction paper (two to three feet long) for each student. Shape depends on preference. For example:

3) It would be best for students to plan their pennant on scrap paper before the art work is done on the construction paper pennant.

Students should include on their pennant:

a) three words that describe what they value. For example: courage, truth, honesty, fairplay, equality, justice, etc.

b) a symbol or drawing of what they like to do now. For example: sewing (needle and thread or thimble), ball, skates, skis and poles, book for reading, etc.

c) a symbol that might depict something their family likes to do. For example: camping (tent), hiking figure, biking figure, fishing pole, boat, tennis racquet, golf club, etc.

d) a symbol of what they would like to be in the future. For example: doctor (medical bag), fireman (hat), teacher (torch of knowledge), etc.

4) Wide end of pennant is rolled around dowel rod and and glued, taped, or stapled in place.

Example of pennant:

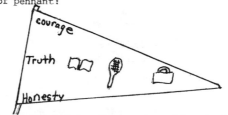

Specific objective: Identifying the meaning of beauty in other cultures and comparing it to one's meaning of beauty.

3. Activity & materials

Sixth Grade Newspaper

when: three weeks

what: materials as needed

how: Students will create a newspaper using beauty as the main theme. Depending on what class is studying, newspaper could feature beauty in ancient civilization, or beauty in Latin American countries, or beauty in European countries, etc.

Jobs:

    a) Editors to interview, write stories, receive
       reports from other student, faculty, or com-
       munity members. For example on Latin America:

           Editor for Brazil

           Editor for Argentina

           Editor for Mexico

           Editor for Colombia

           Editor for Chili

           Editor for El Salvabor

           etc.

    b) illustrators

    c) committee to put final paper together so it
       can be run off (copier, mimeograph, etc.)

A total class planning session should be held to plan
newspaper. Jobs should be assigned or volunteered for.
There should be a job for each member of the class.
Students then should break up into groups for each job
and plan their activities.

4. Activity & materials

    In My Opinion

when: two periods

what: materials as needed

how: Each student picks something that he/she believes is
     beautiful from the past and something from the present.
     For example:

       past--Greek statue
      present--Calder mobile

       past--Parthenon in Athens
      present--National Art Gallery in Washington, D.C.

       past--dress from era of Louis XV
      present--modern ball gown

       past--Coliseum in Rome
      present--Astrodome in Houston

Students must plan how to show their choice.

For example:

    costume dolls
    carefully mount pictures
    prepare a clay model
    prepare a brief slide presentation
    diorama

IV. Purpose: The application of knowledge through active participation.
     Specific objective: Identifying one's own values and
     learning to participate in a group concerned with values.
     1. Activity & materials
         Reaching Consensus

when: one period

what: list of social or community problems

how: 1) Give each student the list of problems and have
       him/her rank the problems in order of priority:
       (1) being problem he/she feels is most in need of
       attention, and (2) being second most important, and
       so on.
       2) Divide class into groups. Each group will try to
       reach a consensus on ranking the problems. Consensus
       is very difficult to reach since every member of the
       group must agree to the order of ranking established
       by the group.
       Suggestions for reaching group consensus:
            a) Don't change your mind just to go along with the
               other members of your group, but "bend" a little
               if you can agree a little with the group's opinion.
            b) Avoid easy solutions such as majority vote, com-
               promising, etc.
            c) Listen to all opinions and use logic.
            d) When group reaches consensus each member should
               mark group's ranking on his/her sheet and then
               record the difference between his/her own ranking
               and the group's. For example:

Individual ranking	Social problem	Group ranking	Difference
6	school safety	2	4
2	women's rights	5	3

3) Hold class discussion on:

   a) Reasons for differences between individual and group ranking.

   b) Similarities and difference between group rankings.

   c) For person in each group whose personal ranking came closest to group ranking--were there reasons for this?

PROBLEM LIST

	Individual ranking	social or community problem	group ranking	difference
1.	_____	school safety	_____	_____
2.	_____	highway safety	_____	_____
3.	_____	pollution	_____	_____
4.	_____	crime	_____	_____
5.	_____	unemployment	_____	_____
6.	_____	inflation	_____	_____
7.	_____	race relations	_____	_____
8.	_____	gun control	_____	_____
9.	_____	women's rights	_____	_____
10.	_____	alcoholism	_____	_____
11.	_____	world peace	_____	_____
12.	_____	cost of medical care	_____	_____

2. Activity & materials

Inquiry--A Citizen's Obligation
in a Democratic Society[7]

Why this concern about inquiry when our interest is in citizenship? Authorities say that the one major goal for teaching social studies is that of developing citizenship. Remember, when we are talking about citizenship, we are not talking about some vague abstraction but we are talking about you. We are primarily interested in your effectiveness as you participate in a democratic society.

It should be clear that an assumption is being made. We ask the question, "Why is it best for a citizen to inquiry?" Not only do we assume an answer to this question, but notice

that we also make a value judgment that there is a best citizen.
We answer, "The best citizens should inquire in a democratic
society because they can discover for themselves the most meaningful properties of their environment." In other words, the
best citizen is the autonomous person who has gained the skill
of checking ideas about the environment--that is, a citizen capable
of making rational independent judgments.

Inquiry as a Method

Some would say that the truth shall make you "free."
Others believe that it is the process of seeking truth that makes
you "free." We cast out lot with the latter belief that it is
the method of gaining knowledge (inquiry) that will assist you
to be an effective citizen, an autonomous citizen.

What Is Inquiry?

Some authorities suggest that one way to avoid bias,
stereotypes and prejudiced type thoughts is to apply the inquiry
method. The method merely provides a step by step process by
which thoughts can be verified. Inquiry implies a particular way
of apporaching life, for a true inquirer is highly skeptical of
pick-up knowledge but sensitive to his/her own felt problems.

The inquiry method has six steps:

1. Experience
    The process of inquiry starts with an experience.

2. State of uncertainty and doubt
    The heart of inquiry is not fact. It is uncertainty.
    It is not the established, symmetrical "givens" that
    generate inquiry. It is that which does not fit--
    the irregular, the confusing.

3. Framing the problem
    The sensing of the problem may lead you to frame
    that which you do not know, and it is that frame
    which becomes the statement of the problem.
    The statement of the problem prescribes the
    boundaries within which the conflict is seen and
    the tension created.

4. Formulating hypotheses

When you frame an hypothesis you are literally "brainstorming the possibilities." The framing of the problem gives you the limits within which you will hypothesize.

5. Experiencing and evidencing

The title of this stage almost explains itself. At this stage you gather and evaluate sources of evidence.

6. Generalization

The final step in the inquiry process is generalization. The generalization is a statement about how well the hypothesis has given meaning to the understanding of the problem.

when: depends on problem studied

what: Inquiry Form, list of issues

how: 1) Student picks issue to investigate.

2) Each student uses Inquiry Form in investigation.

3) Individualized instruction--teacher gives help when needed as students work on forms.

4) Students' conclusions reported to class.

Issues

world hunger

birth control around the world

problems in the "Fourth World" underdeveloped nations

problems in the "Third World" underdeveloped nations

problems in the "Second World" developed nations

problems in the "First World" developed nations

China's role in the world

Middle East conflict

use of power reserves

problems of water and water usage

growing deserts

wars and the threat of wars

mining of the seas

fishing rights

space exploration

control and use of space

atomic proliferation

disease control

pollution control

United Nations

INQUIRY FORM

1. Experiencing: What experience have you had with
   the issue you have chosen from the above list
   that has caused you to be interested in or curious
   about that issue?_____

   _____

   _____

2. Uncertainty and doubt: The issue can become a
   personal as well as a social problem if you feel
   the need to know. Express as best you can the
   uncertainty you feel about the issue. What con-
   fuses you?_____

   _____

   _____

3. Framing the problem:
   What do you know about the issue?_____

   _____

   _____

   What do you think you know about the issue?_____

   _____

   _____

   What is it you do not know about the issue?_____

   _____

   _____

4. Formulating hypotheses: The hypothesis is a proposed point of view on the issue. That view needs
   to be proved or disproved._____

   _____

   _____

5. <u>Exploring and evidencing</u>: Gather and evaluate
   sources of evidence on the issue.
   Circle and then name the sources you will use in
   finding information about your hypothesis.

   books   pictures   newspapers   filmstrips
   magazines interviews personal observations
   other

   _____

   _____

   _____

   List specific pieces of information that deal
   directly with your hypothesis._____

   _____

   _____

6. <u>Generalization</u>: How does your information prove or
   disprove your hypothesis?_____

   _____

   _____

   Evaluating the inquiry: What have you learned? Has the
   inquiry into the issue provided you with an accurate
   point of view on the issue?_____
   Explain:_____

   _____

   _____

V.   INTEREST FORM

You have hust completed the Chapter Sixth Grade and in
an effort to have you identify activities and materials
that seem most promising at this grade level to you,
please fill out the following interest form.

Instructions:

Identify two activities from this chapter. Name the
activities and briefly describe why these particular
activities are of interest to you.

ACTIVITY 1

ACTIVITY 2

NOTES

CHAPTER SEVENTH GRADE

ACTIVITIES AND MATERIALS FOR SEVENTH GRADE

CHAPTER SEVENTH GRADE

I. Advanced Organizer

Each succeeding chapter represents a particular grade level, in this case seventh grade. Each chapter consists of four parts and this is why the introduction is called an "advanced organizer." In other words you ought to know before reading this chapter how it is organized for such knowledge can help you to remember the major parts. The four parts are: part I is a brief discussion on courses, topics, and national trends in teaching seventh grade throughout the United States. The second part is an example of a state seventh grade program. The third part is activities and materials for the seventh grade categorized by the four purposes of teaching social studies: knowledge, processing, valuing, and participation. The fourth part of the chapter is an interest form.

II. Topics Taught and National Trends
in Teaching Seventh Grade

In this book an examination of elementary social studies curriculum is extended to the seventh grade because in many respects what is taught in grades four through six could just as well be found in seventh. For example, some states and cities teach their history in the seventh grade rather than in the fourth. Some states will start American history (studies) in the seventh grade while others will wish to continue the global studies from the sixth grade through the seventh. Some states have mandated the teaching of non-western studies in the seventh grade while requiring state history to be taught at the fourth grade level. If you have a suspicion that the alternative directions a teacher can go with social studies increases from first grade through sixth, then you probably have sensed the trend correctly. We know for sure that the eighth grade will be American history just as we knew fifth grade would be American history because of the recommendations of the Wesley Report. In a sense seventh grade social studies is a catching up, a capstone to all of the global and comparative studies that have preceded it.

There appears to be five distinguishably different courses offered at the seventh grade level. They are: State History, Seventh and Eight Grade American Studies, Old World Eastern Hemisphere Geography and History, World Geography, and Global Studies (with emphasis on area studies of the non-Western World).

Courses, Topics and Themes
most Frequently Covered in Seventh Grade
"State History" and
"Seventh and Eighth Grade American Studies"

The objectives for state history at the seventh grade level are
approximately the same as those offered at the fourth grade level. If you
need to recall both the objectives and the content of state history, then
refer to the fourth grade.

A recent development has been the combining of seventh and eighth grade
into American studies. The course often resembles the following: seventh
grade is state history and early national history, eighth grade is modern
and contemporary national history and American government. The seventh
grade portion of the course is almost exactly the same as the fourth grade
course called "State and United States History."

Courses, Topics and Themes
most Frequently Covered in Seventh Grade
"Old World Eastern Hemisphere Geography and History"

This course is similar in objectives and content to the course
with the same general characteristics wich is frequently taught and has
been described above in grade six. Those schools which teach this course
in seventh grade undoubltedly devote sixth grade to a study of Latin
America or American Neighbors. The historical portion of the course that
deals with foundations of the western civilization are intended to provide
background for the study of United States history in grade eight.

Courses, Topics and Themes
most Frequently Covered in Seventh Grade
"Global Studies (with emphasis on area studies of the non-
Western World)"

With the growth of dependence on and interest of the United States
since World War II in Third World Nations schools have begun to mandate
area studies of the non-west. These studies include areas such as Sub-
Saharan Africa, the Middle East, South Asia, Southeast Asia, East Asia,
and the Soviet Union. The course is designed in such a way that there is
an overview of the area and then one indepth study of a particular country:
Nigeria, Egypt, India, Japan, China, etc. The emphasis is not only upon
the development of these nations but upon how the development of these

nations effect the balance of international power.

Courses, Topics and themes
most Frequently Covered in Seventh Grade
"World Geography"

World Geography has been a traditional course offered at the seventh grade level. Because of the rather standard offering of this course, it may be useful to view objectives and basic content as a means of contrasting this traditional course to a similar course offered in the sixth grade and the preceding seventh grade Global Studies.

Objectives of the course: Developing the students' world view; reinforcing and expanding their understanding of geographic concepts and skills.

Basic content of the course: After an introductory unit on physical geography, selected countries and regions of the world are studied, with attention to physical features, climate, resources, industries and products, and the "way of life of the people." World relationships of the various countries and regions are usually treated. The following list of units is typical: Understanding the Physical World Around Us; Introducing the Caribbean Countries (chief emphasis on Mexico, Canal Zone, Guatemala, Costa Rica, Venezuela); Introducing the Countries of South America (chief emphasis on Argentina, Brazil, and Chile); Introducing the USSR and eastern Europe; Introducing the Far East (emphasis on China, Japan, and India); Introducing the Middle East and Northern Africa (emphasis on Egypt, Saudia Arabia, and Israel); Introducing Africa south of the Sahara (emphasis on Ghana and Union of South Africa); Introducing Western Europe (emphasis on Great Britain, France, and Germany).

Trends in Teaching Seventh Grade Social Studies
1. Seventh grade social studies seems to be the catch basin for all leftover topics, themes, and key concepts which for some reason were not treated in the first six grades. It could be proper to view seventh grade social studies as the place to cap off or tie up loose ends.
2. Some states have made an effort to coordinate seventh and eighth grade into a two year sequence including United States history, geography, civics, and the study of the home state. This effort is an attempt to create the base for a consistent program in junior high rather than having it remain a tail end course for elementary. In many states the middle schools are still unsettled as to what their systematic curriculum ought to be.

3. As some schools devote the entire year of grade six to Latin America or American Neighbors, Eastern Hemisphere Studies, World Geography or Global Studies are apparently taking over grade seven.

4. A course such as World Geography in which a large number of nations are surveyed continues to be a traditional but not necessarily a recommended approach. Courses built exclusively upon the survey tend to pressure teachers into ground covering, rushing from nation to nation in an attempt to cover the world. A contemporary approach of educators is one that calls for a quick survey of a region with an in-depth study of one or two illustrative countries within that region.

III. Illustrations of a State
Seventh Grade Program

There is no one prescribed social studies program throughout the United States. However, one state's description of its seventh grade program will illustrate the content which the state expects to be taught. This illustration is included so that you can identify how a state mandates the teaching of social studies in the seventh grade.

> Global Studies at this juncture, provides an opportunity for students to synthesize concepts gained in prior grades while further extending their knowledge of the world in which we live. An in-depth examination of areas of the world such as Europe, the Middle East, Africa or Asia (depending on the emphasis in prior grades) will provide greater understanding of our dependence on resource available in various geographic locations and how economic, social and political institutions develop in relationship to our environment. Students should be provided opportunities to incorporate current global news into the program to emphasize how the present has been influenced by the past and will affect the future in a global setting.[1]

IV. Activities and Materials Categorized
by Knowledge, Processing, Valuing, and Participation

I realize a rather common practice is to skip purposes and specific objectives which precede the activities, but in this case the objectives are extremely important for an objective in the seventh grade will be found in proceeding grades. This is a developmental program with objectives, activities, and materials organized to build from one grade level to another.

SEVENTH GRADE ACTIVITIES AND MATERIALS

I. Purpose: Gaining knowledge about the human condition which includes
    past, present, and future.

    Specific objective: Learning to recognize geographic concepts.

    1. Activity & materials

        World Wide News 2

    when: three periods

    what: world map, thumb tacks, construction paper

    how: 1) Each student must bring in a news story (magazine
           or newspaper) about some country other than the United
           States.

           2) Each student tells what his/her news story concerns
           then he/she puts the date of the story on a small piece
           of construction paper and tacks it to the map at the
           place where the story took place.

           3) When all students have presented a story, a list
           should be drawn up of all the places the stories re-
           present. Make sure each story is listed under the
           continent of which it is a part.

           4) This activity can be extended to teach students
           how to measure by longitude and latitude. Have each
           student find the longitude and latitude of his/her
           particular story.

           The following are sample headlines about foreign
           countries.

           "Arrests strengthen Somoza's hold"
                                              Managua, Nicaragua
           "Canada, Vietnam to look for oil"
                                              Hanoi
           "Moslems protest against shah"
                                              Tehran, Iran
           "Latest controller slowdown ends"
                                              Paris
           "Argentina head defends regime"
                                              Rome
           "Jerusalem hit by bomb blasts"
                                              Jerusalem

    2. Activity & materials

"It's a Small World, After All"[3]

when: two periods

what: folders from travel agencies

how: 1) Discuss with students the idea of the world seeming
        smaller because of modern travel mostly by plane. Plane
        routes are planned to take the shortest distance between
        two cities. Have students look at globe from the North
        Pole. See how planes may use the polar route as a
        shorter route. For example planes from Los Angeles
        fly over the Pole to reach England and northern Europe.

        In past years students have studied how long it
        took pilgrims to reach America, how   Forty-niners
        moving west to California had to leave early enough
        in the spring to get over the Rocky Mountains before
        the snows of late autumn trapped them. Time of year
        and weather are no longer the major concern of a
        traveler. Quite often we no longer measure how far
        one place is from another in miles, we measure it in
        time. (Grandma lives two hours away)

        2) Have students measure some distance by time.
        For example you can travel:

4 miles in an hour walking
50 miles in a hour by car
25 miles in a hour by ship
500 miles in an hour by plane

        How long would it take to get from Indianapolis to
        Atlanta, Georgia 500 miles away by foot? (125 hours)
        By car? (10 hours)
        How long would it take to get from San Francisco to
        Honolulu 2050 miles away by ship? (82 hours)
        By plane? (4 hours)

        3) Obtain some travel folders from a travel agency.
        Include cruise folders. Have each student pick an
        overseas trip he/she would like to take. Students
        must figure the miles from one stop to the next and
        then figure the distance in hours by car, plane, and
        ship (by whatever means they would be traveling).

3. Activity & materials

    Exploring West Africa

when: one period

what:

how: Divide the class into groups. Each group has been
        given the opportunity to explore a West African country.
        Each group must plan their trip from a port or major
        city and travel across the country. As explorers they
        must keep a detailed record of the trip including land
        forms, weather, climate, vegetation, animal life, etc.
        Examples of trips:

            Bamako to Timbuktu in Mali

            Accra to Tamale in Ghana

            Lagos to Kano in Nigeria

            Conakry to Kankan in Guinea

            Douala to Garoua in Cameroon

            Fort Lamy to Largeau in Chad

        Example of report:

June 1:   Disembarked at Lagos. Large city.

          Water unsafe for drinking.

          Temperature in 90°s, high humidity, heavy late
          afternoon rain.

June 2:   Left Lagos to travel north.

          Temperature still 90°s with high humidity.

          Tropical rain-forest country.

   . . . . . .

June 7:   Crossed Niger river at town of Jebba.

          Temperature still high, humidity less.

          Country has changed from rain forest to savannah.

   . . . . . .

June 31: Reach Kano, city of mud-walled compounds.

          Everything is dry and brown. The edge of the
          Sahara Desert lies to the north.

Specific objective: Identifying the effect of geographic
factors on people and cultures.

4. Activity & materials

The Encroaching Sahara

when: three periods

what: story paragraph below, resource materials

how: 1) Have students read paragraph below and perhaps
some resource materials that pertain to the region
of West Africa.

2) Hold class discussion. Include:

a) geography of area

b) way people live

c) problems faced by expanding desert and
improved standard of living

d) possible alternatives for inhabitants

e) future predictions for area.

Jusif Tanko is a thirteen year old Nigerian boy. He
lives in a compound with his family near Katsina in northern
Nigeria. Jusif's family has always been able to grow enough
yams and peppers to feed themselves and to sell in the market.
But in the last few years the amount of land they could work
has been shrinking. As the standard of living improves for
Jusif Tanko's family more children live and the family grows
in number. The family needs more firewood so more trees are
cut, they own more goats which eat all of the grass at a faster
rate. As the land is stripped in this way the Sahara Desert
advances and takes over the land. The slowly advancing Sahara
is destroying the land of the Tanko family. There is little
rain and in the winter the harmattan winds blow across the
desert carrying sand further south each year. Soon Jusif
Tanko's family will be forced from their land.

Specific objective: Identifying characteristics of a culture.

5. Activity & materials

Concept Wheel[4]

when: one period

what: wheel diagram

how: The following is a method to help students understand
events, trends, ideas, and their implications and

consequences.

Place anything you want to understand (event, trend, idea) in the middle of a small circle in the middle of a paper. Draw lines spoke-like out from your circle. At the end of the lines write what goes with it--its implications, consequences, associations and such. If you wish you can then run out consequences of the consecqueches and so forth. This gives an orientation to the understanding you generate from your original idea in the middle of the circle.

For example:

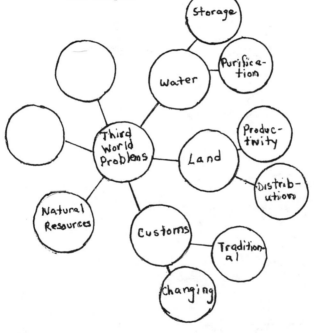

6. Activity & materials

Building a Culture

when: one period

what: Identifying what is common to all cultures. To show how the common elements are related.

how: Using what is common to all cultures a form is built

using triangles to show how characteristics
are related. May make a free-form figure by placing
triangles anyway they fit or may make a specific figure.
For example:

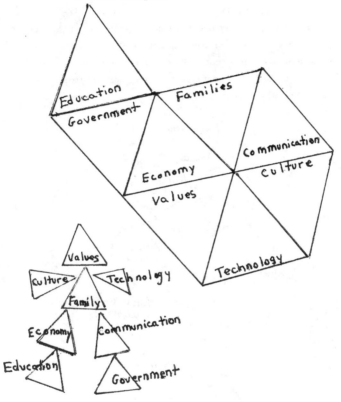

7. Activity & materials

Discovery--Culture [5]

when: one period

what: Artifacts or some means of learning about artifacts
such as pictures or descriptions of a past or present
day culture unknown to students. Artifacts could
cover long time period and if so they should be stated
so. For example:

       pictures of Chinese culture covering all or
         part of 5000 years.
       Egyptian culture, 4000 years.
       Japanese, for the past 200 years.
       India, for the last 2000 years.
       Africa, for the past 1500 years.
       etc.

how: 1) Teacher should scatter (put in several locations)
the artifacts around the room.

2) Divide the class into groups, and have them move
around the room examining the artifacts and discussing
and reflecting on the growth (and possible decline) of
the culture. All students' ideas should be considered.

3) Disclose the culture to the students after they
have had sufficient time to study artifacts and make
deductions. Give a brief history of culture. Compare
actual culture with the students' speculation of
artifacts.

8. Activity & materials

    Ils-o-way[6]

when: three periods

what: description of country below

how: Have students read description of country below.
From this available information students should try
to determine as much about the people and culture as
they can, i.e., family structure, work, technology,
future, etc. Back up deductions with facts or what
you infer from the description of the country.

A small chart may help to clarify understanding of
deductions. For example:

	Cultural inference	Evidence
Family Structure		
Work		
Technology		
Future		

Ils-o-way Culture

Geography:

A cold country with a short summer growing season.
Surrounded on three sides by water. Low coastal area
changes abruptly to hills which merge eventually with the
mountains on its fourth side.
Rainfall is moderate in the summer but the winter snows drift
many feet high.
The country is about the size of Arizona and has a
population of about three million people, and has remained
this size for the past thirty years.
The natural resources are fish and off-shore oil. There
is some trade in furs and wood carving.

Effects of Geography:

Most people make a living that is in some way
connected with the sea.

> fishing 42%
> ship building and trade 15%
> processing fish 9%
> off-shore oil rig 12%
> other 20%
> unemployed 2%

Housing: stone with some wood
Clothing: much use is made of animal skins for their
warmth in the bitter winter cold.
Off-shore drilling has caused fishing fleets to go
farther for their catch. Major harbor nearest
off-shore drilling has been widened and improved.
Most people live along the coast in the major cities.
There are some families who farm the coastal plains in
summer and hunt and trap in the winter. Their numbers
remain fairly constant. The population of the towns has
begun a slow growth in the area of the off-shore oil drilling.

Goals:

Raise the standard of living for all citizens.
Become self-sufficient and independent and remain
somewhat isolated from the rest of the world for citizens
do not want to experience the social change of modern
industrial nations.

9. Activity & materials

Assessing the Future
of other Countries

when: one period

what: information of Ils-o-way from previous activity, chart

how: 1) Record the natural resources, goals, and the

consequences of Ills-o-way on the chart below.

Seeing the information of the chart makes it easy

to hold a class discussion on the following questions:

   a) Name the country's assets and natural resources?

   b) What are the future goals of the country?

   c) Suppose the country were able to reach its ideal
      goal, how would that change the country?

2) Pick two contrasting countries. Chart them the same

way. For example, compare Iran or Nigeria with Ils-o-way.

How do they differ, how are they alike?

Natural resource and assets	Goals	Consequences
fish oil ful wood carving	become independent and self-sufficient raise standard of living.	Stay about the same as they have been over the past 400 yrs.

Specific objective: Identifying the similarities and
differences in different cultures.

10. Activity & materials

Proverbs[7]

when: two periods

what: proverbs and sayings below

how: Almost every culture has "sayings" that express beliefs

or customs of that culture. Often sayings are similar

from one culture to another.

1) Have students examine the sayings listed below.

2) Have students pick African sayings that have the

same meaning as a saying from another country. Is

there a reason why the phrasing is different?

3) Have students pick out the African sayings that have no similar saying in another culture. Explain possible reasons.

By the time the fool has learned the game the players have dispersed.
                    (Ashanti)

When the horse has been stolen, the fool shuts the stable.
                    (French)

Death does not sound a trumpet.
                    (Congo)

Death does not blow a trumpet.
                    (Danish)

Rain does not fall on one roof alone.   (Cameroon)

When it rains, it rains on all alike.   (British)

There is no medicine to cure hatred.   (Ashanti)

Hamte knows no age but death.
                    (British)

No matter how long the night, the day is sure to come. (Congo)

It's always darkest before the dawn   (American)

Knowledge is always better than riches.   (Ashanti)

A learned man has always riches in himself.   (Latin)

When you follow the path of your father, you learn to walk like him.
                    (Ashanti)

Like father, like son.
                    (Latin)

One camel does not make fun of the other camel's hump. (Guinea)

The pot does not call the kettle black.   (British)

One falsehood spoils a thousand truths. (Ashanti)

It is the calm and silent water that drowns a man. (Ashanti)

Wood already touched by fire is not hard to set alight. (Ashanti)

If you are in hiding, don't light a fire. (Ashanti)

The ruin of a nation begins in the homes of its people. (Ashanti)

If the palm of the hand itches, it signifies the coming of great luck. (Baustoland)

She is like a road--pretty but crooked. (Cameroon)

You do not teach the paths of the forest to an old gorilla. (Congo)

Two birds disputed about a kernel, when a third swooped down and carried it off. (Congo)

A close friend can become a close enemy. (Ethiopia)

One who recovers from a sickness, forgets about God. (Ethiopia)

Unless you call out, who will open the door? (Ethiopia)

When spider webs unite, they can tie up a lion. (Ethiopia)

You cannot build a house from last year's summer. (Ethiopia)

A blade won't cut another blade; a cheat won't cheat another cheat.
(Ethopia)

Where there is no shame, there is no honor. (Ethiopia)

(M)

(S.S. BOOK)

Advise and counsel him: if he does not listen, let adversity teach him. (Ethiopia)

If there is no elephant in the jungle, the buffalo would be a great animal. (Ghana)

Knowledge is like a garden: if it is not cultivated, it cannot be harvested. (Guinea)

After a foolish deed comes remorse. (Kenya)

He who is unable to dance says that the yard is stony. (Kenya)

11. Activity & materials

Categorizing Cultures

when: one period

what: pictures from any source representing shelters, food, clothes, family, law, etc., in many cultures.

how: 1) Divide class into groups and distribute pictures.
2) Groups should separate pictures into categories such as shelter, food, clothes, family, law, etc., and further separate them as to whether they are representative of the past, present or future.
3) Hold class discussion on results of group categorizing and observed differences between cultures.

12. Activity & materials

Identifying Culture

when: one week

what: pictures of shelters, pictures of environment, designated locations, resource materials as needed.

how: 1) Show students pictures of different types of shelter preferable from a wide variety of cultures. Shelter is basic to survival. Many factors influence shelter such as environment, technology, money, etc. Have students determine where they would find these various shelters and why. Help them draw up generalizations about shelter.
2)Show students pictures of environment without shelter. Using generalization findings have students speculate about what type of shelter would fit the environment.

3) Expand the exercise: give student locations by longitude and latitude. Have them locate position on globe and determine what kind of shelter would be found there on the basis of research on climate, resources, land forms, etc.

Activities: construct models of shelters

paint mural depicting shelter and environment

research paper on shelter

invite architects or builders to visit class

forecast future shelter designs.

Specific objective: Identifying how cultures and societies are interdependent and interrelated.

13. Activity & materials

Interdependence or Isolation

when: one period

what: review of regions previously studied

how: Most developed and developing countries are economically dependent on one another to some extent. Have students come up with examples from countries studied. Record examples on the board. Have students answer the following questions:

a) Are there any countries that are totally independent? Name country and location.

b) Are there countries that could maintain existence if they were isolated? Explain.

c) What are the countries that might quickly perish if isolated? Explain.

d) Does a higher standard of living mean a more complex interdependence with other nations?

e) How would your life be different if the United States were cut off and isolated from the rest of the world?

II. Purpose: Develop skills necessary to process information.

Specific objective: To identify and practice writing the four different types of questions.

1. Activity & materials

Questioning Skills--Seventh grade

when: two periods

what: practice checklist, practice writing form, textbook

how: Seventh grade questioning skills is a·continuation of
        activities and materials started in the fourth grade.
        In grades four and five categories of different levels
        of questions were limited to open and closed. In
        the sixth grade the two categories were extended to
        include speculation and evaluation as levels of open
        questions and memory and description as closed level
        questions. If there are questions about the differences
        between the different levels of questions, see four,
        five and six grade materials on questioning. The
        reason for emphasis on questioning skills is to
        encourage a variety of levels of thinking in the class-
        room. Memory, description, speculation, and evaluation
        are roughly the lowest to the highest levels of
        thinking, all of which should be used by both teachers
        and students. Have students mark the following
        questions to check their mastery.

Checklist

Mark the questionswith their appropriate letters:
M for memory, D for description, S for speculation, and E for evaluation.

__M__ 1. What is the population of Nigeria?

__D__ 2. Compare Nigeria with Niger?

__S__ 3. What would you predict about the future of Nigeria?

__E__ 4. Would you want to live in Nigeria?

__D__ 5. Explain how the Niger River effects Nigeria's economy?

__M__ 6. Name the largest city in Nigeria?

__D__ 7. Describe where you find the Jos highland in Nigeria?

__M__ 8. Identify Nigeria's major cash export?

__E__ 9. Do you think Nigeria is a powerful African nation?

__S__ 10. How might Nigeria improve its form of government?

            If students have difficulty identifying the type of
            questions in the above checklist use the sixth grade

materials on questioning as a review.
Have students practice writing the four levels of
quesions at least twice over the social studies
topic the class is studying.

<table>
<tr><td></td><td>1.</td><td>Speculation: (for example) What would happen to Nigeria if its oil reserves ran out?</td></tr>
</table>

open
questions

2. Evaluation: (for example) What in your opinion keeps Nigeria as a third world nation?

3. Memory: (for example) What is the name of the largest city in the north of Nigeria?

closed
questions

4. Description: (for example) Describe Nigerians transportation problems?

1. Speculation:_____

_____

open
questions

2. Evaluation:_____

_____

3. Memory:_____

_____

closed
questions

4. Description:_____

_____

Follow up activities

a) As a follow up activity students should examine
their social studies text and other supplementary
materials for examples of the four levels of questions. Questions are usually found at the end of
each chapter.

b) Be sure when evaluating to include all four levels
of questions. The four levels will assume importance
if students find they are used in testing.

Specific objective: To identify the criteria for good
oral and written reports.

2. Activity & materials

Oral Report Checklist and Teacher[8]
Evaluation

when: time length of report determined by teacher

what: oral report checklist

how: 1) Students must choose topic related to what
class is studying.

2) Students must outline report and get teacher's
approval of outline. Students should checkout
anything they do not understand at this time with
teacher.

3) Students must use more than one source to obtain
information from more than one point of view.

4) Teacher should give copy of oral report form
to students so they can use it as a guide.
Teacher will use form to evaluate student while he/she
is giving report and then will give checklist to
student after report.

Oral Report Checklist			
student's name	well done	satisfactory	needs attention
1. Approved outline			
2. Write subject on board			
3. Face class, speak slowly			
4. Identify sources			
5. State time and place of subject			
6. Relate subject to what class is studying			
7. Give report from notes (no reading)			
8. Write difficult names on board or on overhead			
9. Summarize			
10. Be ready for class questions.			
11. Comments:			

3. Activity & materials

Oral Report Evaluation Form
for Students

when: at time of oral reports

what: oral report form for students

how: Students are encouraged to evaluate performance of
       other students presenting oral reports. The following
       form will allow students to evaluate an oral report
       and add comments.

       Have students fill out form either during or after
       report.

Oral Report Evaluation Form for Students	very weak	fair	good	very good	superior
student giving report _____ evaluator _____ 1. Introduction was interesting.					
2. Student related topic to what we are studying in class.					
3. Student was able to make report interesting with personal opinions yet stuck basically to facts.					
4. Student summarized briefly					
Comments:					

4. Activity & materials

Papers Evaluation [9]

when: one period or at end of writing assignment

what: evaluation form

how: This form may be used as an exercise in evaluating
       an essay selected by teacher or students may use it
       to self-evaluate his/her own paper and then check
       evaluation with teacher.

Papers Evaluation

students's name
_____

title of paper
_____

Content:

	excellent	good	suggestions for improvement
1. Sources: number selected and quality			
2. Thoroughness of investigation			
3. Exactness of data			
4. Subject covered to extent required.			
Style 5. Form: table of contents footnotes bibliography titles and subtitles			
6. Spelling and punctuation			
7. Students expression of content			
8. Proofread			

Specific objective: To identify propaganda techniques with which people attempt to influence others.

5. Activity & materials

Propaganda Skills, Seventh Grade

when: two days

what: materials attached

how: We are persuaded to particular points of view and that is what propaganda is all about. Propaganda is a means by which people are influenced to make choices. In a world where media is used so frequently to teach and preach the techniques used by that media to influence should, for the sake of the individual, be identified and understood. Activities and materials on propaganda techniques were identified in Chapter Fifth Grade and Chapter Sixth Grade. Chapter Seventh Grade will conclude the introductory activities on the propaganda techniques.

Have students practice on identifying techniques studied
in fifth and sixth grade as a check on their level of
mastery.

Instruction: match the propaganda techniques by writing the
letter beside the name of that technique on the line by the
sentence which best illustrates that technique.

__a__ 1.	I call Senator Jones a lier.	a. name calling
__b__ 2.	All politicians are crooks	b. glittering generalities
__c__ 3.	You know my grand father was a good man, so you can trust me.	c. transfer
		d. testimonial
__f__ 4.	All the kids have one why I can't I have one too.	e. plain folks
__d__ 5.	This is Billy Carter talking, "Drink this, it's good."	f. bandwagon
		g. card stacking
__e__ 6.	"You all know me, I'm just one one of the folks."	h. wishful thinking
__g__ 7.	Buy this used car, look at all the wonderful things it's got, good tires, no rust, and a radio.	i. oversimplification
		j. slogans
__h__ 8.	I am the richest person in the world because I think I am.	k. prejudice
		l. vagueness
__j__ 9.	"Coke adds life."	m. out of context
__i__ 10.	The reason I failed the test was because a black cat crossed my path.	
__k__ 11.	We just don't like those people, after all they are new comers.	
__l__ 12.	This is really a great wonderful product.	
__m__ 13.	He said, "All girls could be beautiful but many don't try." You said he said, "Most girls don't try to be beautiful."	

---

1) Hand out new definitions to class and discuss with
students these common forms of propaganda.

2) Have students think of examples from TV, etc. and
put them on board.

3) Have each student bring to class at least two
different propaganda techniques to share with class.

May display these on bulletin board.

4) Have each student prepare one original propaganda
example using one of the four techniques learned during
this activity. The example may be whatever they wish,
i.e., TV, magazine ads, etc.

5) Check students knowledge with matching questions.
(see below)

Propaganda Techniques:

1. Arousing feelings: the attempt to persuade others for
   or against a particular point of view by appeal to
   emotion.
   "This is our big rival so go to the game and cheer on
   the team." "This is the big game for our dear beloved
   school."

2. Appeal to rank and status: relating rank or status of.
   the person or event to the object or idea which is intended
   to persuade.
   "The club president, who is a wealthy man, thinks this
   way, perhaps you should." "The greatest golfer in the
   world drives this make of car, perhaps you also deserve
   that elegance."

3. Sales promotion: an appeal is made on the grounds that
   a sale on items will save you money. The sale may or
   may not be real, comparative buying is the only way
   to know if savings is real.
   "Sale, for two days only: all items one-third off."
   "You'll never save more than you will right now."
   "Buy now, save now."

4. Repetition: the technique calls for repeating the idea
   over and over until the name or product is familiar and
   will be recognized at the appropriate time.
   "Vote for George. George will get the job done. George
   needs your support. George is the one."
   "Double your pleasure, double your fun, with double good,
   double good Doublemint Gum."

Instructions: write the letter for the appropriate propaganda
technique on the line next to the most appropriate sentence.

_____1. All the important people have one.   a. arousing feelings

_____2. This is our annual white sale.   b. appeal to rank or
         status
_____3. Think pink, Dad; get pink, Dad;
     be pink, Dad.   c. sale promotion

_____4. The President has it now, do you   d. repetition
     want it too?

_____5. Our lives are at stake, we have
     to fight pollution.

III. Purpose: Develop the skill to examine values and beliefs.

Specific objectives: Identify values of culture other than
one's own.

1. Activity & materials

Contrasting Cultural Values

when: one period

what:

how: students will examine values of a non-west culture
at the end of the study unit on that non-west culture.
Divide students into groups. Have groups list values
that mattered to the people during the time period
studied.

Compare and contrast group lists.

	Japan	Communist China	India	Nigeria
1. Education				
2. Authority				
3. Family				
4. Religion				
5. etc.				

2. Activity & materials

Foreign Film Festival[10]

when: one or two periods depending on length of film

what: foreign film or film highlighting another culture

how: Show foreign film.

Hold class discussion on following questions or have students answer them individually.

1) What action did main character take?

2) What prompted the main character to take action?

3) What values would you imagine the main character believed in?

4) If you (student) had been in the same situation how would you have acted?

5) What values would prompt you to act the way you would?

6) Compare values and actions of main character to that of students.

3. Activity & materials

Identifying Current Global Values[11]

when: two periods

what: newspaper or magazine reports on a country or group of countries selected by teacher. For example:

Tehran, Iran--Many thousands of Moslems protested against the Shah of Iran when they marched through the streets of Tehran. The Moslems were demonstrating their objection to the Shah's plan to try Western style democratic reforms such as extending voting rights, holding democratic elections and supporting a representative legislature. The protesting Moslems favor a return to strict Islamic rule.

Farnborough, England--Britains "air and space bazaar" which is held every two years, opened Monday with many fewer war planes from the United States and none from Russia. Emphasis is on products manufactured in Third World countries and on cooperation between nations on earth and in space.

how: Examine headlines and major points of stories.

What values are inferred. Using sample news stories above for example:

Values Inferred	Support for Inference-
Democratic values (Shah)	Proposed reforms
Islamic values (protestors)	Protests in the streets
Cooperation	Third World products
Peaceful use of space and land	Fewer military planes

Specific objective: Identifying how the values of national
leaders effect decisions in a different time and place.

4. Activity & materials

Time Machine[12]

when: one period

what: chart

how: Imagine that the following people have been carried
through space and in some cases time. Jimmy Carter
finds himself in the Germany of Adolf Hitler. He is
to take the place of Hitler in 1932. Ghandi is be replace
Churchill. Socrates is to replace Mao Tse-Tung in
China. Attila the Hun is declared Pope and the Pope
is the Soviet Premier in the Kremlin. Idi Amin is
King of the Netherlands; the list, of course, is
endless.

What would be the reaction of the above people? What
problems would these men face if they tried to govern
using the methods they normally practice? Use the
following chart:

What are the consequences of an individual applying his values and methods in the times to which he is transported?				
Name	Values & Methods	Location to which transported	Time to which transported	Consequences
Carter		Germany	1932	
Ghandi		England	1940	
Socrates		China	1977	
Attila		Italy	1975	
Pope John Paul I		Russia	1978	
Idi Amin		Netherlands	1976	

Specific objective: Identifying values from what selected
men and women say about each other.

5. Activity & materials

What is Said About Women and Thought[13]
About Men

when: one period

what: materials attached below

how: Every culture has values of some kind. Often the same
        values are held by different cultures and often
        values are passed from one generation to the next in
        the form of short sayings.

        Below are some things that have been said about men
        and women. Examine each example: Do we still hold
        these values? Explain:

WOMAN

"Take my word for it, the silliest woman can manage a clever
man, but it needs a very clever woman to manage a fool."
                                        Kipling

"Choose in marriage only a woman whom you would choose as
friend if she were a man."   Joubert

"I will not say that women have no character; rather, they
have a new one every day."   Heine

"Women better understand spending a fortune than making one."
                                        Balsac

"Being a woman is a terribly difficult trade, since it
consists principally of dealing with men."   Conrad

"I would gladly raise my voice in praise of women, only they
won't let me raise my voice."   Winkle

"Talk to women as much as you can. This is the best school.
This is the way to gain fluency, because you need not care
what you say, and had better not be sensible." Disraeli

"When God saw how faulty was man He tried again and made
woman. As to why he then stopped there are two opinions.
One of them is woman's."   De Gourmont

MAN

He who thinks that he never was a fool is a fool now.

Man is the only animal that can be skinned more than once.

A man who will never change his mind, may not have any mind
to change.

A man is judged by the company he keeps.

A man is valued according to his own estimate of himself.

Men talk wisely but live foolishly.

He who hears forgets, he who sees remembers, he who does learns.

A lazy boy and a warm bed are difficult to part.

IV. Purpose: The application of knowledge through active participation.

   Specific objective: Identifying the relationship between quality and quantity of work and grade achievement.

   1. Activity & materials

      Teacher--Student Contracts[14]

when: recurring

what: contract form

how: student participates by entering into a contract with teacher.

CONTRACT

_____ is contracting for a grade of_____.
student's name

_____ may contract for a higher grade at any time but
student's name   never for a lower grade.

_____ (Twenty points will be subtacted for each day
due date   work is overdue)

                           _____   _____
                           teacher's name   date

- - - - - - - - - - - - - - - - - -

Activities selected from list below to fulfill contract obligations:

Activity selected (describe)   possible points   grade

- - - - - - - - - - - - - - - - - -

Contract Activities for Africa
(example)

possible
points
 50 1. Prepare a chart naming countries in Africa and date they won independence. Include whether independence was gained peacefully or with violence.
 30 2. Do map of colonial Africa in 1920's.
100 3. Write essay on slave trade in West Africa.
100 4. Write essay on early native government including powers of sultans and emirs in Nigeria.
 60 5. Make a chart of resources of West Africa that attracted foreign nations.

50 6. Write essay on how Great Britain could claim Gold Coast
and force Africans to follow their rule.
75 7. Read text_____pages_____to_____.
Answer questions numbers_____on page_____.
75 8. Read text_____pages_____to_____.
Answer questions numbers_____on page_____.
75 9. Read text_____pages_____to_____.
Answer questions numbers_____on page_____.
200 10. Do a biography of an African dictator. Include
bibliography.
90 11. Make a chart of ten Africal tribes giving name,
way of life, and location.
60 12. Make a chart of wildlife native to West Africa.
25 13. Prepare native African food and serve to class.
30 14. Summarize (one page) movie seen in class.
100 15. Write essay on Moslem religion and customs.
50 16. Make chart with drawings of native shelter in various
parts of Africa.
? 17. Student identified activity with teacher approval.
Teacher sets possible points.

_____points = A
_____points = B
_____points = C

Specific objective: Student and teacher identify their roles
in evaluating achievement.

2. Activity & materials

Student--Teacher Activity Evaluation[15]

when: three periods

what: joint evaluation form

how: 1) This activity is one way to involve student in
self-evaluation.

2) How to use:

a) pass out form and have students complete I and II
before activity is begun.

b) have students complete III, **IV,** V, and VI after
activity is finished, and turn it in to teacher.

c) teacher completes VII and gives it back to
student, OR
teacher and student complete VII together during
a conference.

Student--Teacher Activity Evaluation

_____
student's name

  I. Issue being studied_____

_____

 II. My activity_____

_____

III. What I have accomplished specifically_____

_____

 IV. Research materials used:

     titles   authors

  V. What I learned_____

_____

 VI. Students self-evaluation:

     I deserve the following grade_____

     Because_____

     My suggestions for changes in this activity._____

_____

VII. Teachers Evaluation: Grade_____

     Ranking: from 4 representing   Comments:_____
     excellent to 0 representing
     poor work.

     4 3 2 1 0   class work
     4 3 2 1 0   self control
     4 3 2 1 0   use of time
     4 3 2 1 0   research
     4 3 2 1 0   cooperation
                    with others

    3. Activity & materials

        Unit Evaluation: Student Self Checklist

when: one period

what: checklist form below

how: At the end of a unit of study have each student fill out

the self checklist. This activity will help student
to evaluatie his/her own participation and provide the
teacher with necessary feedback from the student.

Unit Evaluation: Student Self Checklist

name_____

date_____

unit title_____

1. I understood the purpose of the unit...
    (check those words that best represent your feelings)
    _____right from the start of the unit
    _____not during any part of the unit
    _____got some understanding, but not much
    _____confused most of the time
    _____knew what I was doing
    _____don't really know what the unit was all about
    _____just never made sense to me
    _____(your own words)_____.

2. I spent most of my time during the unit...
    (check those words that best represent your feelings)
    _____reading
    _____talking
    _____listening
    _____doing very little
    _____working hard most of the time
    _____playing around
    _____with a small group project
    _____learning somethings
    _____learning a lot of things
    _____just kind of messing around
    _____(your own words)_____.

3. The best part of the unit for me was...
    (check those words that best represent your feelings)
    _____working with others
    _____working by my self
    _____finding resources
    _____just sitting around
    _____the class presentations
    _____the small groups
    _____talking with the teacher
    _____learning things that were important to me
    _____(your own words)_____.

4. If I had a chance to do the unit over I would...
    (check those words that best represent your feelings)
    _____work a little harder
    _____work about the same
    _____discourage the teacher from teaching this unit
    _____read more
    _____write more

_____play around more
_____participate in small groups more
_____try to get more out of the unit
_____(your own words)_____.

4. Activity & materials

Student-Teacher Group Procedures[16]
Evaluation

when: one period

what:

how: 1) Divide students into groups of four or five. Leave
enough students so each group has an "observe".

2) Observers must listen to statements made by group
members and categorize them:

    a) statements related to activity: "Explain what
      you mean."

    b) positive statements: "Good idea!"

    c) negative statements: "That's dumb!"

Observers can just make a checklist and mark it off as
they listen to the group. For example:

a--statements related to activity...
b--positive statements.............
c--negative statements.............

If possible observers might want to write some
statements down if they have time.

3) Give groups a topic to discuss. For example:

providing more electrical power for African
    nations
using the natural resources of African nations

human rights in African nations

selling arms to African nations.

4) After a short group discussion have observers report
on their own checklist or on combined checklists to the
teacher and then to the class.

5) Discuss checklists with class stressing how
related statements and positive statements achieve
more than negative statements.

6) Let each group give brief report on their
discussion.

5. Activity & materials
    Student Evaluation of Committee Work

when: one period

what: evaluation form

how: At the end of committee or group work have each student
        evaluate how well his/her own committee functioned.
        The form will help students summerize their participation
        and provide teacher with necessary feedback.

Student Evaluation of Committee Work					
Check the box that tells how the committee worked.					
Evaluation Sentence	most all the time	frequently	above average	not often	did not do it
1. The committee members contributed ideas and suggestions.					
2. The committee shared materials.					
3. The committee did the job assigned to it.					
4. The committee members listened courteously when others were talking.					
5. The committee works together well.					
6. This committee should work together again.					

6. Activity & materials
    Student Evaluation of His/Her
        Group Participation

when: one period

what:- evaluation form

how: At the end of group work have each student evaluate his/her participation as a member of the group. This form will help students identify their own particular contribution to the group effort. Suggest these forms be used by students at least once a week, collected over the period of the grouping and passed back to student for analysis and evaluation at the end of a marking period.

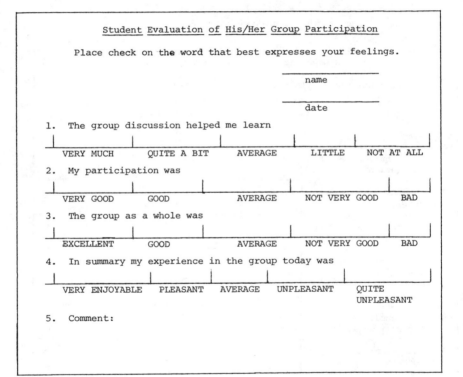

Student Evaluation of His/Her Group Participation

Place check on the word that best expresses your feelings.

_____
name

_____
date

1. The group discussion helped me learn

VERY MUCH   QUITE A BIT   AVERAGE   LITTLE   NOT AT ALL

2. My participation was

VERY GOOD   GOOD   AVERAGE   NOT VERY GOOD   BAD

3. The group as a whole was

EXCELLENT   GOOD   AVERAGE   NOT VERY GOOD   BAD

4. In summary my experience in the group today was

VERY ENJOYABLE   PLEASANT   AVERAGE   UNPLEASANT   QUITE UNPLEASANT

5. Comment:

V.   INTEREST FORM

You have just completed the Chapter Seventh Grade and in
an effort to have you identify activities and materials
that seem most promising at this grade level to you,
please fill out the following interest form.

INSTRUCTIONS:

Identify two activities from this chapter. Name the
activities and briefly describe why these particular
activities are of interest to you.

ACTIVITY 1

ACTIVITY 2

NOTES

CHAPTER EIGHTH GRADE

ACTIVITIES AND MATERIALS FOR EIGHTH GRADE

CHAPTER EIGHTH GRADE

I. Advanced Organizer

Each chapter represents a particular grade level, in this case eighth
grade. Each chapter consists of four parts and this is why the introduction
is called an "advanced organizer." In other words you ought to know before
reading this chapter how it is organized for such knowledge can help you to
remember the major parts. The four parts are: part I is a brief discussion
on courses, topics, and national trends in teaching eighth grade throughout
the United States. The second part is an example of a state eighth grade
program. The third part is activities and materials for the eighth grade
categorized by the four purposes of teaching social studies: knowledge,
processing, valuing, and participation. The fourth part of the chapter is
an interest form.

II. Topics Taught and National Trends
in Teaching Eighth Grade

Eighth grade social studies, much like the fifth grade, as distinct from
other grade levels is "reserved" for American history. Again this did not just
happen, it was planned as part of a fifth grade, eighth grade, and senior high
American history cycle by the 1943 Committee on American history in the Schools
and Colleges commonly known as the Wesley Report. The Wesley Report is
important because school systems by and large have followed the recommendation
of the Committee. The Committee not only established the three cycles but
recommended appropriate historical periods and topics to be taught in each
cycle. The fifth grade was to emphasize discovery, colonization, colonial
period, becoming a nation, and the movement west with in depth study up to the
1850's followed by a rapid survey to the present. The intention was that
history and geography were to be integrated into telling the story of the
development of the North American continent in the seventeenth, eighteenth and
early part of the nineteenth centuries with special emphasis on the United
States and often Canada.

Eighth grade American history was to be concerned essentially with the
nineteenth century with special emphasis upon the Constitution, development of
the nation, sectionalism, slavery, Civil War, industrialization, immigration,
and America's emergence as a world power. This was to be followed by a rapid
survey of contemporary American history. The third and final cycle, senior

high American history, offered usually in eleventh grade, was to emphasize
the twentieth century stressing the World Wars, economic problems, and social
movements with at least one-third time devoted to today's contemporary
problems. The recommendation was that in all three cycles rapid surveys would
be a standard part of each course but the emphasis would be on a particular
historical period. The obvious intention was to discourage teachers form
attempting to cover (in depth) all of American history in each cycle.
Teachers who have attempted the in depth approach from discovery to the
present in one year have found that the school year runs out somewhere around
the depression and the Second World War. If the assumption is that the study
of history would help students to identify appropriate lessons from the past
to be applied to contemporary events, then the course is not achieving the
desired goal because instruction rarely reaches contemporary application.

Courses, Topics and Themes
most Frequently Covered in Eighth Grade
"United States History"

Objectives of the course: Students will identify significant historical
events which have led to the development of the nation's traditions and its
territory. Will develop a critical yet cooperative attitude when examining
concepts such as freedom and democracy. Will continue to develop skills in
decision-making.

Basic content of the course: A chronological survey of American history with
special emphasis (perhaps three-quarter of the text) on the nineteenth
century. Such topics as European origins, discovery, colonization,
ind pendence are rapidly surveyed. In depth attention to fundamental
documents, Declaration of Independence, slavery, Civil War, reconstruction,
industrialization and America as a world power, followed by a rapid survey
of events in the twentieth century.

Courses, Topics and Themes
most Frequently Covered in Eighth Grade
"United States History and Government"

This course is not unlike "United States History," however, it is usually
part of a seventh-eighth grade block that seems to be finding favor in the
middle schools. Emphasis in the seventh grade is on United States history and

in the eighth grade upon United States government. The seventh-eighth grade block usually contains such units (in addition to history and government) as law, career units with special emphasis on jobs and work, and future studies. In some cases states mandate that state and local history be integrated into the American history course. Given the demands on the middle school to cover additional topics such as those mentioned above curriculum committees are turning to greater coordination between seventh and eighth grade social studies.

Trends in Teaching Eighth Grade Social Studies

1. The middle school organization, sixth, seventh, and eighth grades, has helped teachers who are traditionally separated from each other to coordinate their programs. Given the pressures from the federal government to teach units on careers and consumer education, public interest groups such as economics education, law related studies, multi-ethnic studies, economics education, and environmental studies along with the traditional historical events and structures of government have encouraged middle school teachers to consider coordinating their programs. It is perfectly obvious that no one teacher can cover all the topics above in one course.

2. Curriculum planners will continue to follow the Wesley Report. Emphasis will remain on nineteenth century history but will be modified by some of the special interests noted in the first trend.

3. That the American history course as taught in the three cycles will continue to be considered a capstone course, capstone in the sense that the course is a summarizing of social studies up to that cycle. As for example: fifth grade is the capstone for grades one through four summarizing self, family, school, neighborhood, community, region, and state. Eighth grade American history is the capstone for sixth and seventh grades providing a content to which all world and global studies are related.

4. Social studies teachers will probably continue to ignore efforts of the curriculum planners to limit eighth grade American history to an in depth study of the nineteenth century and a rapid survey of the rest. In depth ground covering of "all significant" events will continue to prevail even though that organization continues to receive considerable criticism.

III. Illustrations of a State
Eighth Grade Program

There is no one prescribed social studies program throughout the United States. However, one state's description of its eighth grade program will illustrate the content which the state expects to be taught. This illustration is included so that you can identify how a state mandates the teaching of social studies in the eighth grade.

> This is to be a general overview of American history with the emphasis on pre-twentieth century America. The course should examine the nature and development of forms of government and law, colonialism, democracy, revolution, land acquisition, immigration and assimilation, nationalism, slavery, abolition, civil rights, industrialization, technological development and urbanization. A focus on the state's current development during the development of the United States will help students relate history to their own lives and location.[1]

IV. Activities and Materials Categorized
by Knowledge, Processing, Valuing, and Participation

I realize a rather common practice is to skip purposes and specific objectives which precede the activities, but in this case the objectives are extremely important for an objective in the eighth grade will be found in proceeding grades. This is a developmental program with objectives, activities, and materials organized to build from one grade level to another.

EIGHTH GRADE ACTIVITIES AND MATERIALS

I. Purpose: Gaining knowledge about the human condition which includes past, present, and future.

Specific objective: Identifying the geography of the United States stressing westward expansion and sectionalism.

1. Activity & materials

Comparing and Inferring from
Sectional Population

when: two periods

what: population percentage figures for 1810, 1830, 1860, outline map of U.S.

how: 1) Have students divide the outline map into three section: northeast, southeast and west. Make sure students understand what states or territories are contained in each of the sections.

2) In each section write the date and population percentage figures. Use a different color for each of the three sections.

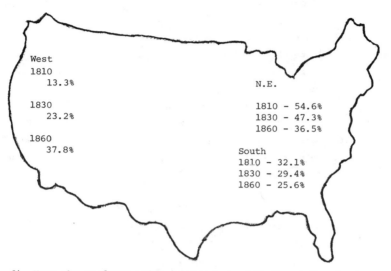

West
1810
    13.3%   N.E.

1830
    23.2%   1810 - 54.6%
                        1830 - 47.3%
                        1860 - 36.5%
1860
    37.8%   South
                      1810 - 32.1%
                      1830 - 29.4%
                      1860 - 25.6%

3) Have the students write questions on what they infer about population shifts from the figures on the map.

    a)   Why did people move from one section to another?

    b)   Suppose one of the sections wanted to secede from the Union, which section would have had the best chance to fight off the other two? Which section would have had the most difficulty?

4) Use students' questions as basis for class discussion.

2. Activity & materials

Acquiring and Sectioning America

when: one week

what: large outline map of U.S. (this can be done by throwing a transparency outline map onto a large sheet of paper and having students trace the outline and cut it out) The map should have the outline of the following:

    a)   U.S. of 1783

    b)   Louisiana Purchase of 1803

    c)   Texas Annexation in 1845

        d)   Oregon Territory in 1846

        e)   Mexican Cession in 1848

        f)   Gadsden Purchase in 1853

how: 1) Divide class into six groups.

       2) Cut map into the six sections listed above and give each group a section.

       3) Each group will cut its section into the states contained in its section. Divide the states among the members of the group.

      (Be aware that the sizes of the groups will have to vary according to the number of the states in the section being researched).

       4) Students should research the following information for each state:

        a)   when it became a state

        b)   size and current population

        c)   capital and major cities

        d)   natural resources

        e)   well known land forms and rivers that run through state or border it

        f)   unusual history.

       5) Starting with the first thirteen states have each group tell about its states and put map together like a jigsaw puzzle.

      Alternative: Forget about land purchases and acquisitions and just divide the states among the students and have them work on them individually.

(Save completed map for display during Social Studies Fair, see last activity in this chapter)

3. Activity & materials

Nineteenth Century in Review

when: two weeks or time established by teacher

what: materials as needed

how: 1) Students are going to produce a newspaper on the 19th century. News magazines usually put out an issue at the end of each year called something like "Year in Review" or "Highlights of the Past Year." The students could name their paper along the same lines:

"19th Century in Review" or "Highlights of the 19th Century."

2) Divide class into groups (or each student could work individually). Each group will develop its own newspaper.

3) Have students look at index of local newspaper and go through the paper to get a feel for the various sections. For example: news stories, editorials, pictures, human interest stories, interviews, ads, cartoons, birth and death announcements, advise columns, woman's fashions, and homemaking tips such as recipes.

4) Groups should develop their papers along the lines studied above confining their news, of course, to the 19th century, on such topics as the Monroe Doctrine, the Forty-niners, Civil War, gay 90's.

5) Have groups compete and get someone in the school to judge the papers. Display all papers but give most prominent display to the one judged best.

(Save newspapers for display during Social Studies Fair, see last activity in this chapter)

4. Activity & materials

Nineteenth Century Bingo

when: two periods

what: blank bingo cards (see Chapter Fifth Grade for example)

how: 1) Have each student write a question and answer for each square of the bingo card. Confine questions to 19th century.

2) Have students write each question on a card and write the answer on a bingo card being sure to mark each space on both card and bingo card with square letter and number. For example:

B, 5 When did Civil War start? Square B, 5 has 1860.

N, 15 Where was gold discovered in California? Square N, 15 has Sutter's Mill.

3) Teacher collects question cards from students and mixes them up. Collect bingo answer cards and pass them out making sure students do not have their own cards.

4) Teacher reads square letter and number and then reads question. The student with the correct answer in the correct square puts a

marker on the square.

5) Winner is the first one to get a straight line completed across, down, or horizontal.

(Save bingo cards and questions for display during Social Studies Fair, see last activity in this chapter)

5. Activity & materials

Eighteenth and Nineteenth Centuries
Review of Eras [2]

when: three periods

what: List of eras

ERAS

a. Progressive Era	g. Age of Sectionalism
b. Age of World Power	h. Era of Good Feeling
c. Age of Imperialism	i. Federal Period
d. Gay Nineties	j. Era of Revolution
e. Period of Industrialism	k. Period of Salutory Neglect
f. Age of Manifest Destiny	

---

how: 1) American history has been divided into general areas. Give each student a list of eras.

2) Each student must establish the years contained by each era (or this could be supplied by teacher) and one event that supports the title for each era and one event that seems to prove the title wrong.

3) List eras and years covered by era on board. Under each era list supportive events chosen by students, then list events that seem to prove the title wrong. For example:

1815-1824 Era of Good Feeling

Support	Prove it wrong
1. East coast prospered	1. Frontier had hard times
2. Nationalism	2. Sectionalism

Count those with similar answers and put number beside event.

4) Hold class discussion on whether the time period deserves the title it has or whether students think another name would be more appropriate.

Specific objective: Identifying cause and effect relationships.
6. Activity & materials

Cause and Effect Concept Wheel[3]

when: several periods

what: list of events, concept wheel (see below)

how: Establishing cause and effect relationship is important because it helps to promote the notion that an event may be part of a number of causes. A cause is usually an event that contributes to or determines a particular effect. For example the causes of the First World War, the cause for liberty, causes of the fall of the Roman Empire. Effect usually means the result of a cause or a set of causes. For example causes are sectionalism, slavery, election of Lincoln; effect is the Civil War. A cause is Manifest Destiny and the effect is westward expansion.

1) To illustrate that complex events have multiple causes and effects have students consider the following events of the nineteenth and twentieth centuries, recalling cause and effect relationships of each:

Independence	Sectionalism	Industrialization
Confederation	The Great Compromises	Urbanization
Constitution	Civil War	Immigration
National Expansion	Reconstruction	World Power

2) Have each student select one of the events listed above and construct a concept wheel visually demonstrating cause and effect relationships. For example the Industrial Revolution:

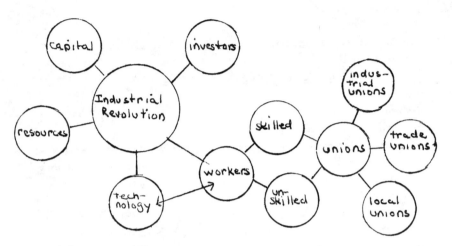

7. Activity & materials

<u>Tracking</u> <u>Cause</u> <u>and</u> <u>Effect</u>

when: recurring

what: construction paper

how: 1) Draw four sets of train tracks one above the other on large
        paper attached to wall or bulletin board. Mark sections of rails
        off into years or decades or half centuries (whatever will work
        best with what students will be studying). Mark top set of tracks
        social, second set of tracks political, third set of tracks
        economics, and bottom set of tracks foreign affairs.

        2) As tracks are being completed students may wish to make small
        "spur" railroad tracks from one track to another connecting events
        that may have cause and effect relationship.

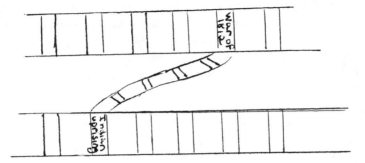

(Save these tracks to display at Social Studies Fair, see last activity in
this chapter)

Specific objective: Identifying status of blacks during nineteenth
century.

8. Activity & materials

What Do You Know about Africa?[4]

when: one period

what: pictures and maps of Africa, list of words (below)

how: 1) Have each student select five words that he/she thinks best
       describes Africa, i.e., hot, jungle, wild animals, primitive
       people, native villages. OR Have students check words they think
       apply to Africa from list below.

_____ 1. beautiful people	_____ 8. poverty
_____ 2. change	_____ 9. mineral wealth
_____ 3. developed	_____10. revolution
_____ 4. enemy	_____11. stable
_____ 5. exotic	_____12. technically advanced
_____ 6. hunger	_____13. underdeveloped
_____ 7. peaceful	_____14. unfriendly

       2) List students' words on board under headings such as climate,
       shelter, animal life, vegetation, food, people, technology, etc.
       3) Have students examine pictures and maps to check their words
       for accuracy.

4) Hold class discussion on reasons for any ideas about Africa that have no basis in fact. For example ask such questions as:

    a) Are there old established universities in African nations?

    b) Are there metropolitan cities?

    c) Do Africans manufacture such products as steel, automobiles, refined oil?

9. Activity & materials

To Be a Slave

when: two periods

what: resource material on slavery, chart (below)

how: 1) Discuss with students or have them read about the reaction of slaves to the conditions of slavery.

2) Have students fill out chart on slaves' reactions and reasons for their reactions and the consequences of whatever actions the slaves took.

3) Have students rank what their choice of reactions would have been (see chart).

4) Hold class discussion:

    a) What action did slaves take most often?

    b) Explain consequences of different slave reactions?

    c) Suppose you had been a slave, what would you have done?

    d) Is it ever right to own another person as a slave?

	first choice of slaves	second choice of slaves	third choice of slaves
Actions taken by slaves	(example) Acceptance		
why slaves took action listed above	well treated by owner afraid of being caught while escaping		
results of actions taken above	remain well treated remain with family		
student ranking of their choice			

Instructions: Below is a list of possible actions taken by slaves toward their condition of slavery. On the chart above list the actions from most frequently taken to least frequently taken. Then fill in the rest of the chart. On the bottom line place your choice of actions from 1 representing what you would have most likely done to 5 which would be least likely done.

     acceptance

     revolt

     escape

     hindering work (passive resistance) on plantation by doing work
         slowly

     hindering work (sabotage) by doing work badly or being destructive.

10. Activity & materials

<u>Civil</u> <u>Rights</u> <u>Time</u> <u>Line</u>[5]

when: four periods

what: resource materials on laws pertaining to blacks: (Slave codes,
         Black codes (Jim Crow), Voting laws, Supreme Court decisions,
         national legislation)

how: 1) Have students look at laws that have affected blacks. Through
         research students, individually or in groups, can learn the reasons
         why these laws came to be passed and the dates of such laws.
         2) Have students find illustrations or make their own (either
         written descriptions or drawings) of the laws in practice.
         3) Have students make a time line on bulletin board of their
         illustrations making sure illustrations are in the order that the
         laws were passed.
         4) Hold class discussion on the results of the legislation and any
         conclusions the students may have arrived at.

11. Activity & materials

Are You Free If...?[6]

when: one week

what: Jim Crow laws, chart (below)
         Jim Crow laws referred to laws that restricted blacks such as:
              Blacks had separate waiting rooms at depots.
              Blacks were required to sit in special Jim Crow sections at the
                  back of trains and street cars.
              Blacks were not allowed in white theaters, hotels, restaurants,
                  or barber shops.
              Schools were segregated.
              Race etiquette: act inferior to whites, doff hat and get off
                  sidewalk in presence of white people, say "Sir" and respond
                  to term "Boy!".

how: 1) Have each student keep a record of all his/her activities
         during a given week, then fill out following chart.

Activities		Those activities prohibited by Jim Crow laws for Blacks	Those activities allowed for Blacks but restricted by Jim Crow laws.
example	ride bus to school		must sit in back of bus
example	ate dinner at restaurant	white only restaurant	
other examples	went to movie drink from public drinking fountain get hair cut walk down street		

Specific objective: Identify present attitudes, opportunities, and restrictions on immigration.

12. Activity & materials

Immigration: A Right or a Privilege

when: one period

what: statements below

how: 1) Have students mark strength of feeling about following statements.

1. The legend on the Statue of Liberty is right for America: "Give me your tired, your poor, your huddled masses yearning to breathe free..."

| strongly agree | agree | neutral | disagree | strongly disagree |

2. I like a lot of mixtures of different races, religions, and in general people who don't look like me.

| strongly agree | agree | neutral | disagree | strongly disagree |

3. The fact is... if you are an American you should adopt American ways
   leaving behind the culture of your native land.

strongly	agree	neutral	disagree	strongly
agree				disagree

4. Idealistically let everyone who wants to come, live in America; but that's
   not realistic. There are some people more valuable than others. We can't
   admit everyone, so admit the valuable people.

strongly	agree	neutral	disagree	strongly
agree				disagree

5. Keeping your foreign cultural heritage is important even though you are an
   American citizen.

strongly	agree	neutral	disagree	strongly
agree				disagree

6. Yes, America is a multi-culture, multi-ethnic, and pluralistic society,
   but there are basic ideas that all citizens should accept if they really
   want to be real Americans.

strongly	agree	neutral	disagree	strongly
agree				disagree

7. My relations immigrated to this country to gain greater opportunity.
   However, if immigration continues to be open to every foreigner, that
   opportunity will be lost.

strongly	agree	neutral	disagree	strongly
agree				disagree

2) It is well known that immigrant groups once settled and
established tend to wish immigration restricted to a qualified
few. Do students follow that wish or do they idealistically
propose to open the door to all who would enter?

3) Determine where class as a whole falls on the scale.
As a final note: when studying unit on immigration refer back
to students attitudes as expressed above.

13. Activity & materials

When Immigration Became a Privilege

when: two days

what: readings on immigration laws

how: 1)· Have students read immigration laws and make a brief outline
giving date and law. For example:

1882 prohibited Chinese workers, insane, diseased criminals, paupers.

1907 prohibited Japanese workers

1917 literacy test demanded

1921 quota system based on national origins

1924 quota revised to 2% of number of people from that nation living
in the U.S. in 1890 (mostly northern European), except for
Canadian and Latin American who were not limited.

1933 Displaced Persons Act.

1952 Allowed small quota for Chinese and Japanese

1953 Refugee Relief Act

1967 Set limit of 170,000 with no more than 20,000 allowed from each
country. Parents, spouses, and children not part of quota. ·
Preserence given those with skills or those who have relatives
in U.S.

2) Discuss laws with students:
a) What were the reasons for the laws?
b) Do you think the present law is fair? If not, what would
be fair? Be sure to refer students to the attitudes
expressed in the above activity. Our concept of fairness
is based on our attitudes, our values.

3) When would following people be allowed to immigrate?
a) nurse from Chile
b) Chinese laborer from mainland
c) baker from Germany
d) Hungarian anti-Communist
e) dental hygenist from Japan
f) gem cutter from Colombia

14. →Activity & materials

<u>Who</u> <u>Is</u> <u>Acceptable</u>, <u>You</u> <u>Decide</u>

when: one period

what: descriptions of immigrants prepared by teacher, see samples below.

how: 1) Divide class into groups. Supply each group with the sample
descriptions of immigrants.

2) The group is to play the role of the U.S. Immigration Bureau
and decide who may enter the U.S. Five out of the eight immigrants
should be allowed to enter.

3) Groups discuss and make decisions.

4) Compile groups' choices on board. Hold class discussion on
reasons for choices. Examine quotas and criteria government uses
for admitting immigrants.

Sample Descriptions:

1. Young University student who has taken part in demonstrations against
his government.

2. Daughter of a minor party official in her native land.

3. Musician who has lost his hand in an accident.

4. Pregnant woman from underdeveloped nation who wants her baby to be
born and raised in America.

5. Medical doctor who speaks no English.

6. Farmer and family who have always been poor for his ancestors, as he,
worked marginal lands.

7. Military officer who took part in an attempted overthrow of his
country's government.

8. A child who lost both parents in a Civil War.

15. Activity & materials

<u>Are</u> <u>You</u> <u>Eligible</u>?

when: one period

what: personal history card, help wanted ads

how: 1) Have students fill out personal history cards. (Do not tell
them what it is for!)

After students have filled out cards give them classified help wanted ads to see if there are any jobs they could apply for. (see below)

```
┌─────────────────────────────────────────────────────────────────────┐
│                        PERSONAL HISTORY CARD                         │
│                                                                       │
│  _____            _____              │
│        (name)                           (age)                         │
│                           ☐ male                                      │
│  _____            _____              │
│      (nationality)        ☐ female      (height)                      │
│                                                                       │
│  _____            _____              │
│        (race)                           (weight)                      │
│                                                                       │
│  _____     _____          │
│      (religion)                   (schooling)                         │
│                                                                       │
│  _____                                             │
│   (languages-spoken)                                                  │
│                                                                       │
│  _____                                             │
│   (languages-read)                                                    │
│                                                                       │
│  _____     _____          │
│      (skills)                 (job in native country)                │
└─────────────────────────────────────────────────────────────────────┘
```

2) Teacher select from newspaper help wanted ads (no more than 10) with specific skills and/or make up your own. Make sure each ad has a restriction such as age (no one over 25), religion, language, etc. Run off copies of ads and give a copy to each student.

   a) How many jobs, given his/her personal history card, would each student be qualified to apply for?

   b) Do some immigrants have a better chance for finding a job than others?

   c) Suppose you were an employer what type people would you want to hire?

   d) Should getting a job depend on "who you are" rather than on your work record?

Sample want ads:

We have openings for dishwashers and bus boys. Must be 18 yrs or older. Also looking for waitresses or waiters, must be 21 or older. Apply in person.	Mature woman wanted to babysit 1 infant in my home, 5 days per week. Must be white and Catholic.

16. Activity & materials

What's in a Name?[7]

when: two periods

what: list of names

how: 1) Discuss with students the fact that Americans have often
modified or changed their names for one reason or another. The very
name America comes from the name of the Italian explorer Amerigo
Vespucci. Foreign students studying in the U.S. often pick a
nickname or shorten their first names for easier pronunciation.
Movie stars often change their names.

2) Below is a list of original names and new names. Give list to
students to see if students can match them up.

original names	new names
Krikor Ohanian	Mike Connors
Suzanne Mahoney	Suzanne Somers
Samuel Godfish	Sam Goldwyn
Norma Jean Mortenson	Marilyn Monroe
Monir Amin-Sichani	Mona Ames
Sopapim Sresthputr Hatayodom	Sophia Hata
Presyanch Apibunyopas	Pat Abby

3) After names have been matched correctly discuss with students
the following questions:

   a) What countries might these people come from?

   b) Why do you think they changed their name?

   c) Are immigrants from certain parts of the world more apt to
   change their names than others?

   d) Do you think immigrants will continue to change their
   names, or do you think it is a trend that has weakened and
   why?

   e) If you changed your name from Giuseppe Marfussgo to George
   Mar, then might you have more opportunity in the U.S.?

17. Activity & materials

Geneology Roots

when: one week

what: geneology chart below

how: Have students research their own family history. Student may trace
both or only one side of his/her family back to time of immigration.
Student may write up the reasons for immigration, where ancestor
settled, and what work he did, etc. OR Student may trace family
back to an ancestor who was perhaps the first to move west, or the
first to move to the city, etc. Student may write up what life
would have witnessed in his day.

The point of this activity is to have students see these ancestors
as real people not just names on a chart. If a student has an idea
for his/her project other than the two suggested above, he/she
should discuss it with the teacher and get approval. This should
be a flexible activity.

Sample family chart
your family

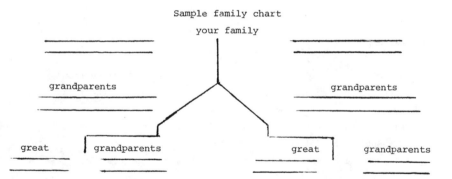

(Save family geneology charts to display at the Social Studies Fair, see
last activity in this chapter)

18. Activity & materials

American Symbols[8]

when: two periods

what: poster board, art supplies, materials suggested below how: 1) Discuss with class what symbols, phrases, etc. are used to describe Americans. What distinguishes an American from other nationalities, such as language, dress, heritage, needs, etc. List suggestions on board.

2) Have each student pick one or more of the suggestions listed on the board as a theme around which he/she will build a poster. For example students may find songs, poems, paintings, cartoons, photos, materials from magazines or newspapers, or create materials of their own. Students use collected materials to decorate their own poster.

3) Display posters around room.

(Save the posters to display at the Social Studies Fair, see last activity in this chapter)

Specific objective: Identifying the technological effect of the Industrial Revolution on everyday life.

19. Activity & materials

Technological Dependence

when: two days

what: Tech Use form (below)

how: 1) Give each student a Tech Use form to fill out. They should list all the technological devices they have used in the last twenty-four hours and what the devise was used for.

2) Ask students to see how many of these devices they can do without in the following twenty-four hours.

3) Hold discussion on reactions and feelings the next day.
For example:

    a) What devices did you give up?

    b) How inconvenient was it without using device?

    c) Suppose you had to give up (teacher can name certain device), how would you react?

    d) What do you think will be the relationship of man and technology by the year 2000?

    e) Is the Industrial Revolution going to continue as the Technological revolution? Is there any sign that people

will want less Technological dependence in the future?
Will your children be more or less dependent?

Last 24 hrs: where used	Tech Use Form name of device	what device used for
(examples) home	blow dryer stereo	dry hair enjoy listening to music
school	projector	see movie on technology
other	bus	transportation to and from school

20. Activity & materials

Does Technology Own Us?

when: one or two periods

what: magazines, art supplies

how: 1) Have each student write down any ten technological inventions. For example radio, TV, lights, bike, etc.

2) Have students cut out a magazine picture or make a drawing to illustrate each of the ten inventions they have named.

3) List inventions from most useful invention to least useful, including a reason beside each invention.

4) Discuss choices and rankings. Some questions to ask:

a) Are there gains and loses when we depend on technology?

b) Does technology own us or do we own technology?

21. Activity & materials

Conserving Power

when: two weeks

what:

how: 1) Students should list and categorize all electrical equipment used by their families. Or teacher can make up a checklist of typical electrical appliances found in home for students to check off.

2) Students should see what they personally can do to cut down on their own use of electricity for one week. For example: turning off lights when not used, going without radio, stereo, TV, etc. when possible.

3) Have students make a written report on how they cut down and their reactions.

4) Students or their parents or relatives may have experienced "brown-outs" or cutbacks or shortages of electricity or natural gas in recent years. Students might report on how family coped with problem and reactions to power cutback.

22. Activity & materials

A Campaign for Technology

when: four days

what: materials as needed

how: 1) Divide class into groups. Have each group select a technological device (invented since 1800). Make sure each group has different device.

2) Groups are to research their technological devices and prepare an oral presentation on what the device has done for man. Groups may use any means available to persuade others that their device is the most important one.

3) Hold class vote for most persuasive presentation.

23. Activity & materials

Which Technology Projects Get Funded?

when: two periods

what: list of funding requests

how: 1) The needs of today's society are many and varied and all seem urgent. There are social problems, medical problems, environmental problems, all need funds for research and development. Hold brief class discussion on above issues.

2) Divide class into groups. Each group must act as a federal government funding agency. Give each group the list of technology

projects.

Each of the ten projects proposed in the President's Budget was to receive 10 million dollars so all projects together received a total of 100 million dollars. The Congress cut the 100 million to 50 million. You must decide from which of the ten projects the 50 million will be cut. List the amount you propose to fund each project, no project should receive more than 10 million.

_____ 1. Project on "wave power" to see if action of the sea can generate power.

_____ 2. Project on "test tube" babies.

_____ 3. Project on car safety.

_____ 4. Project on space flight equipment.

_____ 5. Project on weather control.

_____ 6. Project on new weapons system.

_____ 7. Project on retarding old age.

_____ 8. Project on turning sea water into good drinking water.

_____ 9. Project on producing abundant quantitites of enriched food.

_____10. Project on rat control.

50 million total

3) By majority vote group must decide the distribution of funds.

4) Hold class discussion and compare groups decisions. The following questions might be appropriate:

   a) To what category of projects, people or things, did you fund the most money?

   b) Does your funding tell you anything about what you value?

   c) Are there projects not listed here that should be funded?

24. Activity & materials

Technology Mural

when: time set by teacher

what: large piece of long paper for mural

how: The students will make a mural on the theme of technology and how it has effected our lives and our environment.

   1) Hold class discussion to plan the mural.

Possibilities: a) section it off into time periods.

b) section it off into categories such as land, water, air; or rural and urban; or transportation, communication, etc.

c) class may want to have no predetermined organization.

d) some students who do not like to draw may want to bring in pictures or do lettering perhaps using a stencil.

2) Students might like to post unfinished mural in hall and invite other students to offer drawings that could help complete the mural.

3) Hold informal discussions on facets of technology as they are incorporated into mural.

(Save mural for display at Social Studies Fair, see last activity in this chapter)

25. Activity & materials

Lost on the Moon[9]

when: one period

what: materials included

how: You are in a space crew originally scheduled to rendevous with a mother ship on the lighted surface of the moon. Mechanical difficulties, however, have forced your ship to crash land at a spot some 200 miles from the rendevous point. The rough landing damaged much of the equipment aboard. Since survival depends on reaching the mother ship, the most critical items available must be chosen for the 200-mile trip. The thirteen items left intact after landing are listed below. Your task is to rank them in terms of their importance to your crew in its attempt to reach the rendevous point. Place number 1 by the most important item, number 2 by the second most important, and so on through the least important, number 13.

_____ Box of matches

_____ Food concentrates

_____ 50 feet of nylon rope

_____ Parachute silk

_____ Portable heating unit

_____ Two .45 caliber pistol

_____ One case dehydrated milk

_____ Signal flares

_____ Two 100 lb. tanks of
oxygen

_____ Stellar map of the moon's
constellation

_____ Life raft containing CO_2
bottles

_____ Magnetic Compass

_____ 5 gallons of water

The game can be played in several different ways, depending on the
amount of time the teacher wishes to devote to it or on what special
needs the group has. The quickest, simplest use of the game is for
the group to set to work immediately trying to arrive at consensus
as to how the items should be ranked. Students should be reminded
that their rankings must represent agreement by <u>all</u> members of the
group and may not be arrived at by simply taking a majority vote.
For this simpler use of the game, give the following instructions:

1) Read the problem explained on the distributed sheets.

2) Your task is to solve the problem as a group.

3) The only "catch" is that your answers must be agreed to by
   <u>every</u> member of the group. This will require that you
   spend a fairly long time talking over your ideas about each
   of the items sharing any information you have that could
   help the group. While you should not be unduly stubborn,
   neither should you give in simply to speed the work of the
   group. Often one hard-headed member can save an entire
   group from making a serious error.

4) When you have made a final decision, record your group
   answer on a fresh copy of the problem and compare it to
   the answers prepared by NASA.

Below are the correct rankings for the items, as determined by the
space-survival unit of NASA:

13 Box of matches (little or no use on the moon)

 4 Food concentrate (supply daily food required)

 5 50 feet of nylon rope (useful in tying injured, help in

climbing)

6 Parachute silk (shelter against sun's rays)

11 Portable heating unit (useful only if party landed on dark side)

9 Two .45 caliber pistols (self-propulsion devices could be made from them)

10 One case dehydrated milk (food, mixed with water for drinking)

8 Signal flares (distress call within line of sight)

1 Two 100 lb. tanks of oxygen (fills respiration requirement)

3 Stellar map of the moon's constellation (one of the principal means of finding directions)

7 Life raft (CO_2 bottles for self-propulsion across chasms, etc.)

12 Magnetic compass (probably no magnetized poles, thus, useless)

2 Five gallons of water (replenishes loss by sweating, etc.)

Specific objective: Identifying the cause and effect of America's involvement and growth as a world power.

26. Activity & materials

Take Care of Number One!

when: one period

what: see statements below

how: Have students rank feelings about statements. Compile lists and record results.

Discuss with class the fact that there are always some things people seem to agree on just as there are things people cannot agree on.

Save the findings to see if they hold true when class studies foreign policy.

Rank statements by marking them: 1 for strongly approve, 2 for approve, 3 for undecided, 4 for disapprove, and 5 for strongly disapprove.

_____ 1. It is a nation's duty to take over a neighbor that is doing things that might threaten the peace and safety of the nation.

_____ 2. A nation should give aid and assistance to whichever side they think will win when countries are at war.

_____ 3. I always say "Take care of number one first because no one is going to come to our aid."

_____ 4. One should learn to help others without thinking "what's in it for me?"

_____ 5. Underdeveloped nations should receive only the aid and assistance they request.

_____ 6. When someone doesn't want to do something he should do, our duty is to see that he does it.

_____ 7. If we have defeated another nation in a war, we should help that defeated nation with foreign aid. Turn an enemy into a friend.

_____ 8. A nation should be ready to aid disaster victims in other countries without first thinking how it will be reimbursed.

27. Activity & materials

Going it Alone or Together

when: two periods

what: Newspapers, magazines

how: 1) Discuss with class things people do to stay apart or alone and things people do when they want to share and be with other people. List students' suggestions on board. For example:

Separate	Together
eat alone at lunch	sit with friends
keep to oneself	take part in discussions
don't participate	go places together

2) Broaden discussion to what nations do to stay isolated or to become involved and list these on board. For example:

Separate	Together
Make it difficult to enter or leave country.	Send military hardware to country under attack.
Close countries borders.	Join international organizations, trade agreements.

3) Have students look for examples of America remaining separate (going its own way) or working together with other countries. For example:

    a) Is the Berlin Wall an attempt at separation and isolation?

    b) What about the United Nations and the Olympics, are these examples of separation or togetherness?

    c) Are there countries that seem to wish to remain separate from all other nations?

28. Activity & materials

A Question of Personal and National Values

when: two periods

what: charts (see below)

how: 1) Have students fill out the chart using their own recent actions.

2) Hold class discussion on what students have cited as examples. Which are people most strongly controlled by, the attitude of "take care of number one first," or an idealistic sense of duty, or are both fairly equal?

3) Have students prepare a similar chart on a country.

examples:

What I do for others	Myself What I do for #1	What I do for both
1. Clean up after art work	1. Scrounge food in lunchroom	1. Make batch of popcorn
2. Share class notes	2. Study for test	2. Team sport
3. Give classmate a ride home		

What country does for others	Country What country does for itself	What country does for both
1. send medical supplies to earthquake victims 2. prevent instability among second & third world nations	1. restrict imported goods 2. need to sell finished goods and gain raw material to support standard of living	1. get rid of surplus wheat by sending it to starving countries 2. sale of arms and training armies to prevent invasion and civil war to encourage orderly growth

29. Activity & materials

Do National Values Determine Military Aid?

when: two periods

what: foreign aid chart, see below

how: 1) Discuss with students the meaning of foreign aid and possible reasons for foreign aid.

2) Have students examine the chart on military aid. (below)

3) Hold class discussion:

a) What area in the world received the least military aid from 1945-55? from 1966-75?

b) What area in the world has received the most military aid from 1945-55?

c) What area has received the most military aid from 1966-75? Possible reason for this?

d) From total figures on foreign military aid where would you say America's interest lie around the world?

e) Some say Manifest Destiny did not stop at the Pacific coast but continued across the Pacific, does the chart bear this out?

f) Is military aid provided for countries because it helps the country or because it will benefit the U.S. or both?

g) What do you think the policy of military aid should be in the future? Does our aid follow the areas of the world that we most value? Do you think the U.S. is likely to

value different parts of the world than it has valued in
the past?

Military Aid	Amounts			
Where	1945-55	1956-65	1966-75	Total
Western Hemisphere	1/4 billion	3/4 billion	1/3 billion	1 1/3 billion
Western Europe	9 1/2 billion	6 1/2 billion	4/5 billion	17 billion
Africa	7 million	166 million	1/4 billion	393 million
Near East	2 billion	3 4/5 billion	4 billion	10 billion
Far East	4 2/5 billion	7 2/3 billion	23 billion	35 billion

30. Activity & materials

A Foreign Policy Study

when: five periods

what: List of foreign policies followed or promoted by U.S.

how: 1) Hold class discussion on what policy means.

2) Divide students into groups. Each group must research one
policy (groups must each pick a different policy). Hopefully all
policies on the list can be covered.

3) Each group must make a list of events connected with the policy
they are researching.

4) Have each group give a brief presentation on the meaning of
their policy and events connected with it, and effectiveness of
policy.

5) Activities:

  a) policy time line

  b) world map with flags marking locations where events took
      place

  c) posters graphs, charts (depending on policy and group's
      imagination and research information.

Suggested policies:

Manifest Destiny	Monroe Doctrine	World Policeman
Detente	Domino Theory	Isolation
Shuttle Diplomacy	Good Neighbor Policy	Make World Safe for
Camp David Middle East	Arms Limitation	Democracy
meeting (Spirit of	Containment	
Camp David)		

Specific objective: Identifying social, economical, and political values of the past, comparing them with the present and making predictions about the future.

31. Activity & materials

Values Past, Present and Future

when: two periods

what: student prepared questionnaire

how: 1) Discuss with class the issues that seem important today. List these on the board under the three categories of social, political, and economics.

2) Divide the class into three groups, one for each of the categories. It will be the task of each group to write five questions on the issues listed under their category on the board.

3) When the groups have finished the questions, combine them in a questionnaire.

4) Give each student three copies of the questionnaire. Students should administer the questionnaire to someone their own age, their parents or someone of their parents' generation, and a grandparent or someone of their grandparents' generation.

5) Tally results and discuss:

    a) Are all the answers from one age group similar? How about the other age groups?

    b) What events do you think influenced the answers in each age group?

    c) Suppose you had lived in your grandparents day, do you think you would have answered the questions as they did?

    d) What values seem to be expressed in the answers for each
age group?

    e) How do you think the questions will be answered thirty
years from now? What values will dictate the answers?

32. Activity & materials

Predicting the Future

when: two periods

what: Futures checklist (below)

how: 1) Have students examine predictions of future on checklist. Have
them put a check beside those they believe will happen and +(plus)
if they believe it will be a good change and a -(minus) if they
think it will be a bad change. They may wish to add predictions of
their own. This will give students a chance to examine their own
values.

2) Tally results of checklist on board. Discuss those statements
over which there seems to be strong disagreement.

3) Possibility: have students make own predictions and survey
a group of students, tally results.

Predictions of Change by the Year 2001

√   + −

1. Nuclear power and solar power will be the main sources of energy.

2. Marriages will be by contract only, renewable every five years.

3. Day care centers will be provided for all pre-school children
because most mothers will be working.

4. All medical care will be paid for by the government.

5. No public school buildings, all instruction is individualized and
carried on in student's home.

6. Israel and the Arab countries will have united to become the
United States of the Middle East.

7. Because of medical advances the average life span will be 95 and
the majority of the population will be over 50.

8. No more private homes, only housing built will be 100 story high
rise apartments with all necessities of life built into each of
the high rise complexes.

___|___ 9.   (Student Prediction)

33. ̄Activity & materials

The Year 2025

when: three periods

what:

how: 1) Have students pretend their family is transported to the year
2025. Have them write what life would be like in the areas of
homes, furnishings, transportation, clothes, school, jobs,
environment (climate control), etc.

2) Pick ideas from student essays and list on board. Hold class
discussion on validity and probability of projected ideas.

    a) Do the changes suggested by the year 2025 reflect different
       values and beliefs than we now hold?

    b) Do technological changes effect a society's values?

II. Purpose: Develop skills necessary to process information.
Specific objective: Identify and apply the four different levels of
questioning.

1. Activity & materials

Questioning Skills
Eighth Grade

when: two days

what: materials included below

how: Questions are such a vital part of social studies that activities
and materials have been offered on that skill in this book at all
grade levels since the fourth grade. The skill of questioning,
we have argued, is not the exclusive domain of the teacher.
Students can learn to ask and answer a full range of questions.
Questioning is a skill that can be learned, that can be applied.
Classroom teachers know that good questions from students stimulate
class discussion. What kills discussion and discourages teachers
are students who have no questions. Obviously the skill of asking
and answering different levels of questions does not guarantee
stimulating useful discussion, but it is a step in the right
direction.

Review students' mastery of identifying the different levels of questions.

Mastery Test Survey (Matching)

a	1.	Name one of Columbus's three ships?	a)	memory question
b	2.	Why did Spain support Columbus?	b)	description question
c	3.	What do you suppose would have happened if all three of Columbus's ships had sunk before he could return to Spain?	c)	speculation question
			d)	evaluation question
d	4.	Is it your opinion that the world would have been better off if Columbus had not discovered America?		
b	5.	What happened when Columbus first stepped on shore in the "New World?"		
c	6.	Suppose you were Columbus, would you have made the same decisions about native Americans that he did?		
a	7.	Name the country where Columbus's ship landed when first returning from the "New World?"		
d	8.	Was Columbus a "good" man?		

If students have difficulty identifying the four different levels of questions review Chapters Fifth Grade, Sixth Grade and Seventh Grade for purposes of clarification and practice.

Follow through activities:

a) Have students find questions in back of each chapter of their social studies text. Have them classify the questions they find into one of the four levels.

b) On the social studies topics being studied ask students to write out at least one question at four different levels: Name Columbus's three ships? Why did Columbus take three ships? Suppose you were Columbus how many ships might you have taken? Do you think Columbus's ships were sea worthy?

Specific objective: Learning to identify facts and how a fact can be turned into a biased statement.

2. Activity & materials

Recognizing Bias

when: two periods

what: For introductory treatment on bias see activities and materials in Chapter Fifth Grade and Chapter Sixth Grade.

how: 1) Hold class discussion on bias. For example:

    a) Define bias?

    b) Possible reasons for biased statements?

    c) Suppose you want to get some point of view accepted, would you be apt to make a biased statement?

    d) Do most people make biased statements at some time or another?

    e) Do you think you can recognize a bias?

    f) Ways to recognize bias:

        emotion

        who says it

        author with personal interest in subject.

2) Have students bring in examples of biased writing or biased statements they have heard on TV, radio, or elsewhere.

3) Discuss statements brought in with entire class. Do they all agree that there is bias displayed?

4) As a current events activity have students examine newspapers, popular magazines, and perhaps their own class current events magazine for examples of bias.

3. Activity & materials

Studying Bias

when: two periods

what: newspapers or magazines

how: 1) Divide students into groups and give them copies of newspaper articles about the same subject from two different sources. If different newspapers are not available, Time and Newsweek usually cover the same major stories and they can be used.

2) Have groups compare and contrast the stories. The following form may be helpful:

Additional or inferred information from first newspaper only.	Facts stated by both newspapers.	Additional or inferred information from second newspaper only.
1.	1.	1.
2.	2.	2.

3) Hold class discussion on findings.

   a) Are groups consistent in findings?

   b) Can a writer imply certain feelings by the way he tells the facts?

   c) How can you learn to distinguish between facts of a news story and the writer's feelings?

4. Activity & materials

Pass It On

when: four periods

what:

how: 1) Divide class into groups. Each group is to write a script for some experience that could take place in students' environment.

2) Have group role play experience following their script exactly.

3) Other groups must record as accurately as possible what they saw.

4) Check with script. How close were the other groups' observations to original script?

5) Discuss how observations may differ, reasons for this and how to be more accurate.

Alternative suggestions: Teacher stages an impromptu event which the students are then asked to accurately recall.

An old suggestion but a good one: whisper a description of an event to one student who then is instructed to pass it on, and so on until it reaches the last student who then is asked to repeat the story. Comparing the final version with the original gives a good deal of insight into bias and hearsay.

5. Activity & materials

Persuasion: The Art of Propaganda

when: two periods

what: materials included below

how: The importance of persuasion in the form of propaganda has been
       emphasized starting with Chapter Fifth Grade and continuing through
       Chapter Eighth Grade. The media bombards the society literally day
       and night with a message. To be informed and protected against the
       techniques of persuasion maybe extremely important to a democratic
       society that is obligated if not required to make decisions.
       Below is a matching exercise intended to test students mastery of
       selected propaganda techniques that were identified in earlier
       chapters. If students have difficulty identifying the different
       techniques, review Chapters Fifth, Sixth, and Seventh Grades for
       purposes of clarification and practice.

b	1.	Everyone agrees with Joe, you get with it and make the agreement unanimous.	a) slogans
e	2.	He's not one of us, don't listen to him.	b) bandwagon
a	3.	"There's a Ford in your future."	c) plainfolks
c	4.	Ladies and gents, you can trust me, I'm just like you, born and raised on the east side, worked hard with mu hands like you."	d) testimonial
			e) prejudice
			f) repetition
d	5.	I'm Reggy J. You know I can drive any car but this is the one I want, it's the best.	g) arousing feelings
f	6.	The popcorn stand is open, the corn is hot and buttered. Don't forget to stop at the popcorn stand. We made the popcorn just for you.	
g	7.	This great country of ours has fallen behind the other side. It's about time we as a people take up the challenge and fight to win.	

           Follow through activities:
               a) Ask students to identify at least three of the seven
                   techniques above from TV commercials, newspapers (letters
                   to the editor is a good place to start), radio commercials.

    b) Make up one written illustration of each of the seven
techniques above.

    c) Place students into groups, each group having their own
list of three techniques which they are to illustrate in a
roleplaying. The class should try to guess the technique.

6. Activity & materials

<u>Practice</u> <u>Hypothesizing</u>

when: two periods

what:

how: For an introduction to the inquiry process see Chapter Sixth Grade,
Activity Inquiry: <u>A</u> <u>Citizen's</u> <u>Obligation</u> <u>in</u> <u>a</u> <u>Democratic</u> <u>Society</u>.
1) Discuss the term hypothesis and make sure students understand
it is a "rational guess."
2) Have each student make two personal hypotheses. See example
below.
3) Have students poll rest of class to check hypothesis. See
example.
4) Have students examine the current chapter they are studying in
their text or supplementary materials. Have them practice
hypothesizing by turning chapter and section headings into
hypotheses.

example:

Class poll		
True	False	
ℕ𝕝 ‖	‖‖	1. Girls prefer to wear light colored clothing, boys prefer dark colored clothing.
‖|	ℕ𝕝 ‖|	2. Girls prefer to walk to school, boys prefer to ride bikes.

III.   Purpose: Develop the skill to examine values and beliefs.

Specific Purpose: Learning to identify one's own values and beliefs and predicting whether these values will change as one grows older.

1.   Activity & materials

What Are My Values?[10]

when: one period

what: My Values form (below)

how: 1) Have students fill out the values form below.

2) Discuss responses with students letting them give reasons for their choices. Teacher must be sensitive to the fact that some students may not want to share their choices with the class.

a) How did you arrive at the values you chose as most important?

b) Did you have a hard time deciding how to answer the items in the future?

c) Do some people have a hard time deciding what they value?

d) Are some people afraid to say what they really value and put down what they think others value?

e) Do you think your values are similar to your parents' values?

MY VALUES

Check each item in the appropriate space or spaces.

	Present			Future		
	Value Most	Neutral	Value Least	Value Most	Neutral	Value Least
1. Looks						
2. Good grades						
3. Money for material goods: clothes, car, stereo, etc.						
4. Independence						
5. Religion						
6. Marriage and family						
7. Popularity						
8. Athletic ability						
9. Do what parents expect						
10. Be a success in a career						
11. Have leisure time						
12. Create something (be creative)						
13. Do good for society						
14. Set a goal and work toward it.						

A. Are any of your values going to be difficult to combine?

    Examples: woman with family and career

                leisure and successful career

B. What in the future might make it easier to reach goals?
    example: four day work week and leisure

C. Do you think your values will change when you graduate from high
    school or enter college? _____
    If so, how? _____
    _____

2. Activity & materials

Keeping the Message Up Front[11]

when: one period

what:

how: 1) Have children write down bumper stickers they see on cars and
      bring them to class.
      2) Write bumper sticker messages on board. Examples: "School's
      Open, Drive Carefully;" "I Brake for Animals;" "Hire a Vet;"
      "America, Love It or Leave It;" "Stay off my Case;" "If You Can
      Read This, You're Too Close."
      3) Discuss messages. Do they represent any values? What values?
      Can the different messages be classified into categories such as
      people, places, and things?
      4) If possible get a student with a camera or provide a camera to
      a group who would take slide pictures of bumper stickers. The
      task would be to organize the slides to fit certain categories of
      meaning. The slide show is particularly effective in getting the
      point across that people are trying to deliver a message even if
      it is only on the back of a car.
(Save slide show to display at Social Studies Fair, see last activity in
 this chapter)

3. Activity & materials

The Message Carries the Values[12]

when: two periods

what: newspapers or weekly news magazines

how: 1) Have students cut out newspaper headlines and bring them to

class OR teacher could select headlines and run them off on copier.

2) Have students individually examine headlines and write down

what values they feel the headlines infer and why. For example:

Headline	Value Inferred	Why

3) Hold class discussion. How do students compare on their

inferences?

4. Activity & materials

The Immortality Game:
A Question of Values

when: one period

what: future wheel (below)

how: The "immortality Game" requires the use of a future wheel. It

calls for commitment on serious value questions. It requires a

personal evaluation. It can lead to thinking seriously about

possible consequences of alternative courses of action.

Information Base:

Late last spring the Salk Institute developed a vaccine which,

when injected, will stop aging for one year. It is injected

yearly, then the animal receiving the injection will be frozen in

time and will not age. The cost is 10 cents per shot. It does

not need refrigeration.

Task 1

You sit on a super secret decision panel that will decide
whether or not you will allow this vaccine to be
announced and/or used. There are probabilities that the
information is already into the underground but nothing
has yet been substantiated.

Task 2

If you decide to disseminate the vaccine, you must then
suggest the method for that dissemination. Please be as
specific as you can.

Task 3

If you decide not to disseminate the vaccine, please be
prepared to defend your decision.

Task 4

>Using a futures wheel, please place the vaccine in the
>center and then list the possible effects of the vaccine.
>List the effects of those effects and at least one more
>level beyond that.

Task 5

>Project yourself into a time when the vaccine is
>available for the asking. Write a letter telling why
>you want to use it or why you do not.

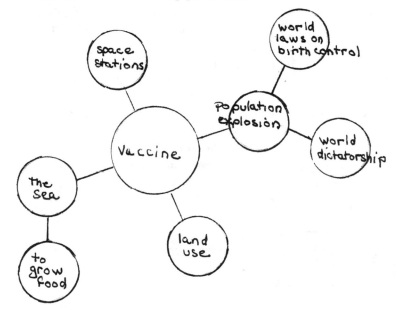

5. Activity & materials

Recognizing Conflicts between Values

when: two periods

what: sets of conflicting values

how: It is quite possible, almost certain, that values will conflict.

Students should be aware having participated in previous activities

in this chapter that they may hold conflicting values. This is

one reason for the emphasis on value clarification. Also values

may be in conflict between nations, organizations and people.
For example: a reporter's right to the privacy of his source of
information. against the government's right to keep national
security secrets from being revealed. These conflicting values
might be explored in the following manner.

  a) Arrive at definition of terms such as privacy, national
      security secrets.

  b) List possible alternatives that might be taken by reporter:
      i.e., report because people have right to know, or not to
      report.

  c) Establish rights of government in this particular case.

  d) What might be the results of possible alternative actions?

  e) What do you think the appropriate actions would be?

Examine another set of conflicting values, perhaps one involving
students.

  a) value earning money but resent having to work which takes
      time away from what they really want to do.

  b) needing sleep, but staying up late to watch a TV program.

  c) wanting a good grade but not caring to do the work.

6. Activity & materials

Does our Country Have Values?

when: two periods

what:

how: 1) Our country's values are found in the so-called "ritualistic
          documents" (Declaration of Independence, Constitution including
          Bill of Rights, Lincoln's Gettysburg Address, etc.) In these
          documents such statements are found as:

We hold these truths to be self-evident: that all men are created
equal, that they are endowed by their Creator with certain
unalienable rights, that among these are life, liberty, and the
pursuit of happiness.
... deriving their just powers from the consent of the governed;
that whenever any form of government becomes destructive of these
ends, it is the right of the people to alter or to abolish

it.

Declaration of Independence

We, the people of the United States, in order to form a more
perfect Union, establish justice, insure domestic tranquility,
provide for the common defense, promote the general welfare, and
secure the blessings of liberty to ourselves and our posterity, do
ordain and establish this CONSTITUTION of the United States of
America.

Preamble, Constitution

Freedom of religion, speech, press, and assembly.

Amendment 1, Bill of Rights

Four score and seven years ago our fathers brought forth on this
continent a new nation, conceived in liberty, and dedicated to the
proposition that all men are created equal.
... that these dead shall not have died in vain; that this nation,
under God, shall have a new birth of freedom; and that government
of the people, by the people, for the people, shall not perish
from the earth.

Lincoln's Gettysbury Address

2) Given these historic statements expressing beliefs and values
of the nation, has the nation, in fact, followed these beliefs
and values?
3) Keeping the announced values of the nation in mind, examine
historical events in the nineteenth and twentieth centuries,
determining whether the event supported or was contrary to the
announced values.
4) Can students answer this? On balance, has the United States
attempted to fulfill its announce values? What evidence is their
to support students' claims?

IV. Purpose: The application of knowledge through active participation.
Specific objective: Identifying and participating in the structure of
government.

1. Activity & materials

Student Council[14]

when: one week

what: Constitution of the student council

how: Students examine student council to see how it affects the
       individual.

1) Examine how student council is organized.

2) Can the student council make changes or must it do as it is
told?

3) Is there true representation of all students on the council,
i.e. special students or handicapped?

4) What actions does the student council consider and how does
this affect each student?

5) What actions should the student council consider?

6) Attend student council meeting.

After students have answered the above questions, they could
examine what values seem to dictate actions of the student council.
Are these values compatible with democracy and citizenship
participation? Explain.

Specific objective: By participating in a Social Studies Fair students
can summarize the activities by displaying materials which they created
during the semester or throughout the year.

2. Activity & materials

Social Studies Fair

when: one week

what: materials from previous activities including jigsaw map, newspapers
       created by students, Bingo·game, cause and effect railroad tracks,
       American symbols poster, technology mural, family geneology trees.

how: The Social Studies Fair should be considered a culminating activity
       that comes usually at the end of the semester or school year. It

offers the opportunity for students in a class or a number of
social studies classes to display the media that they have created
during the semester. Encourage students from the beginning of the
year to save media that they have created. Looking back over this
Chapter Eighth Grade you will note a great many activities that
call for participation through the creation of an object. Many
of these activities ended with a reminder to save the media for
the Social Studies Fair. They include such things as a jigsaw
map, newspapers on nineteenth century created by the students, a
Bingo game, railroad tracks on cause and effect. American symbols
poster, family geneology charts, slide show, etc.
Procedures:
The Fair itself should take one or two days. The planning, of
course, may take several weeks. Planning should include
organization and publicity committees.

> Organization would be in charge of suggesting appropriate
> historic topics, collecting and arranging displays.
> Publicity would be responsible for scheduling the visits of
> other classes, public announcements, posters, and information
> handouts.

Suggestions on organizing the display:

> each class has its own display topics OR organize in terms of
> time periods such as discovery, colonization,
> independence, westward expansion, Civil War, industrialization,
> technology, immigration, world power, future studies.

Suggestions for making the Fair successful:

a) Be sure that the exhibits are supervised by students who
   will by there to answer questions.
b) This is a good opportunity to use a variety of media, such
   as film strips, slides, VTR, audio-tapes. The media
   should be organized so that at least every other station
   the visitor can actively participate such as control the
   viewing of a slide show or taking part in a survey.
c) Music and dress of particular era would help to make
   display more interesting.
d) Provide refreshments that reflect a particular era such
   as corn bread, sassfras tea, corn chowder, maple syrup.

V.   INTEREST FORM

You have just completed the Chapter Eighth Grade and in
an effort to have you identify activities and materials
that seem most promising at this grade level to you,
please fill out the following interest form.

Instructions:
Identify two activities from this chapter. Name the
activities and briefly describe why these particular
activities are of interest to you.

ACTIVITY 1

ACTIVITY 2

CLARIFICATION AND SUMMARY OF SOCIAL

STUDIES CURRICULUM DEVELOPMENT

FOR FOURTH THROUGH EIGHTH GRADES

It is perfectly obvious, if you have read through each chapter of this book, that starting with the fourth grade the chapters become longer and more complex. Obvious because kindergarten through third grade teachers may be required to devote no more than two and a half hours each week to social studies, whereas in intermediate elementary and middle school the requirements are as much as half an hour to forty-five minutes per day. School curriculum directors, state departments of public instruction, and state legislatures seem more willing to prescribe both content to be taught and time to be spent on social studies subjects above the primary grades.

The social studies curriculum fourth grade and above hardly engenders among teachers the feeling that someone in the field knows what should be taught. There is substantial disagreement on the placement of social studies content. Some states teach state history in the fourth grade, others at the seventh grade, while others include state history in the eighth grade American history. Global area studies emphasizing the non-west can be taught at fourth, sixth, or seventh grades. American history normally found at the fifth and eighth grades can also be found in the fourth and seventh grades. Which should it be; history, government, economics, anthropology, sociology? Of course, it is all of these depending upon the program and texts adopted. There continues to be considerable disagreement among authorities in the field. It is easy to get lost in the flow of arguments back and forth on what should be taught. We know that classroom teachers must make decisions, that curriculums be organized, books adopted, materials gathered even though there is no ultimate master plan, no real sure answer to what and how social studies must be taught. For the moment it is important to focus on those trends which may offer guidance on how to think about teaching social studies grades four through eight.

Trends: Grades Four through Eight

1. Kindergarten through third grade foundations were to be set for the study

of current events and comparative studies, with emphasis upon regions within
the country and regions and cities in selected foreign cultures. In fourth
through eighth grades these foundations were to be continued and intensified.

2. An important trend since the early 1960's was for social studies content
to be organized to demonstrate specific key social science concepts, i.e.,
interdependence, conflict, scarcity, social control, etc. In the 1970's in
addition to the social science concepts there is pressure from special private
interest groups and from federal agencies in Washington for career education,
unemployment insurance education, law related education, and courses which deal
exclusively with economics education.

3. The social science concepts will be organized into a social studies
program that emphasizes the integration of those concepts for the purpose
of citizenship education. Clearly the trend is toward integration and away
from fragmentation. Elementary textbook series are emphasizing the role of
all of the social science and are not attempting to teach the concepts from
one social science discipline.

4. A present trend is for students to be introduced to global studies at the
primary and intermediate grade levels, and that introduction should be
followed with an ever increasing emphasis on comparative studies between
cultures. Culture studies in the past tended to emphasize western
civilization. The obvious trend is toward a more comprehensive study which
includes areas of the non-west.

5. The traditional notion that the simple act of gaining information is
sufficient to encourage decision-making is gradually being replaced by an
alternative conterporary notion that equal emphasis should be placed on
processing information, valuing, and participation. Clearly, dicision-
making which some in the field define as the very heart of social studies is
considered a process that requires the skills of validating and valuing.
These are acquired skills, acquired over the length of a kindergarten through
twelvth grade social studies citizenship education program.

FOOTNOTES

Person to Person

[1]Robert D. Barr, James L. Barth, S. Samuel Shermis, <u>Defining the Social Studies</u> (Bulletin 51; Washington, D.C.: National Council for the Social Studies, 1977), p. 69. James L. Barth, <u>Advanced Social Studies Education</u> (Washington, D.C.: University Press of America, 1977), p. 1. Another definition coming out at about the same time defines social studies as "Social studies is an integration of social sciences and humanities for the purpose of instruction in citizenship education." Robert D. Barr, James L. Barth, S. Samuel Shermis, <u>The Nature of the Social Studies</u> (Palm Springs, CA: ETC Publications, 1978), p. 18.

[2]The four purposes were originally identified in <u>Social Studies Guidelines</u> (Washington, D.C.: National Council for the Social Studies, 1971). In recent publications the purposes were referred to as the four objectives in Barr, Barth, Shermis, <u>Defining. . .</u>, p. 69, and Barth, <u>Advanced. . .</u>, p. 2. The four purposes were also used as the rationale for organizing a social studies teachers' guide: Indiana: Department of Public Instruction, <u>Social Studies: A Guide for Curriculum Development</u> (Indianapolis, 1978), p. B-1.

Chapter: A Social Studies Kindergarten through Twelfth Grade Curriculum

[1]Some portions of this chapter were originally published in Barth, <u>Advanced. . .</u>. The portions taken from <u>Advanced. . .</u> have been edited for publication in this book.

[2]The first column on the National Curriculum Pattern was suggested by Leonard S. Kenworthy, "Changing the Social Studies Curriculum: Some Guidelines and a Proposal," <u>Social Education</u>, (May, 1968), p. 485.

[3]<u>Social Studies: A Guide. . .</u>, p. A-4.

Chapter: Kindergarten/First Grade

[1]An abbreviated version of this section is found in James L. Barth, <u>Successful Social Studies Teaching: Elementary and Secondary</u>, (Washington, D.C.: University Press of America, 1977), p. 23-24.

[2]Indiana: Department of Public Instruction, <u>1978 Indiana Textbook Adoption Categories for Social Studies</u> (Indianapolis, 1978), p. 2.

[3]Indiana: Department of Public Instruction, <u>Teaching Social Studies to the Gifted</u> by James L. Barth and S. Samuel Shermis (Indianapolis, 1978), p. 18.

[4]Ibid.

[5]Ibid., 19.

[6]Ibid., and Barth, _Advanced. . ._, 56.

[7]Ibid., 59.

[8]Ibid.

[9]Ibid., 64.

Chapter: Second Grade

[1]Barth, _Successful. . ._, 24-26.

[2]_Indiana Textbook. . ._, 2.

[3]Barth and Shermis, _Teaching. . ._, 17.

[4]Ibid., 19.

[5]Barth, _Advanced. . ._, 59.

[6]Ibid., 60.

[7]Ibid., 69.

[8]Ibid., 71.

Chapter: Third Grade

[1]Barth, _Successful. . ._, 26-28.

[2]_Indiana Textbook. . ._, 2.

[3]Barth and Shermis, _Teaching. . ._, 20.

[4]Barth, _Advanced. . ._, 71.

Chapter: Fourth Grade

[1]Barth, _Successful. . ._, 28-29.

[2]_Indiana Textbook. . ._, 2.

[3]Barth and Shermis, _Teaching. . ._, 23.

[4]Ibid.

[5] Barth, _Advanced. . ._, 67.

[6] Barth and Shermis, _Teaching. . ._, 27.

[7] Ibid., 28.

[8] Barth, _Advanced. . ._, 71-72.

Chapter: Fifth Grade

[1] Barth, _Successful. . ._, 30-31.

[2] _Indiana Textbook. . ._, 2.

[3] Barth, _Advanced. . ._, 80-81.

[4] Ibid., 132.

[5] Ibid., 72.

[6] Barth and Shermis, _Teaching. . ._, 23.

[7] Barth, _Advanced. . ._, 58.

[8] Ibid.

[9] Barth and Shermis, _Teaching. . ._, 24.

[10] Barth, _Advanced. . ._, 64.

[11] Ibid.

Chapter: Sixth Grade

[1] Barth, _Successful. . ._, 31-33.

[2] _Indiana Textbook. . ._, 3.

[3] Barth and Shermis, _Teaching. . ._, 25.

[4] Barth, _Advanced. . ._, 56.

[5] Ibid., 56.

[6] Ibid., 60.

[7] Much of the materials in this activity can be found in chapter length form in Barth, _Advanced. . ._, 30.

Chapter: Seventh Grade

[1]Indiana Textbook. . ., 3.

[2]Barth and Shermis, Teaching. . ., 32.

[3]Ibid.

[4]Barth, Advanced. . ., 70.

[5]Ibid., 62.

[6]Barth and Shermis, Teaching. . ., 34.

[7]Ibid., 35.

[8]Barth, Advanced. . ., 129.

[9]Ibid., 128.

[10]Ibid., 67.

[11]Ibid., 69.

[12]Ibid., 63.

[13]Ibid., 67.

[14]Ibid., 124.

[15]Ibid., 73.

[16]Ibid., 74.

Chapter: Eighth Grade

[1]Indiana Textbook. . ., 3.

[2]Barth, Advanced. . ., 57.

[3]Ibid., 70.

[4]Ibid., 60 and Barth and Shermis, Teaching. . ., 39.

[5]Ibid.

[6]Barth, Advanced. . ., 60.

[7]Barth and Shermis, Teaching. . ., 41.

[8]Ibid., 40.

[9]Barth, Advanced. . ., 130.

[10]Ibid., 65.

[11]Ibid., 68.

[12]Ibid., 69.

[13]Ibid.

[14]Ibid., 73.